Getting and Writing IT Requirements in a **Lean / Agile World**

Business Analysis Techniques for Discovering User Stories, Features, and Gherkin (Given-When-Then) Scenarios

Thomas Hathaway
Angela Hathaway

Copyright © 2020 BA-EXPERTS

All rights reserved. No part of this publication may be reproduced, distributed, or transmitted in any form or by any means, including photocopying, recording, or other electronic or mechanical methods, without the prior written permission of the publisher, except in the case of brief quotations embodied in critical reviews and certain other noncommercial uses permitted by copyright law.

Ordering Information:

Quantity sales. Special discounts are available on quantity purchases by corporations, associations, and others. For details, contact the publisher at books@BusinessAnalysisExperts.com.

The content of this book is also available as an online course at
https://businessanalysisexperts.com/agile-lean-requirements-business-analysis/

ISBN: 9781076481672

CONTENTS

CONTENTS iii
PREFACE ix

I. Requirements in a Lean and Agile World 12
    Agile and Lean Philosophies 16
        Agile and Scrum 17
        Lean and Kanban 18
        DevOps and Continuous Delivery: New Kids on the Block 19
        Testing in a Lean and Agile World 20
        WagiLeanFall or WaterKanScrumBanFall? 21
    Traditional and Lean Requirements 22
        Traditional Requirements 22
        Agile and Lean Requirements Concepts 29
    User Stories Are Stakeholder Requirements 40
        The User Story Paradigm 41
        A Well-Formed User Story Template 44
        INVEST in Your User Stories 47
        User Stories Define the Business Need 51

II. Requirements Elicitation and Backlog Seeding 61
    Common Elicitation Techniques 64
        Start with Open-ended Questions 64
        Analyze Documents 66
        Use Models and Examples 67
    Track Your Progress with a Question File 69
        What Is a Question File? 70

Using the Question File 72

Identifying Stakeholders 76
Basic Stakeholder Identification 76
Use an Org Chart to Identify Internal Stakeholders 78
Stakeholder Groups 79
Exercise: Stakeholder Identification 81

Using Cynefin to Deal with Uncertainty 85
Cynefin Is a Framework for Quantifying Uncertainty 86
Simple Problems with **Obvious** Solutions 87
Life Gets **Complicated** 89
The Situation Becomes **Complex** 91
Chaos Reigns Supreme 95
A Cynefin Success Story 98
Exercise: Cynefin Applied to Proposed Initiatives 100

Reveal User Stories with Business Problem Analysis 107
Define Business Problems 110
Exercise: Define Business Problems 114
Lean Problem-Symptom Reduction Reveals User Stories, Epics and Features 117
Exercise: Problem Symptom Reduction 123

Conversations Are the Core of Lean and Agile 126
Engaging with the Business Community 128
Exercise: What Traits Does a Good Business Analyst Need? . 129
Effective Requirement Discussions 131
Preparation and Planning 132
Types of Requirements Meetings 139
User Story Conversations and Group Interactions 150

Nonverbal Communication 157

Context Clarifies Intent 159
Base Your Assumptions on Clusters 160
Culture Makes All the Difference 161
Congruence: Avoid Mixed Signals 162

Dealing with People 164

Understanding Is Not Enough 164
Dealing with Difficult People 166
Exercise: Problem People or People Problems 171

3 Listening Techniques that Promote Common Understanding 173

Active Listening 174
Informational Listening 177
Highway 350 179

Bias Can Lead Us Astray 180

Confirmation Bias 180
Emotional Bias 182
The Vividness Effect 184
Prepare to End on a High Note 187

Tips for Email and Chats 188

III Agile Requirements Analysis and Backlog Grooming 191

Timing of Analysis in a Typical Agile Lifecycle 195

Just in Time (JIT) vs. Just in Case (JIC) 198
Release Planning 201
Sprint Planning 203
Ongoing Activities During a Sprint 205

Preparing User Stories for Release and Sprint Planning 208

Who Needs Clarity, Anyway? 210

What Are Ambiguity and Subjectivity? 214
Revealing and Removing Ambiguity 217
Ensuring a Common Understanding 224
Exercise: Using Out-of-Box Thinking to Reduce Ambiguity .. 230

5 Common User Story Splitting Techniques **232**
Splitting to Reduce Complexity 233
Splitting Stories by Data Types 239
Splitting Stories by Business Rules 241
Splitting Based on Workflow or Events 243
Splitting by Use Case Path 248

Solution Requirements **250**
Getting to Solution Requirements 251
Data and Information Requirements 260

Non-Functional Requirements, Qualities & Constraints ...**269**
Types of Non-Functional Requirements 272
Split Stories with NFR's 282

IV. Lean Acceptance Testing: The Business Perspective
.... **284**

The New Acceptance Test Paradigm **286**
ATDD/BDD Explained **287**
Acceptance Criteria as Given-When-Then Scenarios 291
Scenarios 293
Defining a Gherkin BACKGROUND 296
Scenario Outlines 297
Examples 299
Exercise: Expressing Scenarios in GWT Format 301
Engineering AGILE Test Data **303**

Minimizing Scenarios and Examples 305
Exercise: Engineering Test Data 313
Lean Analysis to Find Gherkin Scenarios 318
From User Stories to Scenarios 319
Business Rules Identify Scenarios 324
Problems and Symptoms Are Great Test Scenarios 330
From Use Cases to Scenarios 334
Find Scenarios Using Acquire, Abolish, Affirm, Avoid 343
Functional Features Reveal Scenarios 348
Scenarios for Non-functional or Quality Requirements 353

V. Implementing Lean and Agile Practices 359
About the authors 361

FOREWORD

Requirements are often an overwhelming topic especially for the business community. Everyone knows what they mean, but no one really understands them. I suspect that when the pharaoh told the architect of the pyramids his requirements, he may have only thought of a cool summer house, but what did he get?

Every IT initiative benefits from clear, unambiguous, and verifiable requirements that can be implemented by developers with a high degree of confidence.

With the vast amount of knowledge that IT developers need and the growing demand for digital solutions, the challenge of creating high-quality business and stakeholder requirements is increasingly falling on the business community.

It is more and more the task of Product Owners, Product Managers, Project Managers, Business Analysts, Requirements Engineers, and business experts to support Agile or traditional approaches. Therefore, it is of crucial importance to improve their requirements competencies.

We have written this book for this audience. It is our contribution, based on nearly 60 years of combined experience helping organizations around the world improve communication between business professionals and IT professionals.

We hope that it will help companies complete a digital transformation that fits perfectly in the Lean and Agile world.

Thomas and Angela Hathaway
BusinessAnalysisExperts.com

PREFACE

The biggest challenge for companies around the world is how to use information technology to gain competitive advantage. It is not about how to program PCs, laptops, tablets, and cell phones; it is about figuring out what these devices are supposed to do.

The skills needed to identify and define the best IT solutions are invaluable for every role in the organization. These skills can propel you from the mail room to the boardroom by making your organization more effective and more profitable.

Many organizations have moved to a Lean or Agile approach to the development and implementation of information technology. This is an extremely effective and efficient approach to software development.

However, we still have to struggle with the age-old problem that has always plagued IT projects, namely defining the **right** requirements.

What You Will Learn

Agile, Lean, DevOps and continuous software development methods do not change the need for solid business analysis to create high quality requirements. In this book you will learn how the new principles and philosophies in software development influence the discovery, creation, and analysis of requirements.

You will learn how to discover, analyze, and define User Stories, Features, and Quality Requirements (also known as Non-Functional Requirements - NFR) and develop basic Acceptance Tests (Scenarios, Scenario Outlines, and Examples). The latter have become a critical part of many Lean development approaches.

To support the new test paradigm, you will also learn how to identify and optimize Scenarios, Scenario Outlines and Examples in the Given-When-Then format (Gherkin). These form the basis for Acceptance Test Driven Development (ATDD) and Behavior Driven Development (BDD).

After reading this book, you can:

- ➔ Define the capabilities and challenges of Lean and Agile software development philosophies

- ➔ Express business needs and wants in User Story format to optimally support Lean and Agile software development philosophies

- ➔ Reduce the time wasted on miscommunication between Stakeholders of IT initiatives

- ➔ Drill-down Features and User Stories to define Test Scenarios in Given-When-Then statements to facilitate testing

- ➔ Adapt 10 classic techniques of requirements analysis to your Lean and Agile software development process

- ➔ Identify 17 Qualities and develop Given-When-Then (GWT) Scenarios for them

The good news is you do not have to read this book front to back. We try to describe each technique on its own without relying on other techniques. You can jump to any topic in the outline that describes a technique for doing one thing, use that technique, and incorporate it into your toolkit.

Who Should Read this Book?

How organizations develop and deliver working software has changed significantly in recent years. Because the change was greatest in the developer community, many books and courses justifiably target that group. There is, however, an overlooked group of people essential to the development of software-as-an-asset that have been neglected.

Many different job titles in our business world create software requirements for digital solutions. They include Business Analysts, Product Owners, Product Managers, Test Developers, Project Managers, Requirements Engineers, Subject Matter Experts (SMEs), Agile Teams, and Business or Customer-side Teams. This book will help these groups discover, capture, clarify, and confirm the kind of IT requirements that solution providers need to deliver the right digital solutions for the business.

Additional Resources

You can learn more about business analysis techniques by visiting our Business Analysis Learning Store at businessanalysisexperts.com.

We offer a wide selection of books on business analysis, self-study courses, virtual coaching and training, and a selection of FREE business analysis videos.

We welcome all comments, suggestions for improvement, or complaints that you would like to share with us. You can reach us by books@businessanalysisexperts.com.

I. Requirements in a Lean and Agile World

The Lean/Agile approach to software development is a child of the 21st century. Fundamentally, Agile, Lean, and DevOps are all philosophies for delivering working software to end users as quickly and efficiently as possible. Together, they change the paradigm for what we in the industry have long called "requirements".

These new development approaches have significantly changed the process of requirements elicitation and analysis. One of the biggest changes is WHEN requirements should be gathered or analyzed. If you have already followed best practices for defining requirements, the changes may not be as significant.

In any case, you will need a new vocabulary (and may need a different mindset) when defining business needs in a Lean or Agile environment. Lean and Agile requirements are business needs expressed at every level of detail down to the lowest level that developers need to translate them into software code. This process is often referred to as "business analysis", "business needs analysis", or "requirements engineering".

In the past, developers, IT specialists, or Requirements Engineers would define the requirements for an application. In today's world, however, the financial success of a company is intricately linked to the success of its digital solutions. That is why business analysis has emerged over the past two decades a new discipline to improve the business value of digital solutions and ensure greater business agility. But what is the difference between business analysis and requirements engineering?

Business Analysis vs. Requirements Engineering

Business analysis as a discipline is extremely broad and focus of business analysis is on providing solutions business outcomes. Software is often part of the so analysis deals with technology, people, and process pro....ms.

It is about understanding and analyzing the business problem, deriving business needs/requirements, and then providing the solutions for these needs. Activities related to business analysis are related to improving business processes, creating a business case, eliciting, and analyzing requirements, or achieving business benefits.

In contrast, requirements engineering focuses primarily on products and applications and does not include many of the other activities associated with business analysis. Requirements engineering is about defining, documenting, validating, negotiating, and managing the detailed system requirements for a selected solution.

Therefore, the focus of business analysis is on solving problems and achieving business benefits, and the focus of requirements engineering is on manufacturing products with a specified range of Features/Functions. For this reason, Requirements Engineers often report to the Business Analyst. In the past, however, we have also seen in many projects that a single person or team has taken on the role of both the Requirements Engineer and the Business Analyst.

Two different institutions were formed to standardize Requirements Elicitation, Analysis, Communication, and Management. The International Institute of Business Analysis (IIBA, founded 2003 in Toronto, Canada) and the International Requirements Engineering Board (IREB, founded 2006 in Fürth, Germany) accepted the challenge, albeit from different perspectives.

National Institute of Business Analysis (IIBA)

The IIBA focused on defining requirements from a business perspective and usually involved a Business Analyst. They divided requirements into Business Requirements, Stakeholder Requirements, Solution Requirements, and Transition Requirements.

While the first 2 types (Business and Stakeholder Requirements) are related to the business side, the latter 2 (Solution and Transition Requirements) are crucial for the development of software and are very often specified by Requirements Engineers or developers.

International Requirements Engineering Board (IREB)

The focus of the IREB was on the IT product side of correctly structuring and communicating technical requirements that drive the development of software.

Given the profound impact of digitization in an organization, requirements engineering roughly encompasses what the IIBA calls "Stakeholder and Solution" Requirements. As Agile software development gained enormous popularity, the IREB was quickly ready to incorporate new forms of requirements expressions.

For those responsible for business or requirements analysis of IT products/projects, there is an obvious overlap between the two organizations. Starting in 2020 the IREB and the IIBA have signed a "Memorandum of Understanding" for the mutual promotion and further development of the disciplines Requirements Engineering and Business Analysis as complementary approaches. This is helpful to all of us who deal with requirements.

For Anyone Wearing the Business Analysis Hat

In this book the distinction between business analysis and requirements engineering is not important. The goal of our book is to help an organization find out what the business world needs from IT (Business Analysis) and then present those needs in a way that its development teams can understand and program them (Requirements Engineering). We will deal with both.

To make one thing clear: We do not believe that Business Analysts or Requirements Engineers are the only ones in an organization that perform business analysis or create requirements. There are many people who define Business Requirements for IT. These include Product Owners, Project Managers, business experts, testers, teams on the business side and teams on the customer side, to name a few.

Topics Covered in this Chapter

In this chapter, we will answer the question of how Agile, Lean, and DevOps approaches influence the discovery, expression, and analysis of business needs. Since the focus of this book is on requirements, i.e. how to discover, capture, and communicate them in a Lean/Agile environment, we start by creating a common baseline of the new terminology.

We also define requirement constructs in Lean and Agile environments and compare them with conventional requirements forms. We discuss Features, Rules, Scenarios, and User Stories. The good news is that these terms are used consistently whether you are talking "Lean", "Agile", or somewhere in between.

Due to the extreme emphasis that many organizations place on User Stories, we offer an in-depth description of what they are, how to write and structure them, and some guidelines in how to make sure they communicate the business needs as intended.

Agile and Lean Philosophies

A significant difference between traditional versus Lean and Agile requirements deals with timing. When does IT get the level of detail needed to do their job? To answer that, we need to define this phenomenon called Agile or Lean.

There are a thundering herd of philosophies, concepts, methodologies, techniques, or whatever you want to call them that are bandied about in the Lean/Agile universe. Let us explore some of them.

Feel free to skip the explanations of these different software development approaches if you are not interested. However, knowing about them will help you "talk the talk" with your software developers and technical teams. Fortunately, the techniques we teach in this book apply to all Lean and Agile methods.

Agile Methods Unmasked

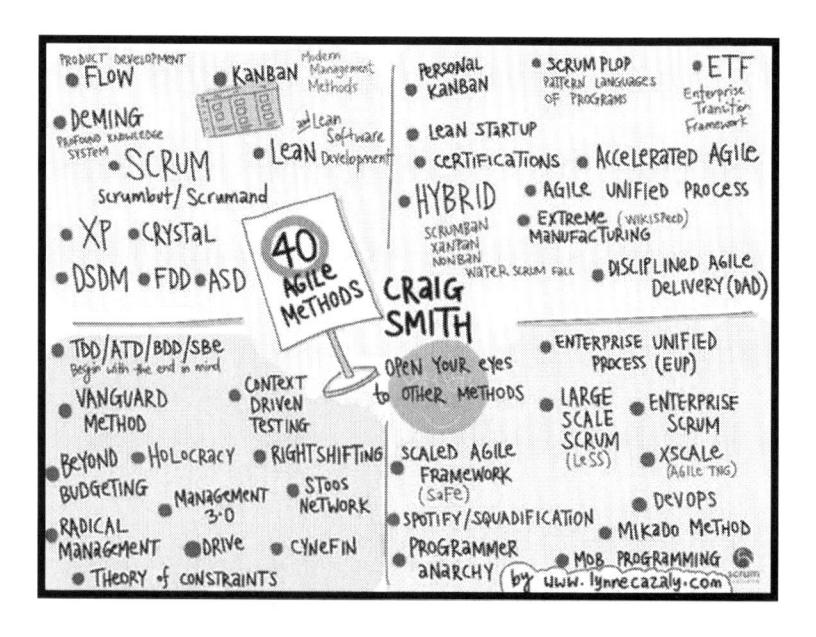

If this chart looks like the biblical Tower of Babel to you, it represents reality. This is why we need to reach agreement regarding what Agile and Lean really are to avoid confusion. The chart presents 40 examples of things that are called "Agile Methods". Each of them is a term used by people when they talk about Agile.

Agile and Scrum

One of the first terms you see in the upper left-hand quadrant is the word "Scrum". Scrum is a methodology that played a role in triggering the emergence of Agile as a software development philosophy. Many "Agilists" call Scrum a framework as opposed to a methodology but for our purpose they are interchangeable. What is the difference between a methodology and a philosophy?

A philosophy is primarily about thinking, abstracting, and attitude whereas a methodology or framework is action focused. A philosophy defines principles and core values whereas a methodology gives you implementation, rules, templates, and sequence.

To learn more about the Agile philosophy, we recommend reading the Agile Manifesto which defines its core principles and values.

Lean and Kanban

You see the term "Lean Software Development" in the chart. Lean, like Agile, is a philosophy but it has a much broader reach. The Lean philosophy in software development is closely related to an older philosophy called "Lean Manufacturing".

The core concept of Lean is simply to eliminate every form of waste in any process by only working on things that you need immediately to get the job done. We will talk a lot more about the Lean philosophy later.

Another term you see in the chart is "Kanban" which is a Lean Software Development methodology. Kanban originated as an approach in Lean manufacturing and just-in-time (JIT) production, where it is used as a scheduling system that tells you what to produce, when to produce it, and how much of it to produce.

A major Feature of Kanban is its focus on visibility. Typically, the workflow of the process is prominently displayed on the Kanban board as a series of essential steps.

| Idea | To do | Doing | Done |

The Kanban board allows visualization of a workflow to expose problems and bottlenecks. To add a new task or work item, simply place it on a Kanban board. The item passes through each column on the board as a step is completed. Everyone can see the status of each step in the workflow. More information about the origins and background of Lean and Kanban can be found on the Internet.

DevOps and Continuous Delivery: New Kids on the Block

"DevOps" is a concept down in the lower right quadrant of the chart. That is where basically software development is heading. It is where most organizations would love to be at – and some of them are already there. If your organization is software driven (which describes most large organizations today), you are either living DevOps or going to very soon.

DevOps is primarily an organizational philosophy in that it combines the historically separate groups of software development (Dev) and operations/maintenance (Ops). By combining the two, organizations can constantly and reliably update production software. Of course, there are many factors that must be considered to successfully implement DevOps.

Continuous Delivery (CD) is the ultimate Lean and/or Agile approach. The premise of CD is to continually create changes, tweaks, or modifications to your product, run them through automated testing (an absolute must in the Continuous Delivery world), and release new Features as often as possible. This allows the product to constantly evolve.

Given the rapid pace of change of business needs in the global economy, software must be just as quick to react. That is the driving force behind DevOps and Continuous Delivery. All requirements techniques and methods in this book support Agile, Lean, DevOps, and Continuous Delivery.

Testing in a Lean and Agile World

One of the key success factors for Lean Software Development is automated Acceptance Testing. Essential components are:

⇨ **Teste-Driven Development (TDD)**

⇨ **Acceptance Test Driven Development (ATDD)**

⇨ **Behavior Driven Development (BTD)**

The original concept was TDD which morphed into ATDD and BDD and all of them are modern software development methods. The process of defining technological business needs for these new methods is different from the traditional Waterfall and iterative methodologies. Because of that it requires a significant change to the analysis of business needs. We will cover these testing concepts and associated tools and techniques in Chapter IV. Lean Acceptance Testing: The Business Perspective.

WagiLeanFall or WaterKanScrumBanFall?

None of the organizations that we have worked with in the past have implemented Lean and Agile philosophies to the full extent. Most organizations try to take the best of all worlds and create something like a "WagiLeanFall" or a "WaterKanScrum". They combine common methods, such as Waterfall, Scrum, and Kanban to come up with the best way of developing and delivering working software to the business community.

We have always maintained that organizations should never go with one single methodology when it comes to developing software. The reasons? Every project or initiative is different. Every organization is different. Every group of people is different. We need to be aware of the different combinations and the pros and cons of each. Then, for any given initiative or project, pick the one that is going to be the least expensive and most effective for that effort.

Traditional and Lean Requirements

Modern software development approaches are all about not wasting any effort. Before we define requirement constructs in an Agile or Lean world, we need to define requirement constructs in a traditional world. That forms the basis for a comparison.

Traditional Requirements

We in the IT world have bandied about the term "Requirements" forever and are constantly trying to redefine what the word means. Talking about a "Requirement" to a business owner or high-level executive is quite different than talking about a "Requirement" to someone who does "real" work down in the trenches. We need a clear definition of what we mean when we use the word requirement.

The International Institute of Business Analysis (IIBA) published their Business Analysis Body of Knowledge (BABOK Version 3.0) in 2015. The BABOK gives us a common definition of terms we should be using to communicate about requirements. The IIBA divides software requirements into three distinct categories – Business, Stakeholder, and Solution Requirements.

Business Requirements

Historically, in a Waterfall approach, **Strategic Business Analysis** has been the preliminary work at the beginning of a project or initiative. The result of the Strategic Business Analysis was to determine the viability of a proposed project and potentially divide it into multiple projects. If a project was deemed viable, Strategic Business Analysis delivered high-level Business Requirements defining the business value of the undertaking.

Even if you believe that business analysis is no longer needed, you still need someone to create Business Requirements and decide whether resources should be approved to solve a particular problem or take advantage of an opportunity.

To do this, you need Business and/or Stakeholder Requirements, which can be formulated in the form of User Stories, high-level Features, or simply as textual requirement statements. The results of Strategic Business Analysis will fill your Product Backlog.

> A "**Business Requirement**" is defined as a high-level goal or objective that benefits the entire organization and not just individuals within it.

That definition puts the Business Requirement at such a high level that there will be only a few of them on any given initiative, project, or even product. Here are a couple of examples:

> **The IRS will increase tax receipts by 15 percent through online spying by December 31st of this year.**

You can debate whether that is a good or bad idea, but as a Business Requirement, it meets our criteria. The requirement names who will benefit *(the IRS)*, what they are going to do *(increase tax receipts by 15 percent)*, how they will achieve it *(through online spying)*, and the time frame *(by December 31st of this year)*. This is a high-level goal or objective and gives us valuable information to start business needs analysis.

Another example of a Business Requirement:

> **Claims processing needs to reduce the time required to process a claim from 10 days to four days.**

This Business Requirement states the benefit for a group within the organization and it gives me measurable numbers.

If you are writing Business Requirements at this level, we highly recommend following the "SMART" acronym which means that these goals should be written to be:

- ⇨ **S**pecific
- ⇨ **M**easurable
- ⇨ **A**chievable
- ⇨ **R**elevant
- ⇨ **T**ime bound

We assume that our readers are familiar with the SMART concept and will not waste your time by going into detail here. Should you need more information, there are many free online resources explaining the SMART technique.

Specific, Measurable, Achievable, Relevant, and Time bound are the five criteria for good core objectives. You can apply them to a project charter or, as in this case, to a Business Requirement that expresses a goal or objective of the product.

Stakeholder Requirements

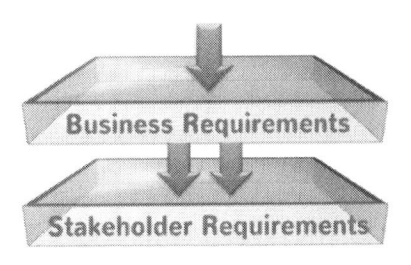

Stakeholder Requirements are the next level of IIBA requirements.

"Stakeholder Requirements"
express what individual or groups of stakeholders with similar duties need or want.

A Stakeholder is either an individual, a group or an organization who is affected by the new software product. They can be within or outside the organization that is sponsoring the initiative or project. A good Stakeholder Requirement expresses a specific need. For example,

---

As an airline passenger,
I can view available seats to select my preference.

This Stakeholder Requirement is written in User Story format, but it could be written in any other textual format. It specifies who the Stakeholder is *(airline passenger)*, what the Stakeholder wants to do *(view available seats)*, and the Stakeholder's purpose *(select my preference)*. It tells me who, what, and why - three key criteria for any good User Story.

To be **HIPPAA compliant**, pharmacy customers will not be able to see other customers' prescriptions.

The Health Insurance Portability and Accountability Act (HIPAA) is a law that was passed in the early 2000s to protect patient privacy and security. This Stakeholder Requirement starts off with the "why" *(to be HIPAA compliant)*, followed by the "who" *(pharmacy customers)*, and the "what" *(see other customers' prescriptions)*.

Those are two good examples of User Stories that express Stakeholder Requirements. You do not have to follow the User Story paradigm but in Lean and Agile environments this format is quite common to express Stakeholder Requirements.

Getting Business Requirements (high-level goals and objectives) and then Stakeholder Requirements (specific needs of groups or individuals inside or outside the organization) is all good and well.

However, developers and other members of the technical teams need more detail to write a program or create an app. They need Solution Requirements.

Solution Requirements

[Diagram: Business Requirements → Stakeholder Requirements → Solution Requirements]

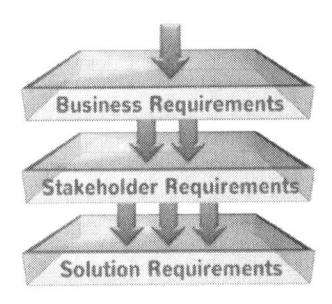

The third and lowest level of detail according to the IIBA are Solution Requirements. This is the level that developers need to start coding. There are two categories of Solution Requirements - Functional and Non-Functional.

> A **Functional Requirement** (FR) expresses what the product, the application, or a user must do or know.

whereas

> A **Non-Functional Requirement** expresses properties of the product or application, such as: "how well", "how fast", or "how many".

Here are a couple of examples:

Functional Requirement:

> Calculate total cost
> including delivery charges and taxes.

This Functional Requirement states that the application must include a function that calculates the total charges and taxes.

Non-Functional Requirement:

> Average response time will not exceed 3 seconds.

This Non-Functional Requirement expresses the maximum wait time for a user who is interacting with the application. In this case, the user should never have to wait more than three seconds for the application to respond.

Solution Requirements are the level of detail that most developers need to start coding. In traditional (e.g. Waterfall) development environments, we created all three levels for the whole project before a line of code was written. Many of these requirements were never implemented. That is an obvious case of unnecessary waste. This changes drastically in Lean and Agile development environments (more on that in later chapters). First, let us explore some new requirements terminology.

Agile and Lean Requirements Concepts

The goal of business analysis is to help an organization figure out what the business community needs from IT and then present these needs in a manner that their IT technical teams understand and can program.

This sounds easy but, as anyone who has worked in this field knows, requirements or business needs analysis is a mine field of miscommunications. With business analysis we put the emphasis on discovering the business needs and wants before we start developing a solution.

Agile has made some major inroads into that. To illustrate Agile and Lean analysis, we will be using "Scrum", the most commonly used method for Agile initiatives.

At the beginning of a project or initiative, you need to have some guidance, some idea as to what you are trying to achieve. Actually, the word "project" is used very seldom in Agile. Agile teams tend to talk about the **product** not the project.

The Shift from Project to Product

One of the major distinguishing facets of Agile is the shift from the Project perspective to the product perspective. Although that change may appear to be minor, it is actually a paradigm shift. To understand this distinction, we need a clear definition:

> A **Project** is a temporal event that has a planned sequence of activities for achieving a specific outcome. It is typically constrained by resources (time and money as defined in a budget and schedule) and quality of outcome.
>
> A **Product** is something that can solve someone's problem or satisfy a need. In the world of Agile Software Development, the

product is primarily a digital solution which is constrained by Features, data, and a wide range of "non-functional" properties. A product evolves over time to meet ever-changing needs. product development is a continuous process involving ongoing adjustments to keep up with changes in the environment.

By changing the focus from "Project" to "Product", the Agile team's primary goal shifts from trying to finish defined tasks within specified time limits to trying to deliver working components of the product to the customer. That shift is significant.

What does the evolution of a typical Agile product look like? We will show this evolution by looking at common artifacts or deliverables throughout the initiative.

The Change in Terminology

As we move into the Lean and Agile world the terminology changes and it changes for a reason. The word "requirement" conjures up the image that "it has to be this way" for many analysts, designers, developers, and system architects. "Requirement" comes from "require", so the inference is difficult to ignore.

In the past, a requirement implied that it was very stable and could only be changed with a formal change request. This rigidness has cost companies millions of dollars in the past. Many IT projects took years and since the requirements were difficult to change, taking advantage of new business opportunities was quite difficult and often impossible.

All Lean and Agile development methods allow for requirements to be changed at any point in the development process. That is a big differentiator and one of the key success factors. The terminology that we use to express requirements in a Lean/Agile World accommodates the diverse needs much better. The terms used are more flexible and not as fixed on the outcome.

It is up to the development team to decide which terminology to use when referring to Lean requirements. For example, Extreme Programming (XP) uses the terms User Stories or Stories to represent Features; SCRUM uses Features, Epics, and User Stories to describe requirements; Feature-Driven Development (FDD) uses the term Features exclusively; and DSDM uses Requirement.

Vision Statements or "the Next Big Thing"

To start an initiative or develop a new product, we need to understand the high-level goals and objectives of the organization so that we can define the business needs that will achieve these goals.

A Vision Statement is a widely used document that expresses what your Lean or Agile initiative is trying to achieve. It is a summary of the idea, intent, and motivation behind the product. It gives everyone a comprehensive picture of the future that the company is aiming for.

Decision makers are responsible for formulating product visions. In Agile methods, this role often falls to the Product Owner (in Lean it can be any role or title).

As usual in our industry, we still have not been able to standardize the terms. In some organizations, "Visions" are expressed as Business Requirements, Goals and Objectives, Project Charters, or simply "the Next Big thing". In other organizations, the vision is expressed in a Product Requirements Document which describes the Features that differentiate your product from existing ones. Regardless what they are called, all of these forms have one thing in common, they are brief, high-level, initial answers to:

- ✓ what the business community will be able to do differently
- ✓ how the product will shape the future
- ✓ what the value of the product is
- ✓ who the primary Stakeholders are

We like Roman Pichler's description best:

> *The product vision is the overarching goal you are aiming for, the reason for creating the product. It provides a continued purpose in an ever-changing world, acts as the product's true north, provides motivation when the going gets tough, and facilitates effective collaboration.*

> By Roman Pichler, 8th October 2014

This book will not teach you how to create a Vision Statement. We are assuming that a high-level business needs description exists and that you have access to it.

The Product Backlog

Regardless what your Vision Statement is called or who creates it, the key question for you is "Where are the business needs articulated?". Every method treats this differently.

In Scrum, a Vision Statement or "the Next Big Thing" as well as Features, User Stories, Epics, Use Cases, work items, and other types of requirements are documented in the Product Backlog. In Kanban, business needs are in a Feature List.

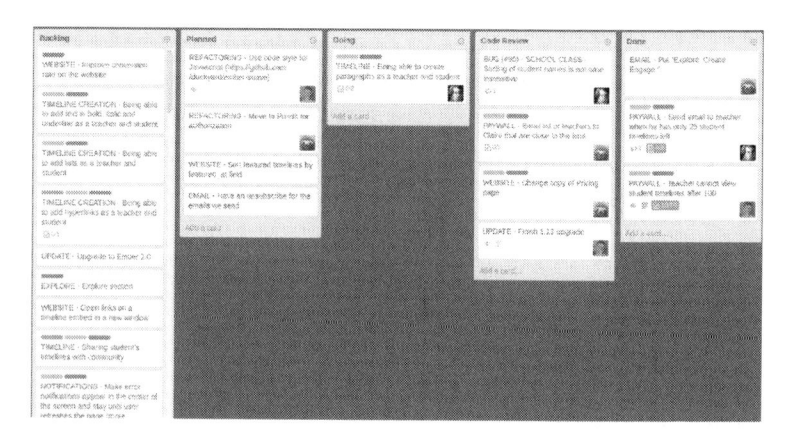

In this book, we will use the term "Backlog" to mean a collection of business needs in various formats (e.g. User Stories, Epics, Features, Requirement Statements, Use Cases, etc.). Each product will most likely have its own Backlog, but we have also seen companies working with one large Backlog.

A Product Backlog contains proposed work items that need to be completed to achieve the desired outcomes. In Scrum, the Product Owner "seeds" the Product Backlog by analyzing the Vision Statement and working with the Product Manager to define a set of Features, User Stories – or more likely Epics at this stage of the game.

The number of items in a Product Backlog will grow in the early weeks of the initiative but over time it should start to go the other way. It is flexible and volatile. It changes constantly.

That is the big plus of Lean and Agile development. You are no longer stuck with Business and Stakeholder Requirements that where defined a long time ago when business was different. Business agility is no longer a desire but becomes reality when you use Lean and Agile methods.

It is important to note that the Product Backlog will never be empty. Based on the Agile philosophy, the work should stop when the customer declares it done. There will be things remaining in the Backlog that are not important enough to warrant the investment needed to complete them.

If the product survives the real world, it will evolve over time and desirable leftover items may be implemented in future Releases.

Types of Textual Requirements

Features and Functions

Many Agile and Lean development efforts tend to be Feature driven. In a Lean environment, for example the Kanban method, the use of Features, Feature Lists, Feature Files, etc. is quite common.

The question then becomes, "What is a Feature?" Experience on many projects and extensive research on the WWW reveals the answer: "Whatever you want it to be".

That means a Feature can be a single function, a behavior, an interface, or anything a Stakeholder wants the product to have or to be when it is delivered. Since there is no consistency in what level of detail a Feature describes, you can never be inconsistent in its use.

Because there is no mutual understanding of the term, Features can be defined at any level. For example, the Features of a website that processes applications for insurance coverage might include Underwrite Policy, Submit Claim, Check Claim Status, Process Payment, Suspend Policy, etc.

Each of these high-level Features would need clarification in User Story format and/or Qualities. Other organizations define Features at the level of application Functions (e.g., Print Check, Get Driving Record, Assign Agent, etc.) As a result, Features are found above and below User Stories.

User Stories

One of the most popular concepts associated with Lean and Agile philosophies is the "User Story". Because it has proven to be extremely effective, even IT projects that follow a Waterfall or iterative methodology may express Stakeholder Requirements in User Story format.

One step in the preparation of User Stories for the next iteration or Release is the definition of Acceptance Criteria which validate the User Stories. The Acceptance Criteria determine when the User Story is completed.

Because of its importance and wide-spread usage, we will offer a detailed description and guidelines for creating User Stories in the next section.

Business Rules

"Business Rules" is a concept that spans both, traditional and Agile methodologies. There is a whole science behind Business Rules. The Business Rules approach decouples the business logic from processes and applications. This book will not go into much depth on this approach, but you will learn techniques to discover and write Business Rules when we explore how to write effective requirements. For now, just a brief overview.

Business Rules are statements that express how the organization wants to function. They can affect multiple applications and should be maintained independently to allow authorized users to change them as needed. Any change to a an externally stored Business Rule should immediately change all affected apps. For example, a good Business Rule might be:

> **We will offer a 10% discount to customers living within 100 miles of our store.**

Management could decide to adjust the discount amount as an incentive to attract customers or decrease the radius to limit losses. If they do, the change should not cause application updates. Whether you create an app that deals with invoicing or one that deals with marketing, you need to be aware of all Business Rules and take them into account.

Constraints

Constraints are absolute limits imposed from the outside environment on the application or a part of it. True Constraints are a universal form of requirement, meaning they are just as legitimate for Agile and Lean projects as they are for traditional or Waterfall methodologies.

Constraints are a type of Non-Functional Requirement. There are distinct types of Constraints. For example, there are legal Constraints; there are environmental Constraints; there are human or people Constraints based upon the talents and the skill levels of the end users, and so on.

The key thing about a Constraint is that no one on the Lean and Agile Team has the authority to change it. Regardless how the business solution evolves, it is essential to ensure that no Constraints are violated. We will have much more on Constraints in the chapter on Non-Functional Requirements.

Use Cases

A Use Case is another construct or concept that spans traditional and Agile/Lean environments.

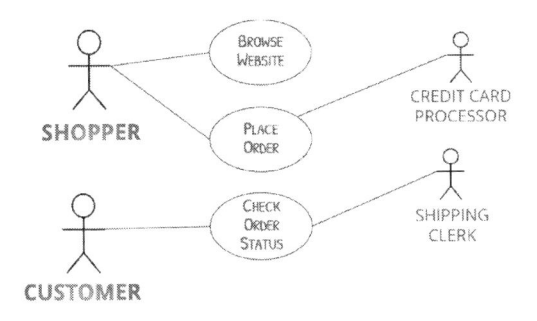

```
       BROWSE
       WEBSITE
  SHOPPER        CREDIT CARD
        PLACE   PROCESSOR
        ORDER

        CHECK
        ORDER   SHIPPING
        STATUS  CLERK
  CUSTOMER
```

Use Cases that show a bird's eye view are called **Business Use Cases** or conceptual Use Cases. They describe a Use Case in technology-independent forms from the user's point of view. For example,

---

Plan vacations, rent movies, organize events

Use Cases that developers create are often referred to as System Use Cases. They are at a much lower level showing detailed interactions of end users with the system or even interactions of one function with another.

Enter customers, change orders, calculate costs

The key word here is "interaction". Use Cases show interactions between an application and someone or something that is external to it. This external entity is an Actor in Use Case parlance.

A Use Case Diagram and textual Use Case Specifications show how people and/or other applications interact with the product under development.

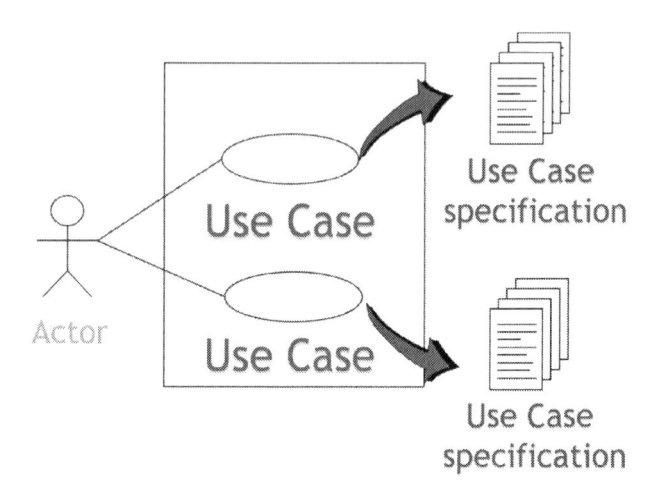

There is a stark difference in creating Use Cases for traditional vs Lean/Agile environments. In a traditional (i.e. Waterfall) development environment, there is a lot of waste when Use Cases are developed for the entire system upfront. Lean/Agile Use Cases take a different approach. Much more on that later in this book.

Scenarios, Scenario Outlines, and Examples

Scenarios and Scenario Outlines with Examples are the ultimate requirements in a Lean and Agile universe. They show the developer what the business needs (requirement) and at the same time, allow the developer and the Stakeholder to validate whether the software does it correctly.

As we already mentioned, testing is a critical success factor for any Lean or Agile development effort. Scenarios, Scenario Outlines, and Examples are the communication tools for business and technical teams. They are part of Acceptance Test Driven Design/Development (ATDD) or Behavior Driven Design/Development (BDD).

Both approaches are based on the idea that it is better to develop Acceptance Tests first instead of creating vague requirements and then trying to extrapolate the right tests. If you have the Acceptance Test first, all developers need to do is write the code that will pass the test. This is a very efficient and effective way of delivering or developing software.

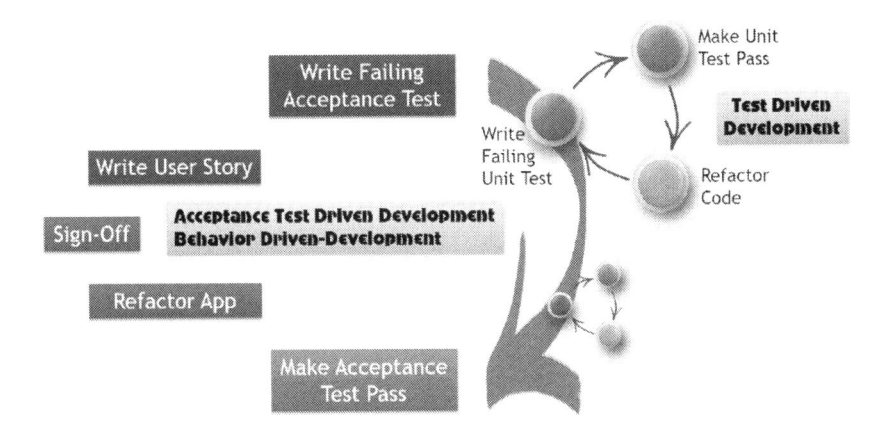

A critical success factor for ATDD and BDD is the use of automated testing tools. One of the most popular ones is Cucumber which understands a language called Gherkin that uses Given-When-Then (GWT) statements. Expressing requirements in the form of GWT statements gives developers a level of detail they could never get out of a traditional textual requirement statement.

This was a brief summary of terms you will encounter in a Lean and Agile world. Features, User Stories, Business Rules, Constraints, Use Cases, Scenarios, Scenario Outlines, and Examples are the new forms of expressing software or IT requirements.

We will explain all of them in detail throughout this book and give you step by step instructions how to discover, analyze and validate **textual** Lean/Agile requirements. Although there are requirements that are of necessity expressed in models and diagrams, those **are not covered** in this book.

User Stories Are Stakeholder Requirements

Agile initiatives often use User Stories, which act as the starting point for further refinement in terms of requirements elaboration, design, risks, and costs. The term "User Story" originated in a methodology called XP (Extreme Programming) where the developers came up with the idea that they needed to know what users expected the application to do **before** developers started to code. What a novel concept!

User Stories express something the business community MIGHT want assuming IT can deliver it in a reasonable timeframe. The emphasis, however, is on simplicity. The User Story just expresses what one role in the business community needs from IT.

A Product Owner works with developers to analyze and prioritize the business need when the time is right (which usually means shortly before the developers are ready to write code for an upcoming Release).

The Product Owner, developers and other stakeholders discuss selected User Stories in detail with the author of each User Story, analyze them, identify Acceptance Criteria, and only stop when consensus is reached. Then the developers can start writing code.

A related concept associated with User Stories is the Epic. Epics are larger bodies of work that hide many User Stories. There is no exact limit to when User Stories become Epics. They help teams create hierarchy and structure. Epics typically take more than one or two Sprints to develop. They are broad in scope, short on details, and will be split into multiple, smaller User Stories before the team can work on them.

The User Story Paradigm

Primarily, a User Story expresses a need from the perspective of a single user, meaning from the point of view of someone who will use the product or the application. That individual expresses the User Story from the perspective of his/her role or set of responsibilities. Each User Story focuses on the outcome of a **single** interaction between a "user" and the application under development.

A User Story is justified by the value it provides and is expressed from the perspective of the person who has the need. The business value must express why this particular User Story is needed to give IT a fighting chance at prioritizing and scheduling it.

The main purpose of the User Story is to replace documentation with dialogue. User Stories shift the focus from writing about requirements to talking about them. We no longer document requirements to the lowest level of detail. They now serve as a reminder to collaborate about the topic of the User Story. The documentation is secondary to the collaboration. This is a fundamental shift in paradigm.

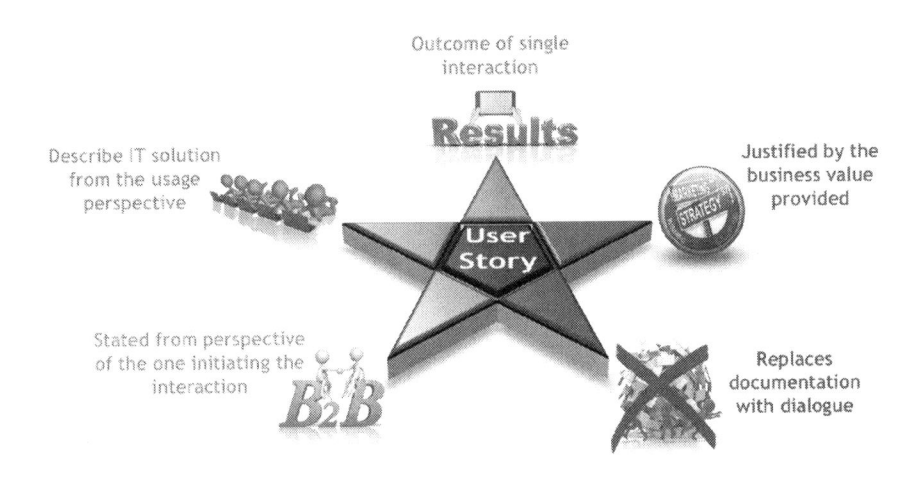

User Stories are a phenomenal new concept because they focus on something we have been trying to achieve for many years in this industry - the business and technical teams working together to create solutions. This approach will get us higher quality digital solutions in a shorter time.

User Stories Define Business Outcomes

Well-written User Stories provide a solid basis for communication and collaboration — focusing on what matters most to **the user**. They help achieve cross-team clarity on what to build, for whom, and why.

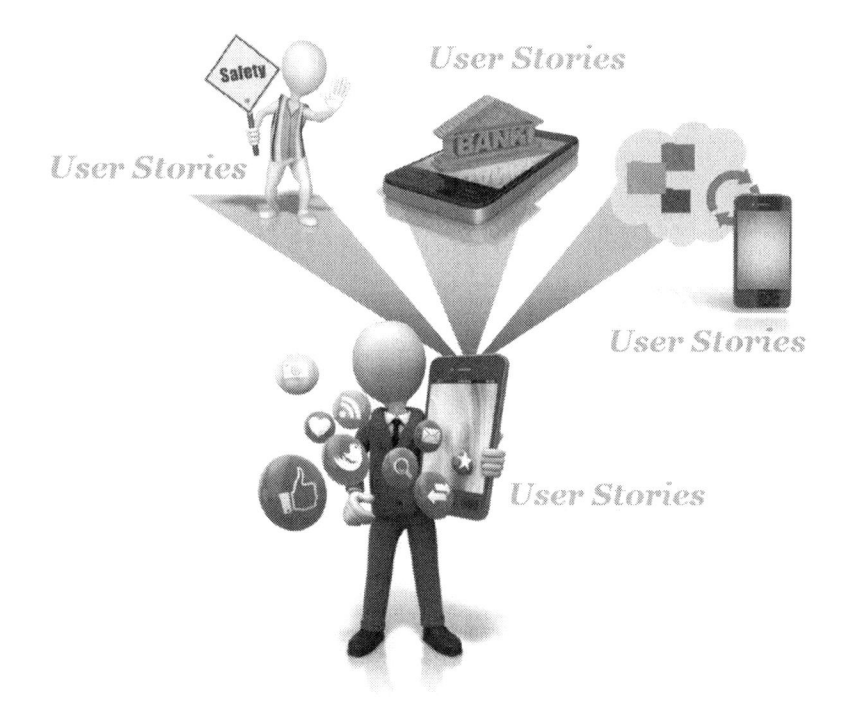

Requirements in User Story format are key elements for Lean, Agile, **and** traditional software development. It is a simple name for a complex idea.

The format of a User Story is straightforward and writing them is easy. But writing great ones might be a bit tricky. Later in the chapter, we will introduce you to several techniques that will make this job a lot easier.

First, however, we will provide you with guidance on how to express things in the User Story format and explain why these guidelines are important.

A Well-Formed User Story Template

When writing a User Story, the first thing you want to focus on is what the end-user is doing (role-focused) or getting out of the story (goal-focused). The role-focused format is more widely spread so we will start there.

User Stories are often expressed in a simple sentence, structured as follows:

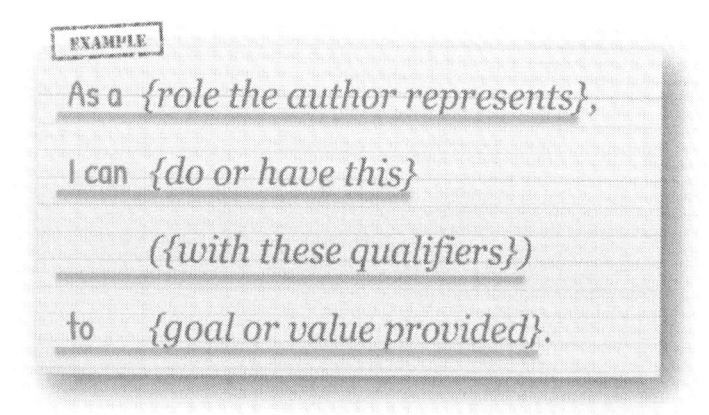

> **EXAMPLE**
>
> As a {role the author represents},
>
> I can {do or have this}
>
> ({with these qualifiers})
>
> to {goal or value provided}.

Who requests something? (role)

A role-focused User Story starts off with the word "As a...", for example, "As a web site visitor" or "As a Sales Manager". Who will be using this? We do not want a job title here, we want the persona of the person, the role this person plays in the story.

What does the requester want? (Function)

It is followed by, "I can...". There are others who recommend "I will be able to"; that seems too wordy. We like to keep it as short as possible. The key point is that you are describing their intent — not the Features they use. What is it they are trying to do? This can be something physical like "I can ship the product...". It also can be new data or knowledge that the Persona needs, like "... I can get a monthly report of customer complaints...".

In addition, you can add **qualifiers** here. Anything that will restrict or clarify exactly how the Persona needs to have or know something.

Why is this Function important? (Business Value)

The "to..." phrase in the role-focused User Story gives you the business value. What is the overall benefit? What is the big problem that needs solving? Product Owners and Business Analysts need answers to these questions to evaluate how the Persona's need fits into the bigger picture. The business value will help the end-users and the technical teams have a better conversation. If the developers understand the "Why" or business value of a User Story, they can create better software solutions.

To finish our example,

"As a Sales Manager,
I can get a monthly report of customer complaints
to review the performance of my Sales Reps."

If there are multiple end users or personas, you should make multiple User Stories. Since these start with the role, we refer to them as "role-focused" User Stories. The only difference to the goal-focused User Story is that it starts off with the business value or goal that this Story will deliver.

If we expressed the example we used with the role-focused User Story and expressed it as golf-focused User Story, it would read:

> **"To review the performance of their Sales Reps,
> Sales Managers
> can get a monthly report of customer complaints."**

As you can see, there is not much difference between the role-focused and the goal-focused User Story. One significant difference is that the role is no longer a single Persona. That can inspire the author to consider other people in the organization doing the same thing and make sure the goal is common to all.

In dealing with difficult User Stories, we have found that asking people to express User Stories in both formats can help them write a complete User Story. Each perspective made them look at the Story differently and looking at it from a role- **and** goal-focused perspective allowed them to minimize missing aspects.

Each format addresses the critical parts of a User Story which is the WHO, the WHAT, and the WHY or business value. You can use the WHY to discover more User Stories. Ask yourself, who else in the organization would get value out of this User Story? With this question, you can find more roles and it might be that those roles need something different.

You do not have to follow a strict pattern like, "As…, I can…, to…" or "To …, roles can …". We have worked with companies that write simple sentences and call them User Stories. Other organizations still use the term "requirements". However, there is one significant difference.

> **A requirement in today's world
> MUST include WHO, WHAT and WHY.**

INVEST in Your User Stories

As you saw in the previous section, the basic structure of a User Story is simple. It seems quite easy to write User Stories once you know that format. However, writing **good** User Stories can be hard.

Fortunately, Bill Wake, creator of the INVEST model, supplies guidance on creating effective User Stories. You can use this nifty mnemonic to guide you in the creation of your User Stories. It is a tool for remembering six characteristics that good User Stories have.

Independent
Negotiable
Valuable
Estimateable
Small
Testable

Independent

The "I" stands for Independent, meaning each User Story should be self-contained to avoid dependencies on other User Stories. This does not mean that Stories cannot have prerequisites. However, it should be possible for a developer to code the Story, test it, and release it into production without having to depend on other Users Stories working first. Obviously, this should be taken with a grain of salt, but every User Story should be as independent as possible.

A good litmus test for this principle is to ask yourself, "If you drastically alter this User Story, would any of the others be invalidated?". If you do find that your User Stories are dependent upon one another, combine them into larger Stories or isolate the dependence into its own User Story.

Negotiable

The N stands for Negotiable. This is a key criterion in Lean and Agile development environments. One of the reasons that Agilists do not like the term "requirements" is because the word implies or, at least suggests, that it is "required" while a User Story is negotiable.

As we mentioned in the introduction to the Lean and Agile world, supporting business agility is one of the big drivers for the Agile movement allowing and even encouraging changing requirements for digital solutions. There is no promise that a User Story in the Backlog will ever be implemented as is. User Stories can always be changed or rewritten up until the point of coding. Once the team has started coding a story, change becomes expensive and should be avoided.

For example, a Product Owner might negotiate the scope and Qualities of a User Story on the fly because of pressing business needs. To support this, your User Stories should never be so detailed or restrictive that they prevent your team from arriving at the best solution. Capture the intentions but leave enough room for team discussion.

Valuable

V stands for Valuable. When we introduced the User Story construct earlier, we talked about the business value that must be part of every User Story. User Stories always must deliver on the value that the role in the User Story needs. Since we treated this topic earlier, we will not dwell on it.

Estimable

Good User Stories are also estimable. This is a major challenge because a User Story should be written from the business perspective whereas estimating the size of a Story is something that the developers need to do. They must estimate how much time it will take to develop the code for this User Story.

This means, that every User Story must have enough information to make a reasonable estimate of the Story's complexity. However, when we talked about "Negotiable", we learned that a Story should not have too much detail as to restrict the developers in solution finding or restrict the business community from changing the Story.

This is where you need to find a good balance. Write your User Story with just enough detail for the team to understand what they are building and why. Err on the side of not enough information. If the Agile team cannot estimate a User Story effort during Release Planning, they will talk to the Product Owner or author until they can.

Small

Good User Stories are small. They hold just enough information to get a software engineer started. Small in this context means it is at a size that a developer can code within a few days or a single Sprint at the most. It should never take more than two weeks to complete the coding.

When a User Story is too large, it must be broken down into smaller Stories. This process is called User Story splitting and we will present several techniques for doing that in a later chapter.

Testable

The T stands for Testable. In Lean/Agile approaches, we have finally recognized that Test Scenarios or Acceptance Criteria **ARE** the real requirements that IT needs.

Scenario languages like Gherkin express the requirements in a manner that developers can more easily understand. Creating User Story Acceptance Criteria (whether in the form of Scenarios or any other form) **before writing the code** is critical for the success of Agile/Lean undertakings.

Because of its importance in Lean and Agile environments, we have dedicated an entire chapter to the new testing paradigm. We will introduce you to the new concepts of Acceptance Test Driven Development (ATDD) or Behavior Driven Development (BDD) and show you how to create Scenarios and Scenario Outlines with Examples.

For every User Story you should always ask yourself, "How can I test this Story to make sure that I get what I want?".

User Stories Define the Business Need

Good Users Stories focus on WHAT not HOW, meaning they avoid preconceived solutions. By avoiding preconceived solutions, we are giving the developers the opportunity to find the best technology for the business need. An effective User Story always allows for multiple solutions to realize the Story.

Focus on the Business Value

To illustrate this point, here is a User Story that deals with booking air travel for one of our instructors. She or he needs to get to the location where the class they are teaching. We could write,

As a traveler, I can book a flight leaving the day before the class starts to be on time for the class.

That sounds like a good User Story. However, the instructor is forced to fly. There is no other possibility.

What happens if the seminar is just a few miles away and flying is not the best choice? The instructor could use a rental car or, if the location is close, take an Uber. What about someone like the authors of this book who like to travel to the customer site in a motorhome. In both instances, the User Story would fall apart.

We want to express the User Story in a manner that eliminates HOW the instructor gets to the location. Flying is a preconceived solution.

Here is an example how you could express this User Story to avoid the preconceived notion of flying.

As a traveler, I can be at the customer site at the designated time on the morning of the first day to begin the class on time.

This is much better. As you can see, this User Story fits with all scenarios that we described. Whether the class happens in the instructor's hometown or on a different planet, the instructor can hold the class.

The key is focusing on the business outcome that you need to achieve and **not** on how developers should program it. This is what it means to express the WHAT not the HOW!

Let us look at another example. If I said something like,

> **As an earth citizen,
> I can install windmills to save the planet.**

That certainly follows all rules for User Story structures. However, it implies that the only way the earth citizen would be satisfied is if the planet were populated with windmills to generate the energy that we need. This makes it a preconceived solution. It tells us HOW we need to solve our energy problems.

**WE NEED WINDMILLS
(THIS EXCLUDES OTHER OPTIONS)**

Windmills are not without a downside: they have their own problems. For instance, windmills kill birds. If there are migratory birds in the area, as they go through these running windmills, several of them will probably die.

There might be better solutions for saving the planet. How about solar or nuclear energy? The decision should be left to the solution developers. After all, their job is to find the best solution.

How can you express this User Story better? You want to save energy, right? So how about,

> **As an earth citizen,
> I can conserve energy to save the planet.**

Or, if you are writing a User Story about heating options, you should be more specific, like,

> **As an earth citizen,
> I can use energy efficient heating devices
> to save the planet.**

Ignore Technology as Much as Possible

A User Story should never stipulate a specific technology because technology is the HOW and not the WHAT. Limits to your technology like, "we have to use platform x or y" are constraining requirements and not User Stories.

For example,

> **As an applicant, I can select my state from a drop-down menu of abbreviations to avoid entering an invalid state.**

This sounds like a reasonable User Story; but the idea of a drop-down menu is not the only way of solving this problem. It is a limiting technology. Even if it is the technology of the day, there might be better ways of doing it. For instance, many modern websites allow visitors to enter their zip code first to enable the app to pre-populate the city and state.

Her is a rewrite that does not include any HOW instructions.

> **As an applicant, I can submit a valid state abbreviation to ensure an accurate quote for insurance coverage.**

This leaves it up to the developers to figure out how they will ensure that the state abbreviation is valid.

Avoiding the "How-to" Trap

To summarize, you can apply three different trains of thought to avoid the "how-to" creeping into your User Stories.

1. Avoid preconceived solutions
2. Focus on the business value not on how to achieve it
3. Express business outcome regardless of technology

This allows software engineers to find the perfect solution to your business needs. In our experience, these three simple ideas will help you focus your User Stories on what the business community needs and wants without trying to tell IT how to do their job. That is a lot more effective.

User Stories Are Not Just for End-Users

Calling them User Stories is a slight misnomer because any Stakeholder can and should write a Story from his or her perspective even if he or she does not use the system. Here are a few examples:

> **As a Business Rules Administrator,**
> I can modify mortgage conditions to allow the organization to adapt to changing market conditions.

This User Story is legit from the Business Rules Administrator perspective which is not an end-user of the product but certainly a Stakeholder.

> **As the CashForecaster App,**
> I need access to the bank's transactions, so I can compare my projections to actuals.

This User Story is from the perspective of another system. The CashForecaster app is a different application. It might play a role if there is the need for an API or information interchange between these applications.

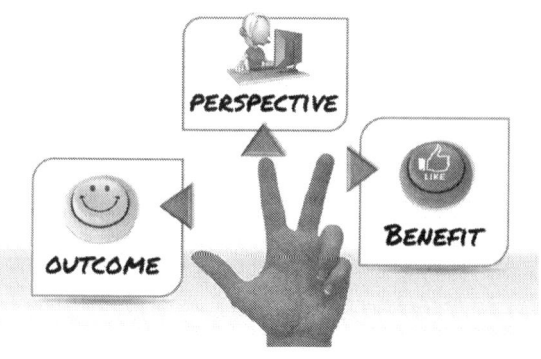

As Webmaster,
I can modify the bandwidth to accommodate surges in usage during peak season.

Here the Stakeholder ("user") is a webmaster making sure that the performance of the website is up to par. And finally,

As Database Administrator,
I can recognize when thrashing negatively impacts performance, so I can redistribute the tables.

As you can see, User Stories are not just for the end-user. Any Stakeholder has a right and an obligation to write User Stories from their perspective. This ensures that the developers have a more complete picture before they start developing each individual User Story.

Now it is time to practice your new-found knowledge.

Exercise: First-Cut User Stories

This exercise allows you to write your own role-focused and goal-focused User Stories.

Instructions:

Based on the Blue Pacific Air Vision Statement, write 3 role-focused and 3 goal-focused User Stories.

Blue Pacific Air Vision Statement

BP Air would like to expand its customer service from traditional phone and in-person to create a customer web site. This expansion would allow customers to manage aspects of their travel from reserving a flight to baggage retrieval at their final destination.

Services include booking flights, making changes to existing flights, checking-in and printing boarding passes. As an added service, we would like to help our customers book lodging and ground transportation from our secure internet site.

Our goals for the website are to:

- ⇨ lower Customer Service inbound calls (or at least shorten the calls)
- ⇨ increase customer Check-in efficiency
- ⇨ improve overall customer satisfaction
- ⇨ reduce the current cost of Reservations sales
- ⇨ increase Customer Retention by making it easy for customers to sign up for our rewards program online

This project will encompass all work related to developing and provisioning the online reservation "booking" system for BP Air customers. However, it cannot involve any modifications or updates to the current airline database system. Also, it must interact with the database modernization project team to ensure compatibility.

For flights booked online, Finance wants immediate full payment (or at least a 20% deposit) to cover all applicable taxes and service charges imposed by government, governmental agencies, airports, etc.

Assignment 1:

Based on the Vision Statement, write 3 **role**-focused User Stories.

Assignment 2:

Based on the Vision Statement, write 3 **goal**-focused User Stories.

Answer Assignment 1: Write 3 role-focused User Stories.

Three possible **role-focused** User Stories are:

- ☑ As a visitor, I can view all flights available for my travel date and destination to select the best option.

- ☑ As a traveler, I can print my boarding pass before I travel to the airport to reduce the time I need to check-in.

- ☑ As a traveler, I can change my itinerary to accommodate changes in my schedule.

If you found others, kudos! There are several User Story candidates that can be extrapolated from the Vision Statement. The key to a well-written **role-focused** User Story is that it follows the structure "As a {ROLE}, I can {do or know something} {with appropriate qualifiers} to {achieve a value or goal}." If your answers follow that format, they are correct.

Answer Assignment 2: Write 3 goal-focused User Stories.

Three possible **goal-focused** User Stories are:

- ☑ To expand our customer base, visitors can book flights directly on our website.

- ☑ To help our customers, travelers on BP Air can book lodging for their destination on our website.

- ☑ To increase customer retention, customers can register for our rewards program online.

As with the role-focused User Story, there are several User Story candidates that can be derived from the Vision Statement. The key to a well-written **goal-oriented** User Story is that it should follow the structure: **To** achieve {a value or a goal}, {**ROLES**} **can** {do or know something } {with appropriate qualifications}. If your answers follow this format, they are correct.

II. Requirements Elicitation and Backlog Seeding

As mentioned in an earlier chapter, requirements in a traditional development environment are documented in a Business Requirements Document (BRD), while requirements in a Lean and Agile environment fill the Product Backlog.

In this chapter we will look at different methods for capturing and collecting requirements. You can use the techniques presented to create a BRD or to seed a Product Backlog.

Requirements elicitation, requirements gathering, or User Story discovery are different terms for the same activity. The results of each are business needs and wants expressed at a level of detail that allow IT to plan, prepare, and scope change initiatives.

Unfortunately, you can rarely look up the technological needs of a company in advance. Most business or technical requirements are not documented anywhere. They exist only in the minds of stakeholders and in feedback that has yet to be gathered from end users.

Therefore, requirements or User Stories must be **elicited** to create a BRD or fill a Product Backlog. That is where the term "Requirements Elicitation" originated. We elicit needs and wants from Subject Matter Experts, from End Users, from Product Owners, and from other Stakeholders, i.e. anybody who has a legitimate right to express a business need or want. This applies to Agile and Lean approaches as well as to the Waterfall approach.

Eliciting can be tricky. Often the business world does not know its detailed business needs or cannot express them in a way that gives software developers the understanding they need to create the digital solution.

3-Amigo sessions, Specification Workshops, User Story Workshops or Requirements Workshops are effective techniques to obtain business or stakeholder requirements. The outcomes of these types of get-togethers can be User Stories, Feature Lists, Use Cases, simple textual requirements or even Process and Data Models.

Topics Covered in this Chapter

The best technique for capturing your level of uncertainty and tracking progress is a "Question File". What do you need to know that you do not know? What answers do you already have? What assumptions do you have to make to keep everything going? The Question File is by far one of the most widely implemented techniques that students of our instructor-led classes mention in evaluation forms.

Before you can elicit requirements or User Stories from anyone, you need to know whom to ask. You need to discover the Stakeholders of your initiative. A Stakeholder is anybody that has a vested interest in the product. The Stakeholder is someone who has a right to say something about what the product does or how it does it.

One of the major challenges in any change initiative is recognizing **all** involved Stakeholders. If you are implementing a new website, who in the organization should you approach? One section in this chapter covers techniques for Stakeholder Identification or Stakeholder Analysis.

Furthermore, we introduce you to a new concept called Cynefin (pronounced kuh-ne-fin). It is a decision-support framework that can increase the probability of making the right decision in any situation. Cynefin forces you to consider the inherent uncertainty of a situation and recommends certain actions depending on the degree of your uncertainty.

Next, we will introduce a technique for discovering requirements by analyzing business problems. Problem Analysis is a great technique that encourages people to think outside the box. It reveals requirements that stakeholders often do not know they have because they are busy with day-to-day operations. Problem Analysis helps them figure out how to find the critical business needs for their domain.

In a Lean environment, business communication must be fast and flexible. The major advantage of all Lean and Agile philosophies is speed and agility. Communication between technical and business-side teams are at the heart of the Lean development approaches. We will show you how to ensure effective communication in your requirements elicitation efforts.

Any conversation or meeting between different functional groups or areas like IT and the business community has a higher chance of success if the meeting is run efficiently and effectively. To accomplish this, you need to prepare for the meeting, know how to conduct the meeting effectively, and recognize that it is not over when it is over. An effective follow-up is essential to a successful meeting.

You will learn tips, techniques, and tricks on how to prepare, plan, conduct, and follow-up any meeting from casual conversations to formal Requirements Discovery (Elicitation) or User Story Workshops. We also present guidelines on dealing with inevitable issues concerning miscommunication.

Common Elicitation Techniques

Start with Open-ended Questions

As "the one wearing the business analysis hat", meaning the person who must elicit requirements, you always are searching for ways to help people discover their own requirements. You are trying to help them figure out what they really want or need. If you help your end-users and other Stakeholders think about the future and how things could be, you are on your way to good requirements. The simplest elicitation technique to get started is to ask questions!

At the start of a conversation ask them,

"What is wrong with the way things work today?"

Your Stakeholders may not have a problem personally, but their manager or boss wants things done quicker or better. It does not matter where the problem originates, any problem or issue is a legitimate answer to that question.

The next question to ask is,

"What is right about the way things work today?"

You also want to capture requirements that your stakeholders would like to keep. What are they doing today that they must or want to do similarly in the future?

The next question is,

"What is missing from the current solution?"

What are the things that you cannot do currently? With this question, you are fishing for opportunities of how you could improve their life.

These are good questions for people who look at the world as a "half empty glass". For the other half, the "glass half full" folks, you should pose the question,

"How can we make things better for you?"

These are fundamental questions and we use them on every project or initiative. Ask them during any type of conversation and jot down your answers. You can use these same answers as memory ticklers for other conversations. They definitively will form the basis for requirements analysis.

Analyze Documents

Stakeholders typically have real jobs, meaning they have a limited amount of time available to answer your question. Leverage the time they grant you by being prepared.

For example, you might start by analyzing documents or other sources to minimize the questions your Stakeholders must answer. The main purpose of document analysis is to learn as much as you can and generate questions for stakeholders. However, you might also find answers to many of your questions hidden in documentation.

Because documentation ages rapidly, do not assume that everything you read is correct or current. Use your document analysis mostly as a source for questions. Business processes and practices evolve and the only way to find out how they are currently carried out is to involve the people who are doing it now.

You also could work with the helpdesk to find out what kind of problems they dealt with in the past or what opportunities for improvement they can see. Ask them for their wish list.

At this stage, requirements in any flavor express business issues the business community needs to solve or opportunities to pursue. These questions will get you started.

Use Models and Examples

However, sometimes words are just not enough to communicate effectively. That is when you need to pull another business analysis technique out of your bag. Visual models, such as process or data models represent workflow or information usage. They will help the Subject Matter Expert (SME) recognize bottlenecks and problem areas to find requirements that address those issues.

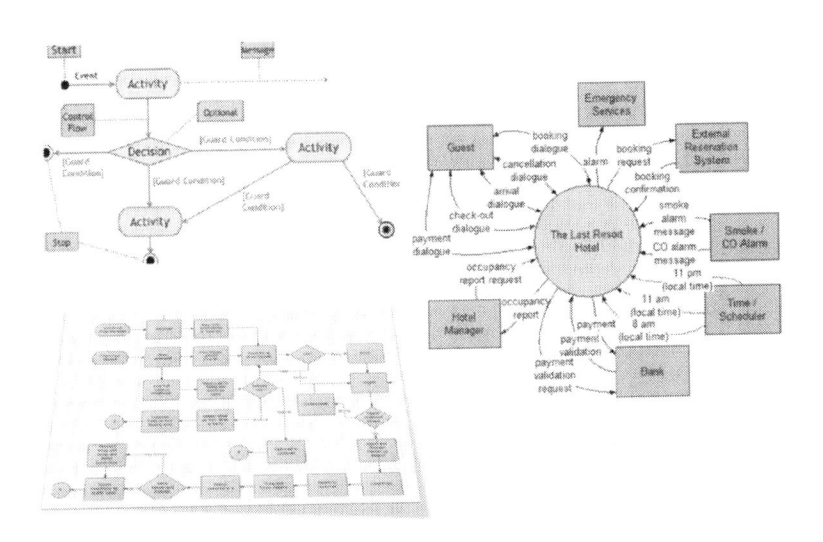

The visual **models** help a good analyst better understand why people are doing what they are doing, and how important it is to keep a certain workflow. Many times, when we have helped SME's visualize their workflow, they found areas they could improve by simply changing the sequence of process steps or by changing how they did things.

The more modeling conventions like BPMN process diagrams, activity diagrams and data flow diagrams that you know, the better you are able to quickly form a picture that helps everyone focus on specific aspects of a process. To support Lean and Agile principles, keep your models simple. Make sure that the model expresses the essence of what you want to communicate and does not go beyond that.

Examples are another great tool for expressing a requirement. Anytime we have a conversation with a SME about their work, we highly encourage them to bring examples that we can walk through. Examples supply context that augment the conversation and lead to more effective communication. They at once move the discussion from the abstract to the concrete.

Track Your Progress with a Question File

Has your supervisor or boss ever asked you how far you have progressed in defining the User Stories or Business Requirements for the new initiative and how much work you have left? Has anyone ever asked, "When will you be done with the analysis?"

If you have previously conducted a requirements analysis or defined User Stories for a digital solution, you know that this question is difficult to answer satisfactorily, especially in the early stages.

Nevertheless, it is important for both your supervisor and you to have that information. If you are not sure how much work you still have to do to meet all the requirements, this can be very unsettling.

We will familiarize you with a simple technique that will help you to answer this question in a more qualified way. It is based on the aforementioned "Question File".

What Is a Question File?

A question file is a place that you keep track of things that you know you know and things you know you do not know. As you can see below, our Question File only has five columns. Each of the columns has a specific purpose and adds value to the process.

Q-Date	Question	Who	Answer	A-Date
12/3	What is the average age of human beings in the wild?	Genome Project Leader	35 Years	1/4
12/5	Will manmade devices exceed the speed of light in our lifetime?	Stephen Hawking		
12/7	Is there intelligent life on other planets?	???		
12/19	What's wrong with my golf swing?	Tiger Woods		
1/1	When will quantum computers be commercially available?	Elon Musk		

The "Question" column is where you capture what you know you do not know. Express the question in a manner that an answer from the person with the knowledge and authority can easily be a new requirement, a new fact, a new Feature, a new User Story, a new Test Scenario, et cetera. Capture anything you need for the success of your project or product.

In the Q-Date column, jot down the date when the question came up to create an instant history.

Next, for every question, consider which of your Stakeholders, can give you a qualified answer. You are looking for the individual who has the knowledge AND the authority to answer the question because either alone is never enough. Document this name in the "Who" column.

Whoever you named in the "Who" column can change as your knowledge evolves. This column is very volatile.

For example, you might put Bill from Accounting in the "Who" column because you think he would be the one to ask. When you talk to Bill, you realize that he does not know the answer, but tells you to talk to Nancy in Marketing. You change the "Who" column to Nancy and she might send you to her boss, Caroline, and so on.

It seems to be a waste of time, but in reality, there is nothing wrong with that. You are like a detective on a mission and this is a big step forward in your hunt for requirements or User Stories.

The next column is the "Answer" column. Obviously, that is where you capture the new knowledge and you should add the date that you received the answer to the A-Date column.

Using the Question File

If you have these five columns in a simple table, you can do magic.

1. **Plan Meetings**

For example, you can sort your table on the WHO column. When you have several questions for the same individual, or even a specific group of people, you can use those questions to prepare and schedule a meeting or 3-Amigo Conversation to get the answers you need.

2. **Document Assumptions**

The other column that we use a lot is the "Answer" column. For example, if you have not been able to get an answer to your question by the time you need it, you will be forced to make an assumption. Write the word "ASSUMED" in this column and then document whatever you feel is the most realistic or most reasonable assumption that you can make for this question.

To be fair and minimize wasted work, we suggest notifying the person in the "Who" column about your assumption. Give her or him a reasonable but limited timeframe to respond before you do any further work based on the assumption. If they do respond and confirm your assumption, remove the word "ASSUMED" and add the date you got the answer. If they respond with a correction, that becomes your answer.

3. **Measure Progress**

Once you have a sizeable number of questions in the file, this simple tool gives you insight into your progress that you can share with your manager. For instance, if you are wondering how much work you have left to do, here is a simple method.

$$(\#ofQ - \#OpenQ) / \#ofQ = Completion\%$$

- ☑ Count the total number of questions (#ofQ) in your file
- ☑ Count all empty cells in the "Answer" column. These are open questions (#OpenQ).
- ☑ Drag the number of open questions (#OpenQ) from the total number (#ofQ).
- ☑ Divide the result by the total number of questions (#ofQ).

Voila, you now have a clearer idea of how much work you have left to do, expressed as a percentage of the total workload.

For example, if you have a total of 100 questions and 30 of them have no answer or acceptance, you can be 70% sure that you have the information you need to proceed.

$$(\#ofQ - \#OpenQ) / \#ofQ = Completion\%$$
$$\text{For example: } (100 - 30) / 100 = 70\%$$

4. Measure Priority and Importance

If you want to know what priority the involved stakeholders attach to your project,

- ☑ count the "assumptions" (#Assu) and the total number of questions (#ofQ).
- ☑ Divide the number of "assumptions" (#Assu) by the total number of questions (#ofQ) and
- ☑ Multiply the result by 100.

The resulting percentage tells you how important this product or project is for the stakeholders involved. It is obvious that the lower this figure is, the less trust you should have.

For example, if you have 120 questions and 40 of them are ASSUMED, simple math shows that 33% of your "answers" are ASSUMED.

$$(\#ofQ - \#Assu) / \#ofQ = Confidence\%$$
$$\text{For example, } (40/120) * 100 = 33\%$$

Any work you do based on your current knowledge has a 33% chance of being wasted. What you do is up to you and depends on your willingness to take risks.

For the mathematically inclined, there are also other formulas that can help you (e.g., comparing the number of answered questions to the number of ASSUMED). This kind of information will enable better go-no go decisions. You could also add a column indicating the magnitude of each question and use that value to adjust the formulas mentioned above.

5. Recognize the Importance of Corporate Policy

There is one more magic trick. Look at the date somebody gave you an answer and compare it to the date you thought of that question. Calculate the duration between them. A long duration is a red flag that this initiative has low the priority for the individual in the "Who" column.

If the answer comes back to you very quickly, it shows that this initiative, product, or project is of high interest to the person in the "Who" column. This gives you a sense of the political environment around this work.

The Question File is a great tool for preparing conversations and gives you valuable indicators of how likely the product or project is to succeed. It is amazing how much you can extrapolate when you are tracking the progress of your analysis efforts towards completion.

If you have a current project or are starting a new one, try this simple technique. It might just be the most important contribution you can make this early in the project.

Identifying Stakeholders

In any project (but especially in an Agile or Lean initiative), finding the **right** Stakeholders is a critical success factor for achieving fast and accurate results. Missing a Stakeholder is one of the primary reasons that IT initiatives fail. Furthermore, it is important that you have all Stakeholders represented BEFORE you start to develop the solution.

So, who are they and how can you find them - where are they hiding?

Basic Stakeholder Identification

If you are looking for Stakeholders start with the end game, namely the **solution**. Ask yourself,

- ⇨ Who is using the product or the application?
- ⇨ Who else is interested in the new digital solution?
- ⇨ Who wants the project to succeed?
- ⇨ Who is affected positively or negatively by the product?
- ⇨ Who can influence the product's success?
- ⇨ Who is affected by manual components of the solution?

Once you have identified the Stakeholders and those who interact directly with the application, take a look at the company org chart. Try to find out if there are other people around these Stakeholders who are not using the application but may need to get data from the application or change the way they work. It is important that you also record their input.

Also, try to think about **anyone else in your organization** who might influence the solution. Remember, a Stakeholder is anyone who can affect or is affected by the application or any of its pieces. This can involve the manual components as well as the automated system. Look at the whole organization and try to find out who else might be interested in this product or who has a personal stake in its success.

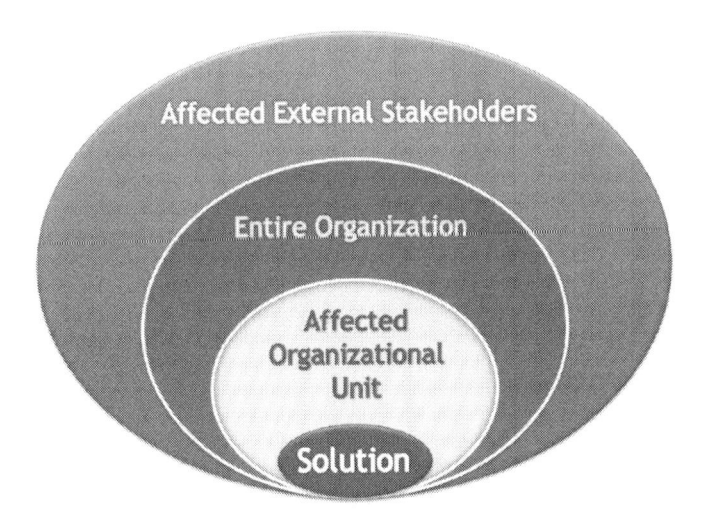

Finally, identify any Stakeholders who are **external** to your organization but might be interested or might have something to say about the initiative or the product.

Regulatory agencies are a good example. They have regulations that might affect you. For instance, if it is a product in the health insurance industry, somebody needs to represent HIPAA (Health Insurance Portability and Accountability Act), the laws that govern patient privacy. Most organizations pay attention to governing bodies that have the power to regulate them. It is a survival instinct.

Never neglect the most important external Stakeholders: your **customers**. The people that are going to buy your products or services. If changes to this product will affect them, you need to focus on their needs, wants, and how they like to do things or your whole initiative could be a bust.

Use an Org Chart to Identify Internal Stakeholders

To find Stakeholders within your organization or department, an org chart is a powerful and easy tool to use. Most organizations have them. If your organization does not have one that is current and up to date, create one. This only takes a couple of minutes, but it can be extremely revealing.

The org chart shows who manages each department, division, group, etc. To identify your Stakeholders, start on the very bottom of the org chart and ask yourself whether there is any way that the folks in that group could possibly be affected by or could have something to say about your project or product. If you think they might, put a check mark on them. That is a group that you must at least consider potential Stakeholders.

Once you have completed the lower level, follow the links upward. If there is anybody in charge of multiple lower levels that are affected, mark them in bold because they might be the ideal person to start talking to.

To summarize, use an org chart to find the people that might have something to say about your initiative, whether it be in the form of requirements, Constraints, or anything else that they have the authority to do. Like we said, it is a very quick and straightforward way to identify your Stakeholders.

Stakeholder Groups

In short, a Stakeholder is anyone who can affect the product or the project, anyone who has the authority to say something about it. That would include organizational groups like the Project Management Office (PMO) if you have one. Even in an Agile initiative, some organizations still have a Project Manager.

The Product Owner is obviously a Stakeholder, but there is quite often also a Product Manager who is the business representative for the product and may or may not be the Product Owner.

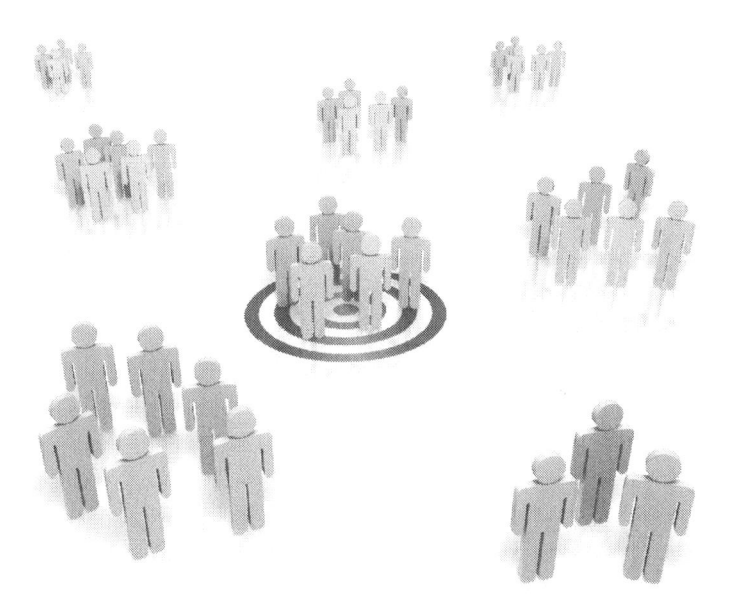

Creator

In addition, anybody working with you on the project is also a Stakeholder. They belong to a Stakeholder group that we call Creators. It includes developers, Business Analysts, solution architects, data architects, testers, the entire Lean or Agile team, and anybody else involved in creating or maintaining the software product.

End-User

When we talk about Stakeholders, many people think about End-Users. Yes, they are an especially important group - no question about it. They will be the ones whose life is affected most by the application. We obviously must be very aware of their needs and wants but we should not neglect all other perspectives.

External Stakeholders

As mentioned before, there are also Stakeholders within your organization such as Regulatory, Compliance, Auditors, Legal, Human Resources, and many others. There might also be external Stakeholders like agencies of the federal, state, or local governments that might have something to say about what your product does or does not do.

Former End Users

Another interesting group of potential Stakeholders is made up of **former** end-users. People that used to use your application but quit. If you are selling software, approaching former users and finding out why they quit can be extremely revealing.

This can introduce a flood of requirements or business needs and wants that your group or your organization never even thought of. These people left because they were unhappy, so whom better to ask for requirements? If you can get to them (which is non-trivial), we would highly recommend making them Stakeholders.

Exercise: Stakeholder Identification

This exercise gives you an opportunity to test your ability to identify initial project Stakeholders based on a vision statement.

Instructions:

Analyze the following vision statement (which you used in the previous exercise) to identify as many potential Stakeholders of the project as you can.

Blue Pacific Air Vision Statement

BP Air wants to expand its customer service from traditional telephone and personal service to a customer website. This expansion would enable customers to manage their travel from booking a flight to retrieving their luggage at their destination.

Services should include flight bookings, changes to existing flights, check-ins, and printing boarding passes. As an additional service, we would like to assist our customers in booking accommodation and ground transportation through our secure Internet platform.

Our business objectives are that this website will:

- → lower Customer Service inbound calls (or at least shorten the calls)
- → increase customer Check-in efficiency
- → improve overall customer satisfaction
- → reduce the current cost of Reservations sales
- → increase Customer Retention by making it easy for customers to sign up for our rewards program online

This project will encompass all work related to developing and provisioning the online reservation "booking" system for BP Air customers. However, it cannot involve any modifications or updates to the current airline database system. Also, it must interact with the database modernization project team to ensure compatibility.

For flights booked online, Finance wants immediate full payment (or at least a 20% deposit) to cover all applicable taxes and service charges imposed by government, governmental agencies, airports, etc..

Assignment:

Identify potential project Stakeholders from the Vision Statement.

Potential Answers: (Kudos if you found more!)

- ✓ Customer Service Reps
- ✓ BP Customers
- ✓ Baggage Handlers
- ✓ Hotels
- ✓ Car Rental Companies
- ✓ Service Attendants
- ✓ Reservationists???
- ✓ DB Modernization Team Rep
- ✓ Finance Department
- ✓ IT
- ✓ Rewards Program Rep

Using Cynefin to Deal with Uncertainty

One of the biggest problems facing any new undertaking is uncertainty. At the beginning of any new initiative, at best you have a faint idea of what it is supposed to accomplish.

If you have responsibility for the project or product, you should have a Vision Statement or some high-level goal or objective that the initiative should achieve. If you do not get that, you need to start there.

Everything else at that time is up in the air. In other words, the only thing you really have in abundance is uncertainty. The Italian Renaissance politician, Niccolo Machiavelli, expressed it very succinctly:

> *"There is nothing more difficult to take in hand,*
> *more perilous to conduct,*
> *or more uncertain in its success,*
> *than to take the lead in the introduction*
> *of a new order of things."*

I think any seasoned IT Project Manager in today's business world can relate!

When it comes to dealing with uncertainty, there is a new sheriff in town. It is a framework called Cynefin. The name itself is a Welsh word meaning something like "belonging to", or "habitat".

Cynefin is one of the most significant new concepts or tools for business analysis. It guides us in the early stages of an initiative or project where we are dealing with a lot of uncertainty. Cynefin is a decision support framework that can increase the probability of making the right decision in any situation. It is an excellent tool for prioritizing and analyzing Features, User Stories, and other types of requirements.

Cynefin Is a Framework for Quantifying Uncertainty

Uncertainty exists everywhere. Assume you are a Product Owner and one of your business associates just handed you a new User Story. As you read the Story, you recognize that there is a lot you do not know about the User Story, meaning you have a high degree of uncertainty.

The purpose of Cynefin is to help you quickly assess a new situation and decide how to best handle it. The recommended actions are based on your **perceived level of uncertainty**. This is a very subjective evaluation as it is based on your personal experience (or, if you are a member of a team, on the team's experience.)

To apply Cynefin, you first need to determine the nature of the inherent uncertainty based on 5 specific decision-making contexts or domains: obvious, complicated, complex, chaotic, and disorder.

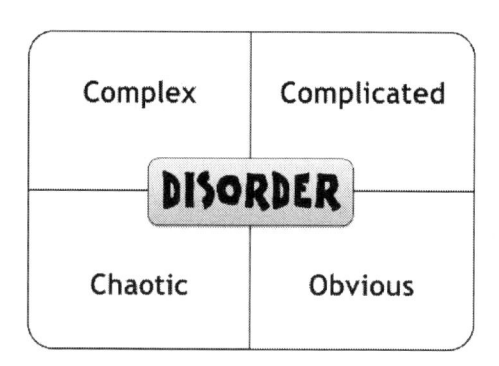

Complex	Complicated
Chaotic	Obvious

DISORDER

Anytime you face a new situation you are facing disorder. Disorder is not bad. It just means that you have not yet had time to analyze the uncertainty in the situation.

You first step is to familiarize yourself with the issue at hand and identify the appropriate Cynefin domain. Once you know which domain the situation belongs to, you have a much better basis for deciding the right course of action.

Simple Problems with **Obvious** Solutions

Assuming your team is developing an application to forecast inventory for a retail store. If you have had similar projects in the past, you know what to do. In that situation, you know how to best react.

You can choose a best practice based on your experience, so just apply it. In the Cynefin framework, that situation falls into a level called "Obvious" or "Simple".

Here are some attributes, examples, approaches, and risks for this domain.

Attributes

- ☑ The problem or challenge you are facing is well-defined and understood.
- ☑ You or your team have relevant experience dealing with this situation.
- ☑ There is consensus about the best solution or response.

Recommended Approach

- ☑ Confirm the simplicity by identifying risks of failure.
- ☑ Implement the accepted best practice.
- ☑ Test and track the outcome over a reasonable amount of time.

Risks

- ☑ Many people have a solution looking for a problem and are quick to grab any opportunity to implement it whether it addresses the real problem or not.
- ☑ Aspects of the situation that are not obvious can be ignored in the rush to solve the problem.

☑ Insufficient understanding of all aspects can cause your solution to tip the situation from Obvious into Chaos.

Example

A friend of yours asks to borrow $1,000 for a new car and promises to pay you back next payday. This same friend borrowed money from you in the past and did not pay you back and besides, you know that he only gets $500 on payday, so your response is obvious, right?

You tell him you lost your checkbook and your wallet including your ATM card, so you are so sorry, but you cannot help him right now. He suggests that you could go with him to your bank and pick it up, so you must remind him that you have no ID because your driver's license was in your wallet. Problem solved, right?

Life Gets **Complicated**

Unfortunately, not everything is as simple as it seems. The second domain in Cynefin is called "Complicated". If you face something that you have never done before, and no one on your team has ever done this, chances are you are looking at a complicated problem or situation.

Another way to recognize this domain is that you know what questions to ask, but you do not know the answers. That situation would be a suitable candidate for the "Complicated" domain in Cynefin.

In the earlier example, your team was developing an application to forecast inventory for a retail store. Since you had many similar projects in the past, you responded that you knew what to do. That put the situation in the "Obvious/Simple" domain.

But what happens if your assessment was not entirely correct? Assume the customer has a different infrastructure than your past initiatives and their infrastructure does not support the programming language or platform with which you are comfortable? Now, there arises a degree of uncertainty that you must consider.

As the saying goes, there is a first time for everything and in the IT world, it feels like there is some hitherto unencountered challenge in every project or product. Technology changes, business practices change, decision makers change. There is always something new and different associated with every product, initiative, or project.

If you find yourself in the complicated domain, you can do some research and ask a few experts. In the end, you form your own opinion based on your research and things you learned from the experts.

Business analysis techniques such as Problem Analysis, Process Modeling, Data Modeling, User Story conversations, and so on are amazingly effective in this domain.

Here are some attributes, examples, approaches, and risks for the "Complicated" domain.

Attributes

- ☑ You have questions that have no obvious answers.
- ☑ Experts have successfully resolved similar situations.
- ☑ Multiple "right" solutions exist but experts may not agree which it is.

Recommended Approach

- ☑ Analyze the situation thoroughly (as mentioned, business analysis techniques excel here).
- ☑ Isolate the factors that cause the complications.
- ☑ Work with multiple experts to develop a "good" practice for dealing with the specifics of your situation.

Risks

- ☑ There may be aspects of your situation that experts overlook or ignore.
- ☑ The different experts you contact disagree on the true nature of the problem or the right solution.
- ☑ The egos of the experts get in the way of unbiased analysis.

Example

Your investment manager suggests you might want to invest $10,000 in a new company that has stellar potential based on her financial analysis and could triple in value in 6 months. Of course, she points out, it is a new venture and there is a possibility that you could lose it all. This is a **complicated** situation because now you must analyze your financial situation as well as your risk tolerance and decide whether the reward outweighs the risk.

The Situation Becomes **Complex**

If you do not know what questions to ask, whom to ask, or even what answers to believe, you have entered the "**Complex**" domain.

You are in a situation with a high degree of uncertainty, meaning you are insecure. At this point, you need to try to find a way of moving out of the "Complex" domain into the "Complicated" or "Obvious" domain. So, how do you do that? By developing "safe to fail" tests.

A "safe to fail" test is anything that you can do that will help you understand the situation. At the same time, anything you do must not make the situation worse. That is what we mean with "safe to fail".

The main difference between all three domains (Complicated, Complex, and Obvious) - is the approach that you use to get to a solution.

- ⇨ In the **Obvious** domain, you are working on getting the job done.

- ⇨ In the **Complicated** domain you first figure out what to do and then just get it done.

- ⇨ In the **Complex** domain, you experiment and investigate potential solutions to figure out how to reduce complexity and move toward "Complicated" or "Obvious" actions.

Typically, at the beginning of a new project or initiative, most people will start with tasks that they know how to do. They are starting with items that are in the "Obvious" domain because that is most people's comfort zone.

Once they run out of easy tasks, they get to the complicated ones. It will take time, very often a lot of time, to find the resolutions. But now comes the real bummer. What if the solution they chose for a complicated task causes them to have to redo tasks from the Obvious domain because those "obvious" solutions no longer work? That would be a violation of the Lean principle of eliminating waste.

To make matters worse, what happens if you had finished all tasks in the Obvious and Complicated categories, but you are dealing with a project that has Complex dimensions to it?

If you cannot find a way to resolve the complex components of your project or initiative, all your work in the other two domains might have been wasted. You could have saved a lot of money by starting with tasks in the "Complex" domain.

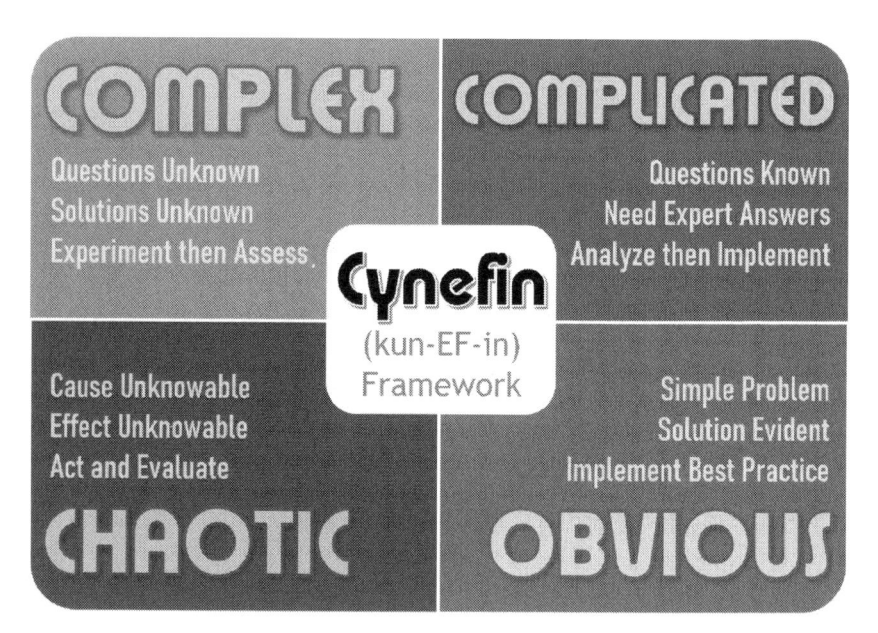

COMPLEX
Questions Unknown
Solutions Unknown
Experiment then Assess

COMPLICATED
Questions Known
Need Expert Answers
Analyze then Implement

Cynefin
(kun-EF-in)
Framework

CHAOTIC
Cause Unknowable
Effect Unknowable
Act and Evaluate

OBVIOUS
Simple Problem
Solution Evident
Implement Best Practice

Our Recommendation:

- ☑ Always work on the complex tasks or problems in the "Complex" domain first.

- ☑ Once these are solved, you can work on complicated tasks in the "Complicated" domain.

- ☑ Obvious tasks or problems should always be the last tasks you tackle!

Here are some attributes, examples, approaches, and risks for the **"Complex"** domain.

Attributes

- ☑ The situation is very fluid, constantly changing.
- ☑ The problem cannot be broken down because your actions change it in unpredictable ways.
- ☑ The right solution evolves with your understanding of the problem.

Approach

- ☑ Initiate actions that will stabilize the situation but not make it worse.
- ☑ Evaluate reactions to your actions and make necessary adjustments.
- ☑ Allow an innovative practice to emerge.

Risks

- ☑ Relying on analysis and the simpler solutions makes the situation worse.
- ☑ Impatience to resolve leads to implementing overly simple solutions that hide the real issue.
- ☑ Managing the situation by mandate preempts beneficial emergence of patterns that could lead to innovative solutions.

Example

Information Technology increases in complexity by an order of magnitude every 10 years (henceforth to be known as Hathaway's Law). We went from stand-alone, monolithic mainframes in the '60's to networked computers in the '70's to client-server platforms in the '80's to the World Wide Web in the '90's to smart devices in the '00's to AI and the Internet of Things (IoT) in the '10's.

As a result, IT projects have increased in complexity as each evolutionary step dramatically increased the number of variables involved. As thousands of data breaches, denial-of-service attacks, and system failures testify, it is nearly impossible to modify any application in isolation without negatively affecting downstream applications and API's.

Technology is constantly changing and as each new technology is rolled out, we discover discontinuities in older, reliable technologies that cause them to fail, often spectacularly. Conventional wisdom holds that "every solution creates its own set of problems". That has never been more apparent than in the current world of IT.

As a result, the vast number of significant IT initiatives nowadays start in the "Complex" domain. Use the guidelines suggested above to minimize your stress levels when you are facing yet another challenging IT project.

Chaos Reigns Supreme

You now have strategies for three Cynefin domains (Complex, Complicated, and Obvious) that we have covered so far.

The fourth dimension **"Chaos"** is quite different from the other three. When you experience a chaotic situation, you often have no idea what is going on, let alone how to solve the problem. You just know there is a huge problem and you must do something about it. In a chaotic situation, pretty much all of the rules fly out the window.

For example, imagine you are supervising the production system in your organization and it has just crashed. You find out that you cannot get it started again. Then your boss tells you that if you do not get it started within a short time, there will be dire consequences for the whole organization. That would be a problem for the "Chaos" domain.

- Nobody knows why it crashed.
- Nobody knows what the cause was.
- You do not know where to start.

According to the Cynefin framework, if you are dealing with a chaotic situation, there is no time to develop "safe-to-fail" tests. You should have done that during a catastrophe planning meeting before now.

The best thing you should do is anything you can think of that could alleviate the problem. Try something to stop the bleeding! Do whatever comes to mind to calm the situation so that you can move the problem into the "Complex" domain and start thinking about "safe to fail" tests.

When you are in a chaotic situation, you do not have time to do analysis. You do not even have time to think. You must react, or bad things will happen.

Here are some attributes, examples, approaches, and risks for this domain.

Attributes

- ☑ No known answers.
- ☑ No recognizable patterns.
- ☑ You do not know what you do not know.

Approach

- ☑ Do something, safe-to-fail or not.
- ☑ Build on whatever helps.
- ☑ Innovate, innovate, innovate.

Risks

- ☑ Decision makers cannot agree, and you get stuck in analysis paralysis.
- ☑ Superman complex when successful.
- ☑ Staying in "crisis mode" after crisis is over.

Examples

The emergence of the novel coronavirus in early 2020 is a prime example of a chaotic situation. Actually, any pandemic-causing virus falls into the chaotic domain. In the early months, nobody knew how deadly the virus was and how severe the outbreak could become. There were no recognizable patterns because every virus is unique in how it affects people. The epidemiologists could only guess based on experience and reports from prior viruses.

As the perceived risks of the outbreak became clear, most countries shut their economy down and issued stay-at-home orders for all but essential workers. The economic impact was devastating and caused many countries to reopen too early which contributed to increased infections and deaths. Vaccine development was fast-tracked, and, in some cases, vaccines were prematurely released which made testing their efficacy and safety challenging. The long-term consequences of these perceived solutions are still unknown and will only unfold in the coming years.

As you can see, this situation has all the hallmarks of the "Chaotic" domain. Applying Cynefin as a tool early in the pandemic could lessen the impact and enable a speedier recovery.

A Cynefin Success Story

We recently applied Cynefin to a customer project, and the results were amazing. We used to start every project with tasks we already knew how to do. We would make great progress, but sometimes we hit a wall late in the project and had to scramble to finish the job.

This time we started by identifying tasks that were "complex" for us because we did not know how to solve them. We examined these complex areas and developed several "safe-to-fail" tests, which all failed.

As a result, we decided not to pursue the project further. Because we were using the Cynefin Framework, this decision cost us less than a week of effort and saved our client months of working on a solution that would most likely fail in the end. The customer appreciated our integrity and rewarded us with 2 more projects that we successfully completed.

Summary

Personally, we believe that Cynefin is one of the best tools ever invented to successfully deal with the uncertainties of a new development initiative.

Cynefin did not begin life as a business analysis tool. It has many applications in many different areas. You can use Cynefin on any problem. Many organizations use Cynefin to prioritize User Stories during Release and Sprint Planning.

First analyze your "Complex" User Stories, Epics or Requirements, then look at the "Complicated" Requirements. What tools or techniques are you familiar with to move your User Stories, Features, or requirements into a simpler domain? Either from "Complex" to "Complicated" or from "Complicated" to "Obvious".

Finally, try to transfer all requests to the domain "Obvious" so that the work can be done. Cynefin is one of the best risk mitigation tools for business or requirements analysis.

Next is an exercise that will test your understanding of the possibilities that the Cynefin framework has.

Exercise: Cynefin Applied to Proposed Initiatives

This exercise will help you use the Cynefin framework to recognize risks associated with an initiative. It will also guide you to select a best-of-breed strategy based on your answer.

Instructions:

If you like tests where any answer is correct, this exercise is for you! Your answers are based on personal experience; ergo, they will be different than those offered by the instructor. That is not a problem and does not mean that your answer is wrong!

We have selected the scenarios to illustrate examples for each Cynefin category and to show how the category determines the best strategy.

Complex Questions Unknown Solutions Unknown Experiment then Assess	**Complicated** Questions Known Need Expert Answers Analyze then Implement
Chaotic Cause Unknowable Effect Unknowable Act and Evaluate	**Obvious** Simple Problem Solution Evident Implement Best Practice

DISORDER (center)

Your Assignment:

Determine which Cynefin domain each of the following initiatives belongs to (remember, your answer will be based on your experience, knowledge, and background; all we can show you is how we answered).

Initiative 1:

Upgrading a website developed in 2005 to support mobile and tablet formats

- ☐ Obvious
- ☐ Complicated
- ☐ Complex
- ☐ Chaos

Initiative 2:

Expanding an e-commerce website to comply with the 2016 EU VAT law

- ☐ Obvious
- ☐ Complicated
- ☐ Complex
- ☐ Chaos

Initiative 3:

Integrating your organization's back-end inventory management system with SAP

- ☐ Obvious
- ☐ Complicated
- ☐ Complex
- ☐ Chaos

Initiative 4:

Your production eCommerce website crashed and will not restart

- ☐ Obvious
- ☐ Complicated
- ☐ Complex
- ☐ Chaos

Initiative 5:

Acquiring and implementing a tool for Automated Test-Driven Development

- ☐ Obvious
- ☐ Complicated
- ☐ Complex
- ☐ Chaos

Initiative 6:

Plan a 2-week vacation to Europe with your extended family after winning the lottery

- ☐ Obvious
- ☐ Complicated
- ☐ Complex
- ☐ Chaos

Authors' Response to Initiative 1: Upgrading a website developed in 2005 to support mobile and tablet formats.

For us, a) OBVIOUS. If you have never upgraded a website or worked with responsive designs, you probably determined this to be COMPLEX.

If you know people who have done it, but you have no personal experience, you should put it into the COMPLICATED domain.

To consider this OBVIOUS implies you have done this type of project several times yourself and you know exactly what you need to do.

We really cannot see it as CHAOTIC since websites abound and there are plenty that can be viewed on multiple devices.

Authors' Response to Answer Initiative 2: Expanding an e-commerce website to comply with the 2016 EU VAT law.

For us, b) COMPLICATED (trust us, we did this recently!). If you have a lot of experience creating and maintaining e-commerce websites but are not versed in international tax laws, you should probably identify this as COMPLICATED at the very least.

If you do not know anyone who can interpret those laws for you, you could list this as COMPLEX.

To consider this OBVIOUS implies you have implemented the new European tax laws for online sales in the past and you know exactly what you need to do.

We really cannot see it as CHAOTIC since there are now many websites where this has been solved.

Authors' Response to Answer Initiative 3:
Integrating your organization's back-end inventory management system with SAP.

For us, b) COMPLICATED.

If you are a certified SAP consultant, this is probably OBVIOUS for you.

If you work on the current inventory management system but are not knowledgeable about SAP, you should probably assign it to the COMPLICATED domain.

But if you do not know SAP from "being a sap", COMPLEX is most likely the right domain.

Authors' Response to Answer Initiative 4: Your production eCommerce website crashed and will not restart.

For us, d) CHAOS because that is what it caused.

Unless you were planning on going out of business or using bankruptcy as an out in a difficult situation, this is probably not OBVIOUS.

Seriously, you are most likely to assign this situation as CHAOS or COMPLEX, depending on your risk tolerance and access to sufficient resources to get it solved before anything dire happens.

Authors' Response to Answer Initiative 5:
Acquiring and implementing a tool for Automated Test-Driven Development.

Since we have done this one, for us it is OBVIOUS.

For anyone who has not had the immense pleasure of studying the Features, costs, functionality, and values of every known test automation tool, we can only hope you never have to. We are, however, ready to offer our support (for a fee, of course).

Authors' Response to Answer Initiative 6: Plan a 2-week vacation to Europe with your extended family after winning the lottery.

We don't know about you but given that our family is spread around the globe and can't even agree on when Christmas presents should be opened (Christmas Eve or Christmas Morning), this one falls into the IMPOSSIBLE category. (Sorry, but we had to sneak that one in.)

Actually, assuming the lottery win was sufficiently large, we could presumably move it into the "OBVIOUS" category by $imply increa$ing the incentive$ for all family member$ to agree to our vacation plans. After all, if you are paid enough, you can afford to buy enough painkiller to put up with your most difficult relatives, can't you? That would make the situation OBVIOUS.

Reveal User Stories with Business Problem Analysis

Defining and analyzing business problems is another effective technique for Requirements Elicitation, both in traditional and Lean / Agile approaches.

Organizations start information technology initiatives for one of two reasons:

1. **To Solve Business Problems:** someone is dissatisfied with the way things work today and expects information technology (IT) to solve these problems.

2. **To Seize a Business Opportunity:** someone recognized an opportunity and they need IT support to take advantage of it.

Seize an Opportunity

If your organization is trying to seize an opportunity, the best approach is Strategic Business Analysis. Together with your Stakeholders, you analyze the situation to find out how products, workflows, software, and business architectures need to be changed or redeveloped to take advantage of the opportunity.

Strategic Business Analysis is followed by Tactical Business Analysis with the start of Requirements Elicitation. In this book, we will not cover the topic of Strategic Business Analysis. However, we will introduce Problem Analysis (a technique from the strategic level) as a tool for eliciting requirements. Defining and analyzing business problems is an effective technique for quickly obtaining high-quality User Stories, Features, and requirements.

Solve Problem(s)

When your organization is trying to solve problems in the business, Business Problem Analysis becomes critical. The problem area needs to be analyzed to ensure that you solve the **right** problems before you start requirements gathering.

If you don't understand the cause of the problem, you can easily come up with a solution that you think is spectacular, only to find that you haven't solved the problem and that your solution might even make things worse.

There is a third reason we recommend using Business Problem Analysis to find your User Stories, Features, and other requirements. There are optimists and pessimists everywhere. Some people view the "glass half-empty", others "half-full" meaning they either prefer positive or negative thinking. It is safe to assume that some of your Stakeholders are "glass half-empty" kind of folks and others think in "glass half-full" terms.

In our experience, if you ask a person who leans toward negative thinking what they want the new application or product to do, you will get a blank stare and maybe a few answers if you are lucky. They do not think in those terms.

However, if you ask them what their problems are, you will get a huge list. Analyzing those problems will lead you to excellent User Stories, Features, and requirements.

We hope we have convinced you of the huge benefits of Problem Analysis as a requirements elicitation tool. So, let us delve into this technique.

Define Business Problems

It starts with Basic Problem Definition. You can apply this technique to any set of problems. We even have applied it to a family situation where the problems seemed overwhelming. Basic Problem Definition is looking at a situation and trying to understand what "**the real problem**" is.

A good analogy to illustrate the concept of "the real problem" is a doctor visit. Your doctor listens to your symptoms and then uses those to diagnose "**the real disease**". If your doctor just treated your symptoms, the underlying disease might kill you.

Basic Problem Definition is a straightforward approach for discovering and understanding the **real problem** before running off and coming up with a solution that addresses all symptoms but kills your digital solution because it does not address the entire problem.

What Is the Problem?

Start by asking all Stakeholders what they perceive the problems to be. We use the phrase "**perceive the problems to be**" very consciously in that sentence. It expresses a fundamental truth for us, which is what one person perceives as a problem, another perceives as an opportunity.

A fitting example of this is if an ATM machine dispenses more cash than the customer requested but the receipt shows the requested amount. If I were to ask the customer, "What's the problem", I doubt seriously that he or she could see one. From the perspective of the bank that owns the ATM, however, I will get quite a different response when they discover the discrepancy.

Once you have compiled a list with all the problems that your Stakeholders perceive, you are ready for the next step.

Whose Problem Is It?

For each problem on your list you need to understand whose problem this is. What is the perspective of the person who gave you this problem? Ask questions like,

- Who suffers because of this problem?
- Who can influence the problem?
- Who cares how you solve the problem?
- Who does **not** want to solve the problem?

By answering these four questions, you could develop a solution that would satisfy all Stakeholders, rather than satisfying one group and possibly irritating another. As a side benefit, answers to the question "Whose problem is it?" will also confirm or expand your list of Stakeholders.

What Is the Root Cause of the Problem?

You want to discover the source of each problem. If you look deeper to figure out what is causing the problem, you might be able to fix the underlying systems and processes so that the problem disappears.

There are many different techniques for Problem Analysis. One of the most popular is Root Cause Analysis, or RCA for short. RCA helps to identify the factors that contribute to a problem or incident. This allows you to get to the root of the problem and then fix it.

The technique assumes that everything is connected in a chain reaction. By tracing this chain backwards, you can find out where the problem started and how it developed into the symptoms you are now facing. If you want to learn Root Cause Analysis, YouTube has a lot of great videos.

Another technique is the "5-why method". This technique is often used in the analysis phase of the Six Sigma method. By repeatedly asking a "why" question, you can get to the actual core or root of the problem. By the way, you do not need to limit yourself to five "whys"; this is just a rule of thumb. There are also plenty of YouTube videos on this technique that can help you.

There is a caveat we would like to attach to the "5-why method", however. Recent neuroscientific studies on how the human brain works show that asking "Why" actually triggers a defense mechanism in the other person's mind forcing them to justify their desire or need. As a result, we consider replacing the question "Why?" with "What is the business value of that?". By focusing them to consider business value, you circumvent the natural defense mechanism.

The Problem Analysis technique that has worked best for us is a modified "Lean Problem/Symptom Reduction". In addition to discovering the root cause or "real problem", this technique creates as a by-product Lean requirements or business needs.

What Is the "Real Problem"?

The expected result / goal of any Problem Analysis technique is to discover the root cause or "real problem". If you have a set of "real problems" then you can focus User Story discovery and other requirements elicitation efforts on solving the "real problem" instead of its associated symptoms. Addressing the root cause allows you to define a solution that will resolve the symptoms quickly and effectively. We will show you how to do this in a later section.

However, before we delve into more detail, we will give you an opportunity to identify problems and create a list that will serve as the starting point.

Exercise: Define Business Problems

Problem identification is not rocket science, but it can be a bit tricky. This exercise gives you an opportunity to test your problem identification skills.

Instructions:

You are assigned a project to modernize the ordering system in a retail store. You asked the Order Entry Supervisor, the Warehouse Manager, and a Customer Service Representative to send you their perceived problems and received the following answers:

Email Response: Order Entry Supervisor
Our company has enjoyed excellent growth the last few years. As a result, the number of orders we are handling per day has increased dramatically. Although we have added staff to handle the load, some of our known deadbeats are getting their orders filled. The Credit Department seems to take a long time to process new customer orders. We also find item numbers on orders that do not exist in our inventory.

Email Response: Warehouse Manager
The number of orders with incorrect article numbers has risen sharply. Sometimes the item number is unknown, other times it is known but the description on the order does not match the description in our system. This should never happen! This leads to delays in shipping because our pickers must leave the warehouse.

Email Response: Customer Service Representative:
Our problems are:

1. We have a lot of new customers asking where their order is.

2. Often, new customers have not received their goods more than a week after placing their order.

3. We have an increase in the number of incorrect invoices. These are invoices charging the customer an incorrect amount.

4. We also see complaints about getting merchandise that was not what was ordered.

Question 1:

After reading the email responses from the three Stakeholders, what "business problems" can you identify? Capture anything that sounds like a problem. Go beyond the obvious to see what you can discover.

Answer Question 1: What "business problems" can you identify?

Here are our sample answers:

1. The number of orders is increasing.
2. New staff is not performing well enough.
3. Known deadbeats are getting their orders filled.
4. New customer orders take too long to process.
5. The warehouse gets item#/description mismatches.
6. Shipping is delayed.
7. Pickers are away from the warehouse floor.
8. Customer invoices have incorrect prices.
9. Orders are incorrectly filled.

If you found any others, they are not wrong. They are just beyond what we need for the next exercise!

Lean Problem-Symptom Reduction Reveals User Stories, Epics and Features

So, now that you have a list of problems, you want to discover "the real problem" using the "Lean Problem/Symptom Reduction" technique. That is a long and fancy name for a simple concept that will help you understand which problems you really should address.

You can use this technique on any list of problems whether these problems relate to an Epic, a single User Story, a Given-When-Then Scenario or even your entire product, initiative, or project.

Identifying the "real problem" is a 4-step process.

1. Create Mutual Understanding

First, get consensus amongst all Stakeholders who are affected by or who can influence the problem. Use your answers to "whose problem is it?" to confirm that this really is a problem that the Stakeholders want to do something about.

Your goal is to create a mutual understanding within the Stakeholder and user community that the problem needs to be solved one way or another.

Some problem statements might need rewriting. Quite often in the creation of a problem list, items slip in that are not really problems. For example, the problem,

> *"It takes 23 minutes to fill out the form requesting insurance coverage."*

Is "23 minutes" a problem or a speed record? As stated, it is just a fact. Restate items like this to express a problem. For example, a good rewrite might be,

> *"We are losing potential customers because it takes 23 minutes to complete our online application form."*

You will recoup the effort it takes to rewrite them later.

2. Does Anyone on Our Team Have the Authority to Solve the Problem?

Next, you need to find whether you **can** solve this problem. Does anyone on the Agile or Lean team or amongst the Stakeholders have the authority and the knowledge to fix this problem?

If you find an item on the list where you find that no Stakeholder has the authority or the means to do anything about it, mark this issue as "Out of Scope". Scratch it from your list and add it to an "out-of-scope" problem list.

This "out-of-scope" list could be useful for your management, your customers, or any other party you can think of. Let them know that your team has identified these issues, but that they do not fall within the scope of your initiative. Someone might be grateful that you informed them about this existing problem. This leads us to the third step.

3. Separate Problems from Potential Solutions

Now that you have eliminated problems that are out of scope from your list, the remainder of the items are either "**real** problems", symptoms of "real problems", or potential solutions.

What are potential solutions? They are a welcome addition to our list of preliminary requirements that will later lead us to User Stories, Epics, Features, Scenarios, etc. Removing them from our list will also make it easier to separate the "real problems" from the symptoms in our last step.

Some of the problems you get will say things like, "We don't have a blog". Is this a problem or a potential solution?

An easy way to distinguish a proposed solution from a problem is to ask: "Can you imagine several solutions that would solve this problem?" If the Stakeholders can think of at least two or more solutions, then you have a problem that must remain on your list.

But here comes the difficult part. Many Stakeholders will give you multiple solutions that are ONE solution in disguise. For example, assume the Stakeholders give you the following three solutions:

- → We can develop the blog inhouse
- → We can outsource blog development
- → We can buy one off the shelve

Each of these "solutions" expresses a different option on HOW to create the blog but the outcome is the same. Your company will have a blog. That makes this a potential solution (and it might even be a great Business Requirement), but it is not a problem.

Instead of labeling it a potential solution, you could also restate this item as a problem. For example,

> We are losing traffic to dynamic websites that stay fresh by constantly posting new material on their blog.

Note the shift from the solution "do not have a blog" to the problem "losing traffic". There are potentially many solutions to the problem of losing traffic and not all of them will result in adding a blog.

Let your Stakeholders decide whether they want a Business Requirement stating that the organization needs a blog or whether they would rather investigate all potential solutions to the restated problem.

Anytime someone starts a problem with "we don't have…", "there aren't any…", or "we need…", they are not expressing a problem; they are expressing a potential solution, maybe even a future requirement, or a problem that requires a rewrite.

At the end, remove all proposed solutions from your problem list and add them to your potential requirements list. This list will come in handy when you start writing and analyzing your User Stories or IT requirements.

4. Will the "REAL PROBLEM" Please Stand Out!

You have gone through the problem list twice. You have removed "problems" that were out of scope and you have removed "problems" that were solutions in disguise (or potential requirements). This is the last time you will go through this list and, yes, finally, you get to identify the "real problems".

This time, for each remaining problem on your list, ask your Stakeholders,

"Assuming we could solve this problem, would any of the other problems go away without additional effort?"

If the answer is yes, then the problem that would disappear is a symptom. This step can be time-consuming because you must compare each problem on your list with every other problem below it. Nonetheless, it is a critical part of identifying the "real" problem.

Make the symptom a subpoint of the "real problem" to form a set. When you are done with your entire list, you can analyze each real problem along with its associated symptoms to create User Stories and requirements.

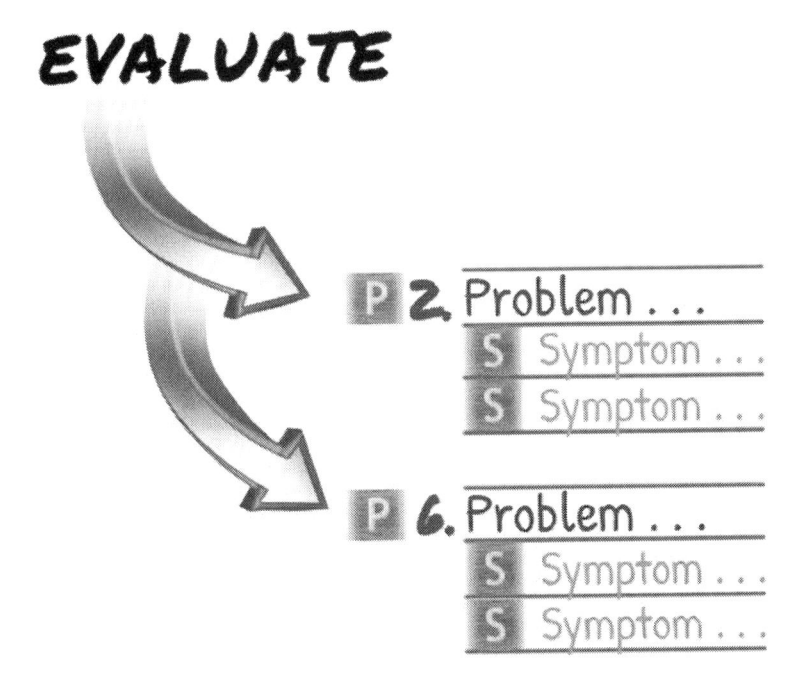

EVALUATE

P 2. Problem . . .
    S Symptom . . .
    S Symptom . . .

P 6. Problem . . .
    S Symptom . . .
    S Symptom . . .

When you apply this technique in real life, you often find that one part of the problem goes away by solving another problem, but a different part of the same problem does not. If this happens, split the problem statement in two, one that expresses the symptom and another that expresses the remaining problem. Move the new problem to the bottom of your problem list.

At a later stage, you define User Stories, Features, or requirements for solving these "real problems" and all related symptoms should disappear. If they do not go away, this is most likely another partial problem that requires restating. Instead of a rewrite, however, you could also just add a requirement that addresses the part of the symptom that would not be solved.

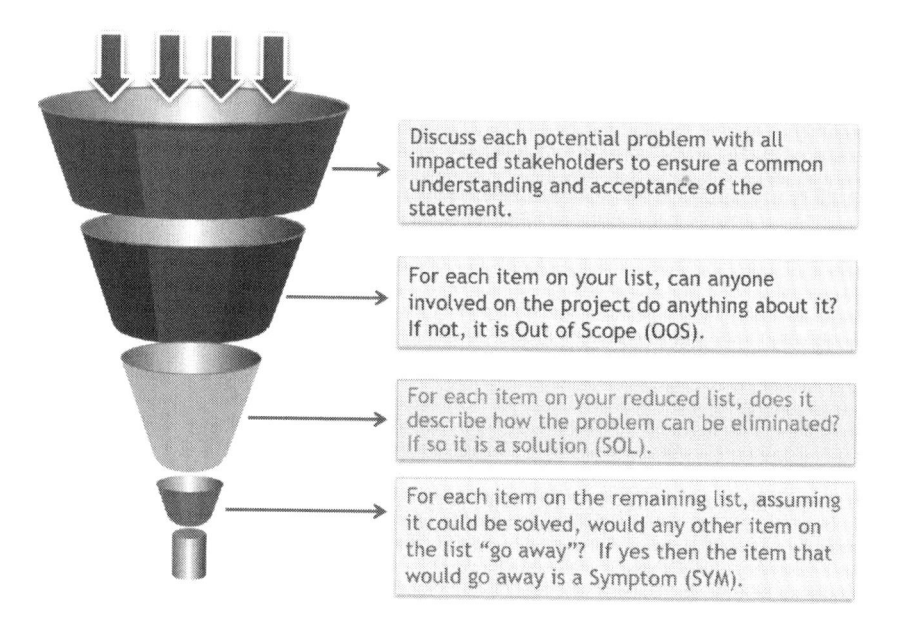

> Discuss each potential problem with all impacted stakeholders to ensure a common understanding and acceptance of the statement.

> For each item on your list, can anyone involved on the project do anything about it? If not, it is Out of Scope (OOS).

> For each item on your reduced list, does it describe how the problem can be eliminated? If so it is a solution (SOL).

> For each item on the remaining list, assuming it could be solved, would any other item on the list "go away"? If yes then the item that would go away is a Symptom (SYM).

We have used this technique on hundreds of projects and initiatives over the years. To give you an example, on one project we assembled a problem list of 105 problem statements in response to the question, "What is wrong with your current process?".

After we applied Lean Problem Symptom Reduction, we ended up with **3 real problems**. Everything else was either a symptom, a solution, or a problem that was out of scope.

With this simple technique, we were able to simplify perceived problems very quickly, speed up the elicitation of requirements **and** significantly improve the completeness and accuracy of our User Stories and other requirements.

Exercise: Problem Symptom Reduction

This exercise gives you the opportunity of trying to distinguish symptoms from problems and finally identify the "real" problems.

Instructions:

Using the problem list from the last exercise, see if you can recognize which items are out of scope, solutions, symptoms, or real problems.

Question 1:

Which problems (if any) are out of scope (assuming your project sponsor is the manager of order entry)?

1. The number of orders is increasing.
2. New staff is not performing well enough.
3. Known deadbeats are getting their orders filled.
4. New customer orders take too long to process.
5. The warehouse gets item#/description mismatches.
6. Shipping is delayed.
7. Pickers are away from the warehouse floor.
8. Customer invoices have incorrect prices.
9. Orders are incorrectly filled.

Question 2:

Of the remaining list, which problems (if any) are solutions in disguise (i.e., there is only one solution)?

Question 3:

Of the remaining list, which problems (if any) are symptoms of other problems on the list?

Answer Question 1: Which problems (if any) are out of scope (assuming your project sponsor is the manager of order entry)?

You may have noticed that the first problem on our list is not necessarily something that top management wants to fix, even if it is a problem for the ordering department; ergo it is outside of their area of responsibility (OOS):):

1. The number of orders is increasing.

Answer Question 2: Of the remaining list, which problems (if any) are solutions in disguise (i.e., there is only one solution)?

None.
An example of a potential solution would be if you had a problem stated as "We don't have enough people to process the orders". If your problem statement implies that if you had something different, the "problem" would go away, it is a solution in disguise.

Answer Question 3: Which of the following items (if any) are symptoms of other problems on the list?

If you have different answers, do not despair. The true value of this exercise is getting a group of Stakeholders to follow these simple steps thereby increasing their awareness of the issues that need to be addressed.

Getting them to agree can be challenging, but in our experience, the process is invaluable.

Here are our analysis results:

1. The number of orders is increasing.
   (OOS)
2. New staff is not performing well enough.
   (REAL PROBLEM)
3. Known deadbeats are getting their orders filled.
   (Symptom of 2)
4. New customer orders take too long to process.
   (Symptom of 2)
5. The warehouse gets item#/description mismatches.
   (Symptom of 2)
6. Shipping is delayed.
   (Symptom of 5)
7. Pickers are away from the warehouse floor.
   (Symptom of 5)
8. Customer invoices have incorrect prices.
   (Symptom of 2)
9. Orders are incorrectly filled.
   (Symptom of 5)

Conversations Are the Core of Lean and Agile

Defining business needs down to the level of software requirements is the most difficult, most error-prone, and most communication intensive part of software development. Nowhere does the adage "garbage-in-garbage-out" fit better than in the definition of business needs. Extensive experience shows that inadequate requirements caused by miscommunication are still the prime reason for software failures.

In Lean and Agile software development environments, the added challenge is to continuously refine and further elaborate the requirements as the product is in progress. This refinement happens at various stages, for example, while grooming the Product Backlog, during Release and Sprint planning, and during conversations between developers and end-users, just to name a few.

During Agile/Lean development, the requirements discovery process must be coordinated with the development effort so that when the development team is ready to start a Sprint, the User Stories or requirements in any form for that Sprint are defined sufficiently to start development.

The main advantage of all Lean and Agile philosophies is speed and agility. Communication between technical and business teams is at the heart of Lean development approaches. We show you how to ensure effective communication in requirements elicitation.

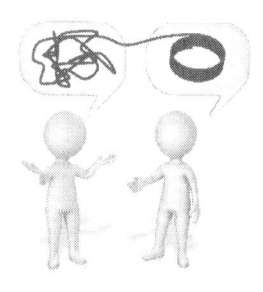

Any conversation or meeting between different functional groups or areas, such as IT and the business community, has a higher chance of success if the meeting is conducted efficiently and effectively. To achieve this, you need to:

- ☑ prepare for the meeting,
- ☑ know how to conduct the meeting effectively
- ☑ and realize that it is not over when it is over

An effective follow-up is essential for a successful meeting.

Engaging with the Business Community

People skills (the ability to deal with people) as well as in-depth knowledge of many business analysis techniques are crucial for successful meetings and workshops. It helps your self-confidence (and the quality of your analysis results) if you are familiar with as many business analysis or requirements gathering techniques as possible. Besides, it does not hurt to have a few tricks up your sleeve.

In addition, you will often need to talk to people above your pay grade while defining requirements. Do not be afraid to ask tough questions. If that intimidates you, you must find a way to deal with it.

A key factor in the success of any conversation is making sure you ask the right questions to the right Stakeholder. If you ask a sales consultant about your company's long-term strategy, he may have an opinion, but management may not share it. Make sure you ask questions that are appropriate for the person you are talking to.

Explain the Purpose and Scope of the Conversation

One of the things that we highly recommend in any conversation is ensuring that all parties understand the purpose of the conversation. You want to communicate why you are meeting AND what the scope of the discussion is.

At the beginning of a conversation, let everyone know the topics you want to address and what you expect the others to contribute. This sets expectations and avoids wasting each other's time.

In the following sections, we present techniques, tips, and tricks that we have learned over the last 30 years. We pass them on to complement your individual toolkit, not to replace it. At the beginning we offer a simple exercise to set the course for a good business analysis.

Exercise: What Traits Does a Good Business Analyst Need?

This exercise is designed to give you time to think about traits, behaviors, or characteristics that would qualify someone to successfully extract information from other people.

Instructions:

Set a time limit of 4 minutes. Write down as many personality traits, attributes, skills, or attitudes that you think are important to guide others to discover and express their business needs and User Stories. NOTE: There are no wrong answers, only potentially different perspectives.

Question:

What are the characteristics of a good Business Analyst in the requirements gathering phase?

When you are ready, go to the next page to see common answers from students in our instructor-led classes (no peaking!!!).

Answer Examples: What are the characteristics of a good Business Analyst in the requirements gathering phase?

1. **Good listener** (understands and applies active and informational listening techniques)

2. **Personable** (makes other people feel comfortable)

3. **Well-spoken** (speaks clearly and distinctly with vocabulary suited to target audience)

4. **Competent** (understands the language of the Subject Matter Expert)

5. **Sense of humor** (self-deprecating, likes to laugh and appreciates good stories that do not denigrate others)

6. **Open-minded** (unbiased, willing to listen to new and different ideas from any source)

7. **Curious** (driven to learn new things and new perspectives)

8. **Focused** (able to devote the right time and focus to each topic)

9. **Organized** (asks the right questions and captures responses)

We are not implying that these are the only important traits for a good elicitor, but based on empirical evidence, working on improving these skills will improve the odds that your elicitation efforts succeed.

Effective Requirement Discussions

A critical success factor for Lean / Agile business needs analysis is effective communication between the business community and IT. Whether you are conducting a 3-amigo conversation with an end user, a formal requirements meeting with the business team, or a User Story Workshop with the Agile team, you should follow these 3 steps:

1. **Plan and Prepare**
2. **Present Like a Pro**
3. **Follow-up**

In this section, we give you some tools, techniques, tips, and tricks on how to effectively prepare, plan, moderate, and track diverse types of collaborative requirements gathering.

Although we will not go into depth on follow-up, we want you to recognize that a requirements meeting is not over when it is over. It does not matter how productive the conversation, meeting, or workshop was, not following up with the individuals afterward can wreak havoc with your initiative.

The benefits of a follow-up are that you can measure the satisfaction of the participants and at the same time make them think about their business needs. Follow-up allows you to gather information that may have been overlooked. Follow-up ensures that you get the most out of your collaborative requirements efforts.

Preparation and Planning

Although the Agile principles emphasize simplicity and directness in conversations, that does not mean that you do not need to be prepared.

Lean principles dictate that you must do everything possible to achieve the required quality outcomes with minimal effort. Without planning and preparing the conversation, meeting, or workshop, you will not follow the Lean principles because you are wasting the time of all participants.

Prepare the Right Questions and Agenda

Before you start planning a conversation, meeting, or workshop, take the time to prepare the questions. Think about what you need to know from this individual or group. For an informal conversation, create a list of questions. If you plan a requirements workshop, draft an agenda.

For example, if you want to discuss a User Story, make sure you understand the User Story before the meeting. Write down everything that is unclear. If you use the "Question File" technique mentioned in the last section, pick out the questions that relate to that User Story and add new questions that come to mind.

You also want to have the "right" questions for your participants. If your User Story is:

> **As a Janitor, I need to be able to order new cleaning supplies to clean the facilities,**

you might want to talk to the Janitor about schedules and supply volumes. However, you should not ask that person how to set up a budget for maintenance. Make sure that the questions for your participant(s) are limited to their areas of responsibility and knowledge.

When you plan a Story Workshop, create an agenda with all the items for which you need answers. Decide upfront which business analysis techniques you will use to get the answers or requirements you need.

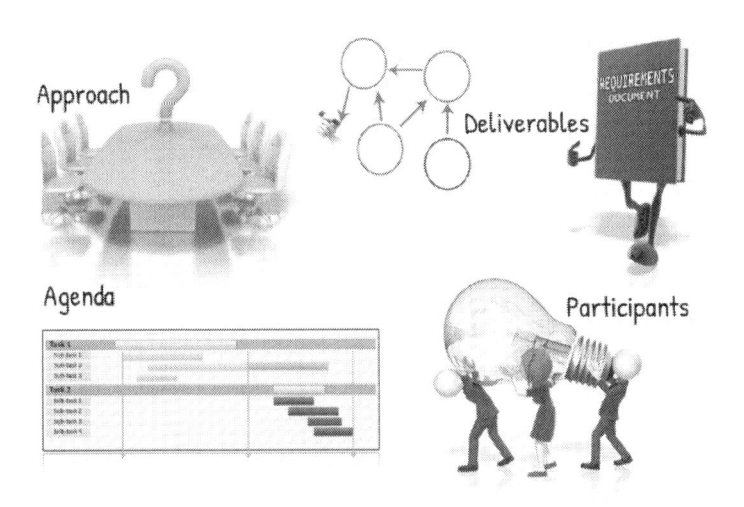

Obviously, the preparation for a workshop is much more complex than for a conversation. We will not go into workshops in detail in this book as that exceeds its scope. For comparison, we teach how to run effective requirements meetings in 1-2 hours, but we teach how to plan, prepare, and facilitate a Requirements Workshop in a 2-day class.

Invite the "Right" Stakeholders

Always invite the author of the User Story for a 3-amigo conversation. This person can give you insights that you would not get from anyone else. If you are the author, you should take the time to explain your User Story to the developers to ensure mutual understanding.

When you read the User Story in preparation for a meeting, the "Who" in the User Story is another person you should talk to. If the User Story starts with "As a sales rep" look at your trusty org chart and find the names of people that perform this role in the company.

In addition, ask yourself who else might be interested in this Feature. You might have questions for them and should invite them too.

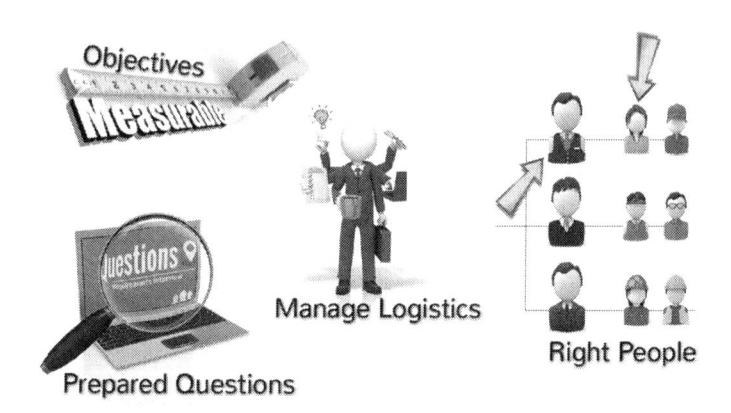

Manage Logistics

Prepared Questions

Right People

Manage the Logistics and Communicate the Goal

Consider the logistics of the workshop or meeting, i.e. when and especially where to meet. We strongly recommend meeting Subject Matter Experts either at a neutral location or at their workplace.

Asking them to come to your workplace can be intimidating. It is important to make your participants feel empowered, make them feel like they are in control by giving them home team advantage. Meeting at their place goes a long way towards that. If you meet them on their home turf, they will be more willing to share what they know. In addition, they have access to resources, if needed, that they only have at their workplace.

If you are planning a workshop, you must decide whether it should take place online or onsite. If onsite, should it be inhouse or external? All variants require a lot of effort to get the logistics right.

Set Goals

Most importantly, let everyone know in advance why you want to talk to them. Tell them what you are trying to achieve (the goal of the conversation) and what you expect them to contribute.

Always add the meeting objectives to the invitation. Explain to the participants why they should give you their time. Set expectations correctly and make sure during the meeting or interview that you keep or exceed your promise.

Determine the Right Level of Detail

In Lean/Agile lifecycles we need different layers of User Story detail at different stages of the lifecycle (more about this in a later chapter). For example, the User Story details you need when filling out the Product Backlog differ significantly from the details you need when planning a Sprint or Release. For this reason, it is critical to plan the level of detail that you want to target in your upcoming conversation.

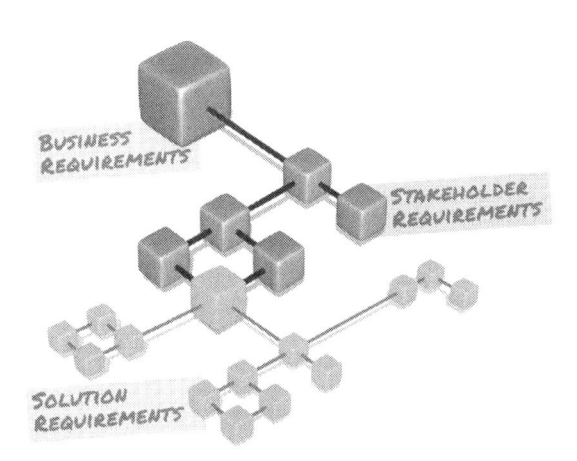

BUSINESS REQUIREMENTS

STAKEHOLDER REQUIREMENTS

SOLUTION REQUIREMENTS

When developers are ready to code a User Story, they need answers that will help them define solution-level requirements (software specifications). They need to understand what function the application supports from an IT perspective. What data does the application need and what are the Non-Functional Requirements for the digital solution? In our experience, having a conversation with the Subject Matter Expert about this level of detail is very fruitful - **at the right time**! You can exchange ideas that will improve the product drastically.

You definitively do not want to talk about this layer during an initial User Story Discovery session. Do not waste time drilling down to the lowest level of the User Story or Feature (specification level) until the decision to implement it has been made, meaning during Release or Sprint Planning (more on this later).

Always make sure that your prepared questions aim at the right layer of User Story detail for the moment in time. This follows the Lean principle to decide at the "last responsible moment".

Agile Documentation

You also need to think about how you will keep track of the information the participants give you. I know that most of us have perfect memories, right? ? Well, maybe not! Sure, there are folks who have an excellent memory. However, they, more than anyone else, need to think in advance about how to capture responses because people with great memory are usually the worst notetakers (as Tom can testify).

With Scrum and most other Agile and Lean approaches a User Story conversation also includes the validation of a User Story. For example, if you have a discussion with a Subject Matter Expert about a User Story, you should ask the Subject Matter Expert how to make sure that the software does everything right. You should capture User Story Acceptance Criteria, Test Scenarios, or even a few Examples.

In the early days of Agile development, this information was written on the back of the User Story card. Nowadays, you would most likely use a computer or mobile device to capture the details. However, it always depends on where the conversation takes place. If you are talking to a SME during your lunch break, you could use a cocktail napkin.

Use the Right Representation Mode (Visual, Verbal, Textual)

Sometimes, writing things down is not enough. Often, we need notes in the form of diagrams. Pictures say a lot more than words. As Gabe Arnold reports:

> ... According to marketing industry influencer Krista Neher, the human brain can process images up to 60,000 times faster than words. With a picture, you can convey so much more information than you can with words. In fact, it can take a thousand words just to describe what is in one picture. And, pictures have the ability to convey abstract and complex concepts ...

At the end of the conversation, we want to be sure that we have a mutual understanding of the information we exchanged.

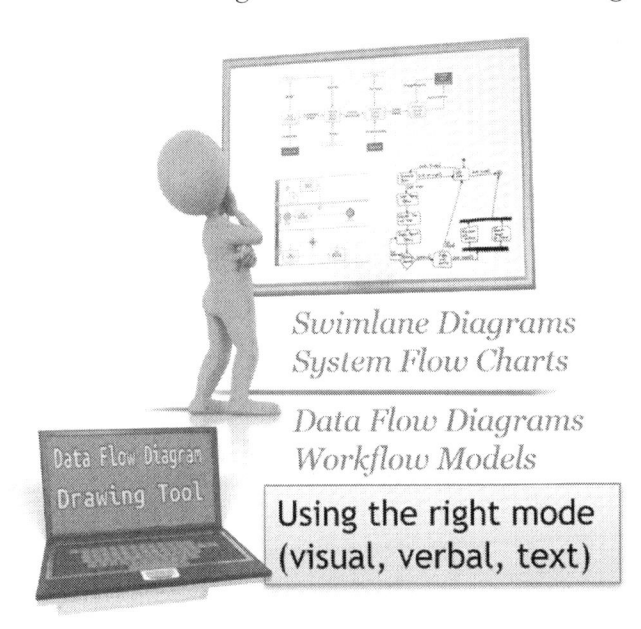

Swimlane Diagrams
System Flow Charts
Data Flow Diagrams
Workflow Models

Using the right mode (visual, verbal, text)

To support this goal, use the communication mode that is most effective for your audience. Some people like to talk; they love verbal communication. For others, visuals help them better. These people would benefit from diagrams, such as Swimlane Diagrams to illustrate workflows or Data Flow Diagrams to show data transformation.

And then there are the readers. Some people just communicate best when reading. Since we often have more than 15 people in our Requirements Discovery Workshops, we always make sure that we have every mode of communication covered.

For the readers, we have a scribe in the room who takes notes that are displayed on a large screen in the front of the room. For more visually oriented participants and for the listeners/talkers, the facilitator draws diagrams and discusses them.

Types of Requirements Meetings

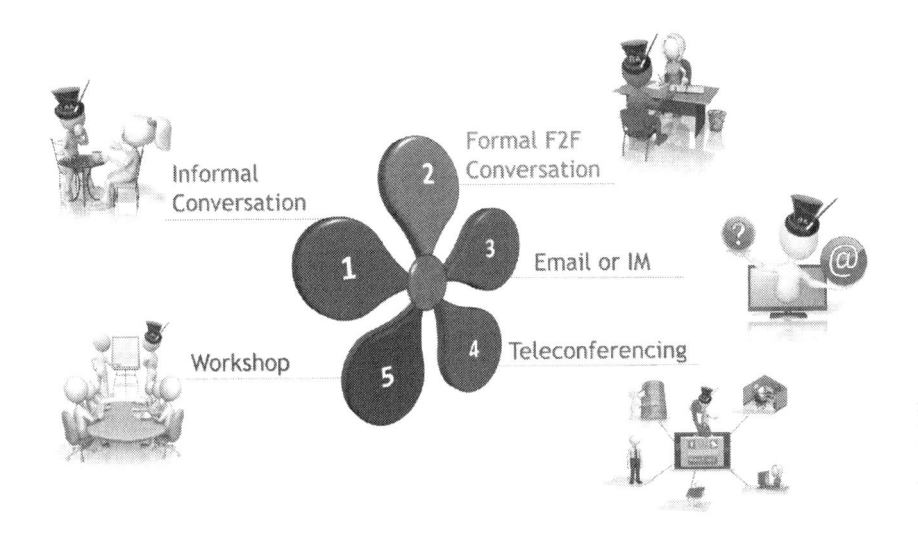

- Informal Conversation
- Formal F2F Conversation
- Email or IM
- Teleconferencing
- Workshop

So, what type of conversation should you choose?

Informal Conversation

First there is the informal conversation. This is the kind of situation where you might be walking down the hall and bump into somebody that you have been trying to contact for a couple of days. You might say, "Hey Fred, wait a minute. While I have you here, can I ask you a few questions?". Just make sure you always have your prepared questions with you. Laptops and cell phones make life here a lot easier.

Face-to-face Conversation

The next stage of a conversation is a personal interview, where you set a date and time when you will meet. As we have already mentioned, we recommend that it be conducted in your Stakeholder's office if possible, because if he or she needs something to clarify a matter, he or she will have immediate access to it.

E-mail or Instant Messaging (IM)

You can also use e-mail or instant messaging (IM). They are especially popular if you just want to ask a quick, clarifying question. Limit this communication mode to brief questions and answers. Consider this mode as well when you want to ensure that you have their responses captured electronically so you do not have to type it (and potentially mistype it).

Videoconferencing or Online Meetings

An increasingly collaborative, networked working environment is driving the rapid growth of virtual meetings. As with everything in life, there are advantages and disadvantages.

For some, the idea of going through a video conference or an online meeting to collect and analyze requirements or User Stories seems like torture. This can be the case if the event is insufficiently moderated. However, online meetings have their advantages. For example, it is much easier to share all kinds of documents in an online meeting and even annotate them.

The critical success factor for successful online User Stories and Requirements Discovery meetings is knowing what to do if something goes wrong. Take the time to prepare and plan the video conference. If you have never moderated an online meeting before, you should take a course in online meeting moderation before you venture into your first conference call.

Workshops and Large Groups

Large groups, Requirements Workshops and User Story Workshops are the preferred approach to start an Agile initiative. The workshop is an excellent tool to deliver initial User Stories or Features that lay the foundation for the Product Backlog.

If your IT team uses the Kanban method, a workshop can deliver a Feature List for your Kanban board. The large group approach has also proven to be remarkably successful for Product Backlog Grooming (more about this later).

Use the Stakeholder Identification techniques we have already presented to invite the "right" Stakeholders. Having the right people, in the right place and at the right time together, combined with good online facilitation skills, ensures the success of your workshop.

The intensive discussions in a workshop also spark new ideas. The participants tend to think outside the box. If you are looking for innovative solutions and requirements, a workshop is the best choice.

Exercise: Requirements Meeting Types

This exercise gives you an opportunity to contemplate the pros and cons of the 5 most used business needs discovery approaches.

Instructions:

For each of the listed conversation / meeting types, find 3 things that are good about it and 3 things that are difficult and could threaten the project.

Assignment 1:

List 3 advantages and 3 disadvantages (pros and cons) of informal (unscheduled) meetings with a Stakeholder.

1
2
3

1
2
3

Assignment 2:

Name 3 advantages and 3 disadvantages (pros and cons) of Face-to-face Conversations with one or more Stakeholders.

1
2
3

1
2
3

Assignment 3:

Name 3 advantages and 3 disadvantages (pros and cons) with a larger group of Stakeholders (e.g. User Story or Requirements Workshops).

1
2
3

1
2
3

Assignment 4:

Name 3 advantages and 3 disadvantages (pros and cons) of video conferencing to elicit or gather requirements.

1
2
3

1
2
3

Assignment 5:

Name 3 advantages and 3 disadvantages (pros and cons) of using email or instant messaging (IM) to capture requirements.

1
2
3

1
2
3

Examples of Past Answers to the Exercise

We provide these as food for thought and to augment your responses.

Answer Assignment 1: Informal Meetings
Potential advantages and disadvantages (kudos if you found others!)

PROS

1. The informal nature puts the Stakeholder at ease.
2. These are quick and do not need extensive preparation.
3. You may get information the Stakeholder would not share in a more formal setting.

CONS

1. The Stakeholder may feel "ambushed".
2. He/she does not have time to prepare.
3. The information may not be well-thought out.

Answer Assignment 2: Face-to-face Conversation
Potential pros and cons (kudos if you found others!)

PROS

1. You have time to prepare and prioritize your questions.
2. The Stakeholder has time to contemplate and research the right answers.

3. It allows everyone to manage their time more efficiently.

CONS

1. In today's busy work environment, it can be difficult to schedule busy Stakeholders.
2. It requires adequate facilities.
3. The more meetings you schedule, the less effective each one becomes.

Answer Assignment 3: Workshops

Potential advantages and disadvantages (kudos if you found others!)

PROS

1. All attendees can listen to each other's needs.
2. Group synergy can generate ideas that combine aspects of different Stakeholders' ideas.
3. The group that creates the requirements owns them and will defend them to their colleagues.

CONS

1. There is a risk of "group-think" (mob mentality).
2. Scheduling facilities and participants can be next to impossible.
3. The volume of responses you capture can become overwhelming.

Answer Assignment 4: Videoconferencing

Potential advantages and disadvantages (kudos if you found others!)

PROS

1. They are much easier to schedule than face-to-face meetings.
2. Participants can be wherever they want.
3. You can easily record the sessions for later analysis.

CONS

1. You have no control over what other people are doing (losing focus).
2. Technology issues (lost connections, recording does not work, etc.).
3. People start to talk over each other more readily than face-to-face which can lead to communication problems.

Answer Assignment 5: E-mail / Instant Messaging

Potential advantages and disadvantages (kudos if you found others!)

PROS

1. The entire conversation is captured electronically by default.
2. They are time independent, meaning people can answer whenever.
3. Stakeholders have more time to think about problems and requirements before they respond.

CONS

1. Written communication is all-to-easily misinterpreted.
2. You have no control over when you get a response.
3. The casual nature of IM can cause people to not take it seriously.

User Story Conversations and Group Interactions

You have spent the time planning and preparing for the conversation. Now it is time to do it. Whether it is a meeting, a conversation, or a formal interview, all of them can be incredibly stressful for the participants. To get the results you need, it is critical that you interact well with whoever the Stakeholder is. You want them to feel relaxed and at ease; so, they can be themselves.

Try to minimize misunderstandings during each discussion. Your goal is to achieve a mutual understanding of User Stories, Features, and requirements.

If at any time you feel that someone is saying something that does not correspond to what you have understood, speak up! It is no good simply ignoring it while thinking something like, "Well, that sounded a little strange, but it's probably right". If you were wrong and your gut feeling was right, you could end up with the wrong requirements.

Build Rapport

For many people, the beginning of a conversation with a stranger can be a stressful experience. Maybe we are missing the words, or we feel uncomfortable with our body language and peculiarities. However, as soon as we have a certain agreement with each other, everything goes much more smoothly. So, what is "rapport"? Here is an interesting definition:

> *"Rapport is a connection with someone.*
> *It as a state of harmonious understanding*
> *with another individual or group."*

The time you invest building a strong rapport with your Stakeholders is the best investment you will ever make. But how do you build rapport with someone?

For starters, small talk (i.e., chatting about things that are not terribly important). Obviously, you want to avoid topics that could be controversial. We always recommend against any political or religious topics or you might just set off a firestorm that you will never be able to control.

Find common ground and be empathic. Small talk is a way to make a human connection. It is allowing people to recognize, "Hey, we're just people here". Unfortunately, because of the nature of people, there is only one very safe topic you can talk about when it comes to small talk and that is the weather. No one can do anything about it. We are all stuck with whatever we got. You can always talk about that if you cannot think of another topic.

SHARED TRUST

If you happen to know the other party, you may know their attitude to questions or some of their favorite topics. If you do not know them, you may know someone who knows them. Take a few minutes to chat with that person to get some background information. Small talk is all about being relaxed, making the right choices, and making sure everyone feels comfortable before you start.

Stay on Topic

Once you start, it is important to remember that you have a goal. You want to come out of this meeting with a better understanding of the User Stories, the Epics, the Features, the requirements or whatever it is that you have planned.

To achieve that, you need to stay on topic. This can be quite a challenge because as human beings we quite often get sidetracked. Many of us are fighting ADD (Attention Deficit Disorder) in today's world which makes it even tougher. Both authors suffer from it. We can easily wander on to a topic that is fascinating, but it is not getting us any closer to achieving our goals.

Display the goals visibly throughout the meeting so that everyone can see them. Hang them on the wall or have one display dedicated to showing them. Whenever participants wander off on a tangent, you can point out the goals to lead them back to the task at hand.

Use Open- and Closed-Ended Questions

One of the techniques recommended for conversations about requirements or User Stories is asking open-ended questions.

However, before we delve into the topic, we need to understand the differences between open- and closed-ended questions.

For closed-ended questions, the potential answers are often predefined (e.g. "yes/no/not sure"). However, a closed-ended question can also offer options for selecting an answer.

Open-ended questions offer the possibility to answer in a digressive way. They encourage discussion. An example of an open-ended question would be: "What problems do you have with the current solution?" The answer to this question varies from one to another and usually leads to a longer discussion.

Although we have mentioned that open-ended questions are recommended for requirements discussions, in our experience both types of questions are equally important.

If you want to have many details, ask an open-ended question. To make sure you understand what Stakeholders have said, closed-ended questions are especially useful. With a closed-ended question you confirm what the Stakeholders have said and make sure that all parties agree.

The Human Factor

Being human means that you can sense if a person you are talking to is even interested in what you are saying. This is based on reciprocity. If you are not interested in what the other person is telling you, they will feel it. And if he or she is not interested in working with you, you will notice. It is about a genuine interest in what the other side is saying.

There are people who have a natural talent for it. They are often person-oriented, but more importantly, they are curious by nature. When they are dealing with a topic and the other person knows more about it than they do, their interest is aroused, and that comes across very clearly. The better you manage to be genuinely interested, the more successful your conversations will be.

There is an interesting TED lecture called "Your Body Language May Shape Who You Are" which deals with body language and how it affects our minds. We have long known that our mood influences our body language. However, there are now some studies that show that it is possible to put yourself in a certain mood by assuming the posture or body language of that mood.

When you run a meeting, you want to make sure that everyone recognizes your authority from the start. According to this TED lecture, you can put yourself in the right mood by making yourself really big before the meeting (when no one is looking). Studies show that if you can pose convincingly for two minutes in front of a mirror, the hormones in your body build up to the point where you become more dynamic, assertive, and confident.

If you expect a participant to be less talkative and more hostile, you can still have a successful User Story conversation if you put yourself in the right mood before the meeting and are genuinely interested in what the other person has to say during the meeting.

Humor and Authenticity

Humor is a great tool if you use it properly. Of course, it must be politically correct; it must be sensitive. In our experience, there is no better way than to tell a story about yourself. Tell something silly about yourself. Something you did wrong, or a funny accident. If you tell it in a self-ironic way, it is not offensive.

You do not have to be a comedian to tell a humorous story. For instance, when one of the authors (Tom) is presenting to a group, he often tells a true story of how his wife portrayed him as "a mindless professor" at a meeting with a group of potential customers. Angela was born and raised in Germany and at that time was refining her knowledge of the English language. She meant to convey the American idiom that he was an "absent-minded professor" which is somewhat different.

If you bring in jokes about a different race, gender, religion or politics, there is a substantial risk that this meeting will be doomed to failure. We cannot emphasize enough that humor can be a life saver in a meeting, but we strongly recommend that it be used with care. Always make sure that all participants appreciate the humor.

But beware! We all think that everyone likes to have fun. Is that true? Although the general advice is to make meetings entertaining, have a few laughs and add some small talk, there are people who consider this a waste of time. Some people think that fun is not the purpose of a meeting.

Have you ever heard something like: "Meetings already take up too much time anyway", "Our job is to do what needs to be done and get back to work", "I hate pointless chatter and nonsense". Get to know your participants, and if you have participant(s) who think like this, leave the humor at home.

Our final advice for interacting with your Stakeholders:

Just Be Yourself!

Remember that you are conducting this meeting for a good reason; you have a clear goal. You are trying to understand what each Stakeholder needs. You are the one who has this meeting or conversation under control. You should be the one who leads the Stakeholders, the Subject Matter Experts, and even the technical team, because they do not know what you need. You are the only one who knows what **you** really need.

Since you are in control, you must feel comfortable. The best way to feel comfortable is to be yourself. The closer you can be to yourself, the more successful your meetings will be - that is a promise!

Nonverbal Communication

A huge part of the way we communicate occurs through nonverbal cues in conversations. Nonverbal communication refers to gestures, facial expressions, tone of voice, eye contact (or lack thereof), body language, posture, and other ways people communicate without using language. These cues can reinforce or undermine your message. How you communicate nonverbally can mean one thing to you and convey a completely different message to your audience.

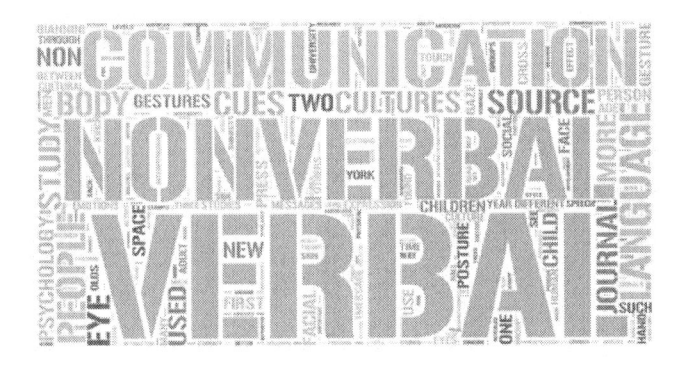

Used in conjunction with verbal communication, nonverbal skills can help punctuate, reinforce, emphasize, and enliven your message. Nonverbal cues help create shared meaning in any communication.

Negative body language creates a negative impression and tends to impede progress. Someone glancing at their watch, playing with their pen, and doodling during negotiations can come across as disinterested or uncooperative.

In this section we present tips and suggestions on how you can use non-verbal communication skills to have a successful conversation with a Stakeholder about their User Stories and requirements. You will learn how to interpret more effectively what the Stakeholder **does not** tell you. You will also learn what your own non-verbal messages could mean to your Stakeholders.

The newest studies show that there are four dimensions that you must pay attention to, to understand what the other person is saying. We call them **"the four C's of nonverbal communication"** and they are Context, Cluster, Culture, and Congruence.

Context Clarifies Intent

The first C stands for "Context". You must be careful to interpret the non-verbal clues your Stakeholders give you in the right context. As a facilitator, you need to be familiar with non-verbal communication to interpret the signals correctly. You must also ensure that what you present comes across in the right context.

Suppose you are talking to someone who avoids eye contact and glances at her phone. Based on the rules of non-verbal communication, you could conclude that this person is bored, but this is not necessarily true. She could just check her cell phone because when she left home this morning, her child was sick. So, think about what is happening around the non-verbal message (in the context of the message) before you come to a conclusion.

Another classic symbol for non-verbal communication is someone who listens to you with crossed arms in front of the body. Most of us have learned that this usually means that this person is not open to discussion or is not willing to discuss the subject. By crossing your arms, a barrier is created as a kind of protection. Sometimes crossed arms can also mean that the person feels vulnerable or insecure.

But it could also be that the room is cold, and the Stakeholder is just trying to stay warm! Make sure that you interpret the non-verbal signals in the context of the meeting. If you understand the context, you will save yourself unnecessary trouble.

Base Your Assumptions on Clusters

The second C in nonverbal communication is "cluster". Clustering means that you should never rely on a single signal to interpret nonverbal communication. A cluster is a group of signals which together lead to a conclusion. For example:

Don't speak to me in that tone of body language

In this picture, it is obvious that the young lady on the left is either angry or aggressive towards the other lady. Why? She gives us several different nonverbal clues,

1. the way she stands
2. her hands on her hips
3. the look in her eyes

A cluster is a group of non-verbal communication signals that all point to the same thing. Always look for three to five behaviors that fit together before assuming you know what the nonverbal message is.

Culture Makes All the Difference

The third C of non-verbal communication is "Culture". The meaning of a nonverbal message varies from culture to culture. If you talk to someone you grew up with or who has a lot in common with you, you are likely to interpret their nonverbal communication accurately.

But what about someone from another country? In most Western cultures, moving the head up and down is understood as an expression of agreement (YES), while moving the head back and forth expresses rejection (NO).

However, this non-verbal communication is not universal. If you are talking to a person from Bulgaria (or from another Balkan country, for that matter), you should be careful with the use of non-verbal "yes" or "no" signals. Nodding means "no" in some countries, while shaking your head up and down actually means "yes".

For example, if you are talking to someone from Greece, tilting your head sideways while your eyes are slightly closed means 'yes'. This is similar to the gesture Americans make when they are confused about something. Funnily enough, "naí" in Greek means "yes" in English, a sound that is remarkably like the English "no". Confusion guaranteed.

Another important point to note is that while you are reading the other person's body signals, they are reading yours as well. So, guess what a Greek or Bulgarian understands when you nod your consent. Nonverbal communication, like any other communication, is a two-way street. You send out nonverbal signals and try to interpret what the other person says.

Congruence: Avoid Mixed Signals

The fourth C of non-verbal communication is "Congruence". Imagine a sales representative trying to sell you a new dishwasher. His words should win you over, but the body language makes you feel that you cannot trust the person. The words are not consistent with the actions. If words and deeds tell the same story, they are congruent.

A study on human communication conducted in the 1960s is often misquoted. The reason: congruence! This study was based on a presentation method in which the visual, verbal and vocal messages were **incongruent**, i.e. they conveyed mixed signals. **Under these circumstances,** about 7% believed the message verbally (what was being said), 38% vocally (how the voice said it) and no less than 55% believed the visual messages (what the speaker saw) most. The take-away was that we believe more what our eyes tell us than the words we hear.

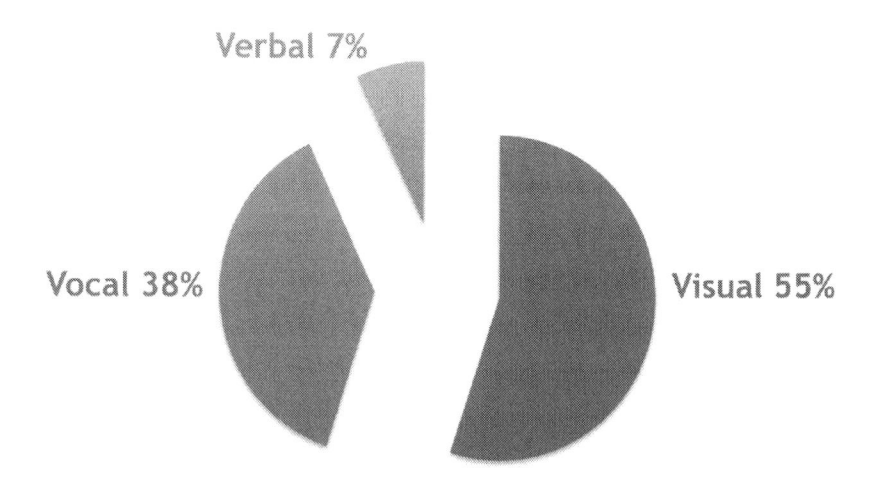

Verbal 7%

Vocal 38%

Visual 55%

The study is only correct if the spoken word conveys a different message than the supporting visual messages, i.e. there is no congruence between the verbal, visual and vocal messages.

From the perspective of requirements elicitation, however, we can use this study to our advantage. If there is an inconsistency between what someone says and their body language during a conversation, you should believe their body language. It probably says more about reality than the words.

By the way, the study is also a perfect indication of how we choose politicians. If they look good and sound good, who cares what they say? They will win anyway, because their words only make up 7% of the message and politicians are almost always incongruent.

Dealing with People

The goal of any communication related to capturing requirements, be it a 3-amigo conversation to get User Stories, a planned requirements meeting with Stakeholders or a facilitated workshop, is to fully understand the Stakeholders' requirements and wishes for their new digital solution.

The primary goal of the discussion is to minimize misunderstandings. For the past 50 odd years, almost every study about why IT projects fail indicates that missing and misunderstood requirements are the number one cause of project failure.

Understanding Is Not Enough

Misunderstanding is a big waste of time and who would not want to minimize misunderstandings? The challenge we face is different folks have different interpretations of the same word. A fitting example is the word "account".

If you talk to someone in the Finance about an "account", they think of bank accounts, credit card accounts, debit accounts and so on. If you talk to someone in Sales about an "account", they think about a customer account. For both, it is the correct interpretation or the correct meaning of the word "account". Yet another meaning of "account" is an e-mail account. Most people, no matter what they do in life, have a definition of what the word "account" means to them.

It is not enough to believe that we understand the Stakeholder. What we really need is **mutual** understanding. You can walk away from a conversation convinced that you know exactly what the other person meant. The other person leaves with the conviction that they understood exactly what you meant, only for one or both of you to realize later that you did not have the same interpretation at all.

Mutual understanding is the big challenge. People are people. There are many people with whom you have a quick connection and others who are exceedingly difficult to understand.

If you want to have a meaningful conversation about Business Requirements, User Stories, Epics, Features, etc., you need to be able to deal with all the different behaviors and terminology.

Dealing with Difficult People

A comedian once quipped: "The earth would be such a beautiful planet if it weren't for all the people". Whether you agree with this comment or not, it is obviously not a good attitude for someone who tries to elicit User Stories and requirements.

We all have problems with certain behaviors of other people, especially when we try to get a certain outcome from our interaction. The good news is that there are ways to deal with any behavior if you only have time to think about it and plan ahead.

You need strategies for difficult people

There are some people with whom you have instant rapport; there are other people that seem difficult. Difficult people will upset the balance of any meeting, kill the momentum, de-motivate people, and keep you from achieving your goal.

There is a significant difference between people who engage in lively discussion, question conventional thinking, and contribute to the pool of ideas - and those who become negative, make it personal and thereby create unpleasant feelings. If you do not deal with them promptly and effectively, it will not be long before they have made it impossible for you to achieve your goals.

What are the best strategies for dealing with people who are belligerent, disruptive, negative, or simply do not contribute? Since every situation is different, there is no "one-size-fits-all" approach. You need to develop a method that works for you. The best we can do is to give you some general suggestions, but your strategy must fit your specific situation.

Dominators

A group with which many facilitators have problems are Dominators. The Dominators want to take the helm. There is nothing wrong with that (there is nothing wrong with any of the behavioral concepts we present here). It is not that these characteristics are bad. It is about recognizing them and finding ways to deal with them when they are about to put a discussion on the wrong track.

If you are holding a workshop or a multi-Stakeholder meeting, the Dominators will talk the most. However, it is important that you integrate everyone's feedback into a coherent set. You must ensure that **everyone** contributes their thoughts and ideas.

A tip that works very well for us is to call every attendee by name and ask for his/her opinion. Groups tend to adapt to the leader's style. Asking a general question without specifying who should respond is an open invitation for Dominators to take over.

If the group notices that you are calling on each of them by name, the Dominators have less of an opportunity to jump in. In extreme cases where that does not work, the Dominator may jeopardize the success of the meeting and you may be forced to ask him or her to leave the meeting.

You will never have a problem getting the Dominator to tell you what he/she wants. The problem will be making sure everyone else contributes as well. Otherwise, the results of the requirements workshop can be a disaster for your future IT solution.

Quitters

A Quitter is someone who starts a sentence and stops in the middle of the sentence. Their eyes glass over, or they look away. They wander off into space somewhere thinking about something that may or may not be relevant. What were they trying to say? Was it important?

Another form of Quitter's are people that suddenly quit taking your calls. They seem no longer interested in the product or project. They are not willing to have another conversation, so you have no choice but to define your own interpretation of their requirements. Good, bad, or indifferent.

One effective way to deal with Quitters is to talk to them outside the group setting. Try to find their motivation for "quitting" and figure out how to make them realize the importance of this initiative or product for their future. As facilitator of the meeting, you must be the chief motivator. Find out why they quit and try to explain how contributing in the meeting will address their issue.

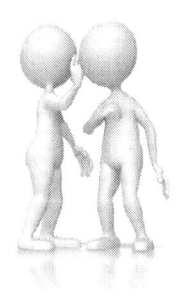

Distractors

Another group of "problem children" are Distractors, which also includes Talkers and Whisperers. Anybody who does anything that gets the group sidetracked, leads them astray, or gets them off topic is a Distractor.

Again, not a bad trait necessarily. Sometimes, it can be productive especially if they bring humor or tell a joke. That can be positive as well as negative. In general, what we mean with Distractors are people that disrupt the flow of a conversation.

For example, we talk about topic A and Distractors start talking about topic B or C, then they get everyone else to talk about F, and suddenly everyone has forgotten about topic A. If the Distractors get out of control, it can derail the entire meeting.

To counteract this, try to make the group understand the importance of achieving the goal. For example, promise that if everyone focuses on topic A, everyone will be able to go home earlier.

Everyone knows Talkers and Whisperers. When you are in a meeting with several people and a subgroup in a corner of the room is quietly talking about something else, everyone focuses on the whispering, which distracts the entire group.

To deal with these types of Distractors, ask them to repeat aloud what they have said so that the whole group can benefit.

Resistors and Doubters

Resisters and Doubters are against everything. Often, they show up in a workshop and when they hear an idea, they will say something like, "Oh, we tried that here. It didn't work in '05. It isn't going to work now". Or they might say, "I don't think that makes any sense in our company. It doesn't really provide any value for us". Resisters and Doubters most likely will hold you back.

The best way to deal with them is a preventive strike. Ask at the beginning of the workshop if there is someone in the room who has worked on similar projects before. Let them recapitulate their experiences briefly. Then encourage them to use these experiences in the evaluation of all ideas developed in this workshop. By leveraging their negative experiences, you might just win them over.

Disinterested

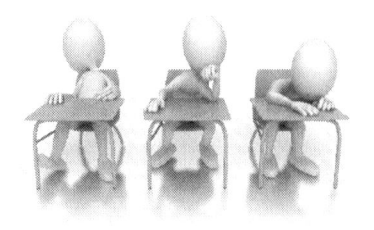

The Disinterested are the group that poses a challenge for many people. They simply do not pay attention. They do not feel any urgency. They are not aware of the importance of the topic. Often, they do not see how it will affect them and therefore cannot imagine how or why they should be involved.

Because of that, they are off in space doing other things. Their disinterest can affect the whole group. They can become Distractors simply because they are not interested in what the group is talking about.

Our main strategy with the Disinterested is to actively involve them, challenge them with somewhat provocative questions and praise their contributions individually (sometimes offline, depending on the norms of the environment).

A Simple Technique to Rule Them All

An excellent tool for managing the group is to post the rules of the meeting so that they can be read by everyone, wherever they are sitting. Present the rules at the beginning of the meeting and, whenever the situation gets out of control, remind the group of the rules. Sometimes, simply pointing to the rule that is violated suffices to make the group aware of the situation.

The most important rule: never embarrass individuals in front of the group, as this will have a negative impact on productivity and their contribution.

Exercise: Problem People or People Problems

Sharing ideas on how to deal with tricky situations will give you an advantage when you are in the moment.

Instructions:

Assuming you are trying to elicit business needs from Stakeholders, name personality traits, quirks, or behaviors that you find challenging.

Question 1:

Which personality traits, idiosyncrasies or behavioral patterns do you find challenging when dealing with Stakeholders?

Question 2:

What would help you to deal with these characteristics more effectively?

Answer Question 1: What types of personalities or attitudes are most challenging for you?

For the authors, the most challenging personality types are Dominators and Distractors.

Answer Question 2: What would help you to deal with those traits more effectively?

When dealing with Dominators, we acknowledge their contributions and then call out other people to solicit their contributions to the topic at hand. If the problem persists, the next level is to chat with the Dominator offline during a break and ask that they allow others to participate as well. Final level (only had to use it one time) is to ask the Dominator to leave the session and talk with his manager to get a replacement.

When dealing with Distractors, the most effective technique we have discovered is to position ourselves close to them to make them aware that their behavior is counterproductive.

3 Listening Techniques that Promote Common Understanding

One way to achieve mutual understanding is to use good listening techniques. How well you listen has a major impact on the effectiveness of your efforts to elicit requirements.

- ☑ You need to listen to the sponsor to find out what the initiative or project is about.

- ☑ You need to listen to your stakeholders to understand what their needs and wants are.

- ☑ You need to listen to the technology folks to make sure that they understand what the requirements really mean an.

- ☑ You need to listen to your manager to ensure that your actions are consistent with the company's objectives.

Everyone must listen to other people sometimes. But as a product Owner, Business Analyst, Subject Matter Expert, or anyone else who defines Features, User Stories and other requirements, listening is one of your most important skills. How can you hone this skill? What business analysis techniques are available to improve your listening skills?

We will introduce you to three listening techniques that you should practice: **Active listening**, **informational listening**, and **Highway 350**. Each technique helps independently. Taken together, they give you the priceless ability to hear not only what the other person is saying, but more importantly, what they are NOT saying.

Active Listening

Active listening has been around for some time, and many of you have been trained in some form or another. Nonetheless, we want to mention it here because it is a critical element in achieving mutual understanding. It is about making sure that the other person knows that you are listening and are interested in what he/she is saying. For that reason, it is also called "Engaged Listening".

Active listening is a two-way communication, which means that you not only have to read the body language, but also "speak" it. You must send out the right signals with your body language because you should assume that the other person can read it whether they have had the training or not. Body language is read by the nonconscious mind, meaning it is laced with nuances and cultural interpretations. Of course, after the third drink on a date, we all slur our body language just as readily as we slur our words but that is a different story.

In addition to many nonverbal components, active listening involves paying attention, withholding judgment, discarding prejudices and biases, reflecting, clarifying, summarizing, and sharing. Here is a summary of the most important components.

Maintaining Eye Contact

Eye contact during a conversation is of crucial importance. Sustained eye contact is a sign of trust: if you do not look away, you have nothing to hide. It gives us information about what is going on in our conversation partner or whether we consider him or her trustworthy and credible. But be careful! There are cultures in which it is considered impolite to look the other person directly in the eye. What we should actually say here is "maintain culturally appropriate eye contact".

Friendliness

Use smiles to show that you are paying attention to what the person says or as a way of agreeing. Combined with nods of the head, smiles can be amazingly effective in affirming that messages are being listened to and understood.

Verbal Cues

Verbal cues are simple things like "aha", "yeah", "very good", "really?" They give the other person signals that you are truly listening; that you are processing what they are telling you. However, overuse of these words and phrases can become irritating. Sometimes it is better to elaborate and explain why you are agreeing with a certain point.

Paraphrase or Summarize

Paraphrasing or summarizing are great techniques for active listening. They let the speaker know that you really understand what the other person is saying. Both can go a long way to achieve mutual understanding.

The word "paraphrase" does not mean to repeat the words you heard verbatim. You might get very strange reactions for repeating something back word for word. It only fulfills its role as great communications tool if you use different words to express the same point.

Sum up what you think they said in your own words. Start with, "What I'm hearing is…," or "Sounds like you are saying…,". Those are great ways to start a paraphrased sentence. If they listen to your words and agree that that is exactly the message they were trying to get across, you are a whole lot closer to having achieved the "holy grail" that is mutual understanding.

Ask Relevant Questions

Show your stakeholders that you have been paying attention by asking relevant questions that will help clarify the situation. By asking relevant questions, the listener also emphasizes that he or she is interested in what the other person said. However, it is important to give each speaker the opportunity to finish his or her point before you ask questions. As a rule, do not interrupt anyone to clarify a question unless it is critical to the intent of the conversation.

Informational Listening

When you listen to learn something, "informational listening" skills can make this task much easier. This is listening with the goal of understanding and grasping information. It is about making sure that you are not just hearing the words but recognizing the relevant information out of what the other person said.

These skills are crucial for people in the espionage or secret service industry, as often certain words can tip the scales for an entire conversation. Although we do not recommend covert operations for Business Analysts, sometimes it is beneficial to adopt techniques from that arena to achieve our ultimate goal, namely ensuring a mutual understanding.

While listening informatively, you concentrate on capturing the essence of the conversation. You only want to pick out the parts of the conversation that you really need. Especially in conversations about requirements and User Stories, careful informational listening is critical. You want to listen with the aim of evaluating what you have heard and extracting the specific information you need.

Informative listening gives you the information you need, despite all the other things the person may have said that did not necessarily contribute to your question.

This is a new concept and we therefore recommend that you take a closer look at it. It will help you to get more relevant facts out of your requirement interviews and workshops than just Active Listening. By listening informatively, you will get the answers and insights you need, regardless of what else has been discussed.

Informational listening is the difference between a dispute and a discussion, between confrontation and negotiation, possibly even between war and peace. As the one who defines the product, you should be emotionally distanced. After all, who could get emotional about business solutions involving information technology?

Nonetheless, if you want to make sure that you are gathering the User Stories and Features that your Stakeholders are trying to communicate, you just might want to give informational listening a chance. It might not change your life, but it could just change your project — which could just change your life.

Highway 350

Another concept while listening is "Highway 350". It is based on your capacity to listen to someone at a speed of 500 words per minute and understand every single word. This is based on studies conducted on English speakers. We do not have relevant statistics for other languages.

The average English speaker, however, speaks at a rate of 150 words per minute. The difference between the two is 350 (500 minus 150 - go ahead, you have a computer; check our math). This means that you have a listening capacity of 350 words, which you do not use while you are listening to someone speak.

The concept is called Highway 350 because it is down that road that your thoughts go zooming off toward the horizon, even while you are listening to every single word that the other person says. That is neither good nor bad. It just is. The questions is how you use Highway 350.

If you use it to think about other topics, such as how to end the conversation, what is for dinner or who is coming for dinner, the other person will notice. This is a major cause for misunderstandings. If, however, you use Highway 350 to apply the active and informational listening techniques we presented above, it becomes an immensely powerful tool in your listening arsenal.

Bias Can Lead Us Astray

There are a few other things that get in the way of listening effectively. Amongst them are Biases. Cognitive biases affect your communications and decision making. Recognizing and knowing how to deal with cognitive bias during requirements elicitation might just be the difference between great or poor User Stories. We will show you three types of bias and give you a few tips on how to combat them.

Confirmation Bias

Confirmation bias is our tendency (we all suffer from it) to filter out and focus on information that confirms our existing beliefs or ideas while ignoring anything that contradicts them. A famous quote from Warren Buffet hits the nail on the head,

> *"What the human being is best at doing is interpreting all new information so that their prior conclusions remain intact."*

When someone says something that confirms something you already "knew", your brain goes on a short vacation. It obviously celebrates the fact that there is someone else who is as intelligent as you and who recognizes this important fact.

The result is that you "switch off" and no longer listen properly. Of course, your razor-sharp mind immediately "fills" the gap with what you remember, what the other person just said, and you leave with the impression that you heard every single word of the conversation.

For example, a study recently found a confirmation bias in chess players. The players were selected from all levels, i.e. from beginners to world champions. The study presented the same challenge for beginners and experts alike. Participants were given a well-known chess configuration in which the player could achieve checkmate within five moves.

The study showed that although there was a better move that led to checkmate in three moves, most players at once recognized the familiar setup and used the five-move solution. The experienced players were more likely to fall into this trap than beginners! The main problem with confirmation bias is that it blinds us to alternatives.

Confirmation bias is a significant cause of misunderstanding and unfortunately difficult to ignore. To counteract it, you need to recognize when it happens. Whenever you are in a conversation and realize that you really do not know what the other party just replied, your mind went on a little vacation. When that happens, you should politely interrupt the other person and ask them to repeat what they had said.

In addition, you should always question your deeply held beliefs so that you can rationally evaluate new information. Recognize the other person's point of view. The payout will be immediate in how the other person perceives you and how you can more quickly achieve that "mutual understanding".

Emotional Bias

You do not need to be a Facilitator or Requirements Engineer to experience emotional bias. Imagine you are involved in a discussion to which there is a significant amount of emotion attached. For instance, a conversation with your spouse (not that it ever happened to us), or your boss (same disclaimer), or someone with an opposing political view (but who gets emotional over politics?).

As soon as an abundance of emotions is involved, our nonconscious mind gets real busy "feeling" things and that apparently takes precedence over "listening". We get so busy trying to convince the other party of the rightness of our viewpoint that we are incapable of extracting the informational content of their message.

Avoiding emotional involvement is incredibly challenging. That is why so many books have been written about it. It is why psychiatrists live in expensive mansions. Of course, recognizing it in the heat of the moment is difficult, but whenever you recognize it, the first step we recommend is a cooling off period as a first step.

After that, you need to decide whether a follow-up is desirable (highly recommended if the situation involved your spouse or boss; for the political discussion, you are on your own). If you decide that a follow-up is needed, then we recommend trying to change the physical setting before you cautiously restart the conversation.

But what can you do if this happens in a conversation with one of your stakeholders? It is probably not the best idea to leave the meeting to cool off. If, on the other hand, you are not able to deal with your emotional bias, this may cause the meeting or even the workshop to fail.

Recognize Your Own Feelings and Those of Others!

One solution is to enhance your emotional awareness. Become aware of your own emotions and the possible effects these emotions have, both on yourself and the others. Pay attention to the ways in which your emotions affect your behavior. Being able to accurately assess yourself will allow you to make the necessary changes, diffuse the situation, and get back to creating a productive environment.

The other side is recognizing and dealing with the emotions of others. Avoid being biased towards them. Become aware of their emotions but do not judge them. If they are angry, do not think they are unprofessional. That constitutes a high emotional bias towards the feelings of others. Instead, use empathy to identify with the situation. To reduce your emotional bias, you must be more accepting and understanding of the emotions of others.

If you need to deal with your own emotions first, you could recommend a short break to everyone or switch the topic. Sometimes, simple mindfulness techniques can be your best friend in those situations.

The Vividness Effect

A final disruptive factor for active and informational listening is the vividness effect. This is what happens in your nonconscious mind when someone mentions something that has made a deep impression on you in the past.

For older Americans, events like Pearl Harbor and the Kennedy assassination are memories they will never forget. For those who were emotionally aware when it happened, a more recent event like 9/11, the attack on the World Trade Center, was one of those moments. Every American certainly knows exactly where they were and what they did on that day. Currently, dealing with the Covid-19 pandemic is creating scars in all of us that will be with us for the rest of our lives.

In the course of an ordinary day these events are just that - memories. However, if someone mentions one of these topics or even uses a term that activates that memory, your nonconscious mind starts reliving it and makes your conscious mind aware of the memory.

If you are talking and someone brings up something that triggers the vividness effect, you will at least be a little distracted. As a result, you "switch off" and must leave it to your perfect brain to "fill in" the gap afterwards.

Recognize When It Happens!

The best remedy here is the same as for confirmation bias. Recognize when it happens and ask the other person to repeat what they said earlier. Do not simply accept what you think you have understood. Our marvelous mind is always able to "fill in the blanks" with whatever it thinks is right.

The Vividness effect, however, is not only about simply switching off and being distracted. Since the Vividness Effect also depends on how vivid or horrible the images of the event were and how much they were intensified by the media in recent decades.

For example, a year after the Columbine High School massacre, about 60 percent of Americans who responded to a USA Weekend survey said they thought a shooting at their own school was likely. This did not correspond to reality.

What does this have to do with your requirement discussions about User Stories? Glad you asked!

Imagine you are conducting a conversation with a legislator who defines the User Stories or Features for a new gun law. Do you think that reporting on mass shootings that you see online and on television today would influence your decision making? Would you remain neutral and recognize that the legislator is the expert in the field, or would the vividness effect cause you to make assumptions and judgments?

By now, you may feel that because of these obstacles you cannot succeed with active or informational listening or even with Highway 350. The main reason to bring them up is not to discourage you, but to make you aware of them.

Recognize confirmation bias, emotional bias, and the vividness effect on yourself as well as on others and do not let yourself be distracted from the goal of your requirements conversation, meeting, or workshop. Knowing these obstacles will enable you to create high quality User Stories, Features, Epics, etc. based on mutual understanding with your stakeholders.

Prepare to End on a High Note

At the end of a conversation with your stakeholders, try to follow the adage: "always leave them laughing". This may not be appropriate in all situations, but if it fits, it is our preferred method of ending interviews, meetings, and workshops.

In the end, make sure that all parties are satisfied with the results. Your stakeholders should feel that this was a productive conversation that made progress. That you got the information you needed. Make them feel that they have made a valuable contribution to your project.

Make Results Available to All Participants

Capture the conversation - record it, write it down, enter it into your computer or whatever. Then either share the results at the end with all participants or let them know when they can expect the results.

Let the person or group know what you have learned from the conversation. Inform your stakeholders that the results obtained will be part of the official record, i.e. they will become part of the product Backlog (User Stories, Epics, etc.), the Feature list, or another requirements repository, depending on the approach your company takes.

The participants need to be able to look at your results and to confirm for themselves and for you that everything is as they meant it. Allow them to make changes if they feel that you missed something or interpreted it incorrectly.

Having closure to your conversation is an effective way of ending on a high note. Make sure all participants recognize the value the session added. And by the way if it is appropriate, we still like the saying, "always leave them laughing".

Tips for Email and Chats

Given the global reach of many organizations or the widespread distribution of a company within one country, face-to-face conversations (online or in person) are not the only means of communication. Email, chat, and IM are widely used in the business environment. This has become even more widespread since the pandemic struck.

Exchanging emails or chat messages is a convenient way to gather information for your User Stories, Features, or other requirements. If you are closing in on a deadline, email and messaging can be an ideal approach for multitasking. They are also especially useful to confirm and clarify questions.

However, there are some things you must pay attention to since misunderstandings in these formats are even more common than in personal conversations. Here are some tips that we have successfully applied in the past.

1. State Your Purpose

Before you ask questions (especially open questions that allow a longer answer), let the recipient know what you need. What is this e-mail or chat about?

Express your goals in the subject line if you use e-mail. Most people look at the subject line first when they receive a stack of email. If that does not get their attention, they might just skip your email and move on to the next one.

2. Let the Recipient Know Your Role

Make sure that your Stakeholder understands your role quickly. They need to know:

- → Who you are
- → Why you need to know this information
- → Why you are authorized to ask these questions
- → Why you can be trusted with the answers
- → Why they should take the time to respond

3. Keep your questions clear and short

All questions should be clear and concise. We like to use examples that show what kind of answer we expect. For example, if you ask them for a User Story, a question like "What are your User Stories?" would not produce good results. However, if you give an example of what a User Story looks like and what exactly you need from them, your chances of getting something useful will increase drastically.

4. Limit the Number of Questions

Keep the number of questions between five and nine if you want them to respond quickly (or at all). If you are presenting a huge list of questions to recipients, they will have to spend a lot of time on it. And who has the luxury of time in today's world? However, most people can find the time to answer a few questions. Make it as easy as possible for them to answer them by numbering the questions and leaving space for the answers.

5. End with a Matching Final Question

As a last question, we recommend something like: "Can you think of anything I forgot to ask?" Give them the opportunity to expand their answers and bring in aspects and issues they consider important.

Before you end the chat or email, let them know when you need the answer. If you do not receive a response from your stakeholder by that date, send a follow-up reminder. If you still do not receive a response after that,

- make assumptions,
- communicate them to the stakeholder,
- and let them know that unless they correct your assumptions by a specific date, you will be forced to conclude that the assumptions are correct.

Finally, you should not forget to thank the recipients in advance. Let them know that you appreciate their time to keep the project on track. The little word "thank you" can make an enormous difference and be very motivating.

As soon as you have received an answer, follow up with further questions you might have. You should apply all the concepts we mentioned earlier about effective conversations to your email and messaging discussions.

III Agile Requirements Analysis and Backlog Grooming

"Agile" or "Lean" does not eliminate the need for solid analysis. However, compared to traditional approaches, these modern development approaches significantly change when and to what level of detail analysis is needed. Whether you use conventional or Agile methods, digital solution initiatives will fail if the technical team does not understand the true business needs of the organization.

In the last chapter, you learned how to use elicitation or discovery techniques to **seed or replenish a Backlog**. In this chapter, we will look at User Story Analysis (**groom/refine Backlog, elaborate selected User Stories**).

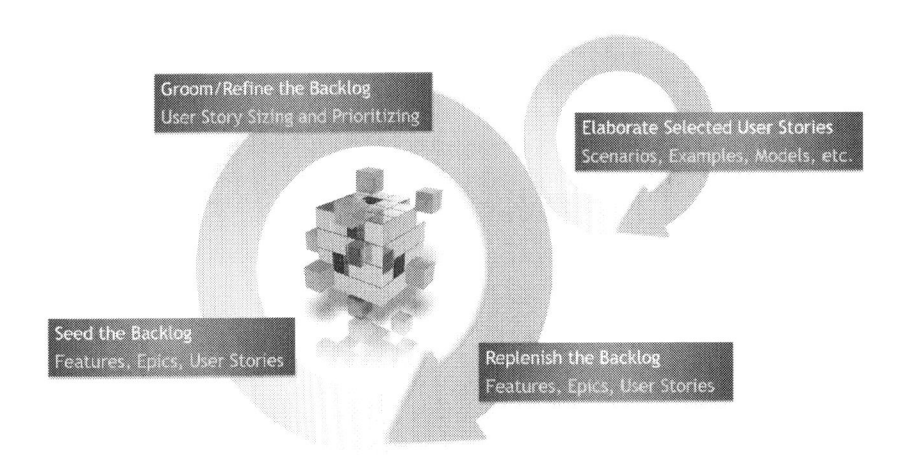

In line with Lean principles, it would be a waste of time to analyze and perfect User Stories or Features as you capture them because you cannot know if they will ever be implemented. For this reason, requirements elicitation and requirements analysis in modern development approaches are usually far apart in terms of time.

Requirements Analysis is needed to groom or refine the Backlog, to plan the next Release or Sprint, or in 3-amigo meetings to support developers during the Sprint.

Traditionally, requirements analysis has been the responsibility of Requirements Engineers, Systems Analysts, Business Analysts, or developers. In Lean/Agile approaches, whoever is best qualified takes over this role in the Agile Team. As a result, everyone, from the Product Owner to the Business Analyst, Subject Matter Expert, Project Manager, and even the entire Agile and business-side teams, needs analysis techniques like the ones we will cover in this chapter.

As facilitators and management consultants we have experienced many different constellations and role assignments in different companies.

The heart and soul of this chapter is User Story Analysis or, in general, analysis for textual requirements. The outcome is User Stories and Features that are ready for the next Release or Sprint.

This book does not cover Requirements Analysis using visual representations such as Process and Data Models as those are special cases that should be handled separately (and require another book).

Topics Covered in this Chapter

First, we explore the timing of analysis in more depth in a Lean and Agile environment. We will be using the Agile method "Scrum" to show the timing of business needs / requirements specification. You will learn the evolution of a Lean requirement from the Product Backlog to the Sprint where the developers code the next Release.

We will introduce you to another important concept of Lean/Agile Analysis, namely "Just in Time (JIT)" communication. Gone are the days when we delivered a flood of low-level solution requirements or specifications that were outdated as soon as we delivered them. JIT Analysis cuts waste and improves software quality.

Our next focus is on making sure that User Stories, Features, or other textual requirements are clear, correct, consistent, complete, unambiguous, verifiable, and at the level of detail that the developers need to code the solution. You will learn several techniques to remove ambiguity and subjectivity from your User Stories and Features. This will strengthen the team's ability to deliver the RIGHT product or solution for the business. In addition, it will shorten the duration of conversations with the technical team saving everyone time and resources.

The "Small" requirement in the INVEST model drives us to break large User Stories apart. That process is known as User Story Splitting. Each User Story must be small enough that developers can complete it during the current iteration, but it still must deliver value to the user community. That consideration makes User Story splitting extremely challenging. To make this task easier, we will present 5 User Story splitting techniques that have worked best for us.

During Sprint Planning, the developers or the Agile team need much more detail to ensure mutual understanding. This is the right time for developers, testers, and the business community to further analyze upcoming User Stories and define technical specifications, i.e. to make sure they are ready for programming.

To design a solution that meets defined User Stories or Features, developers need help from the business to get to the right level of detail to make the right design decisions. This chapter describes a technique called Story Decomp (Feature Drill-down). It is one of the best techniques we have ever used to decompose a User Story into Functional Features (a.k.a. Solution Requirements).

Even in a Lean and Agile environment, most developers use something like Story Decomp either intuitively or consciously when they design the solution for a User Story. Functional Features define what the software must DO (Business Functions) and what people using the software need to KNOW (Business Data).

Last, we present ideas for discovering Qualities that the solution must deliver expressed in the form of Non-Functional Requirements (NFR). We present common types of NFRs that you need to consider for any attempt to automate business processes.

Whether the business community, Business Analyst, or Product Owner is involved in the last two steps depends on the experience of the technical team and the standards of the organization. We have included these techniques for the readers involved in defining the technical specifications.

Timing of Analysis in a Typical Agile Lifecycle

Conventional Software Life Cycle

A traditional software development lifecycle (i.e. Waterfall) follows strict phases, sticking to the original requirements and design plan created at the beginning of the project. Waterfall is a step by step process with several phases, for example, Analysis, Design, Testing, Implementation. The output of one phase becomes the input of the next phase. In short, there is little to no overlapping phases in a strict Waterfall model. Each phase of a Waterfall model is unique and well organized.

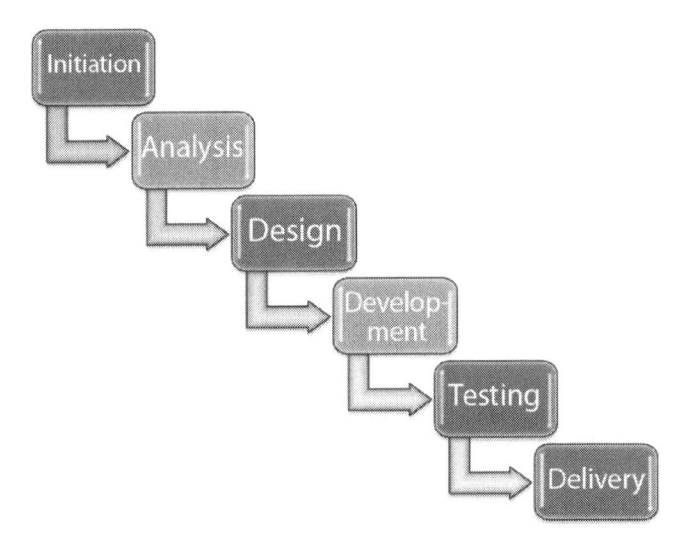

The analysis phase (requirements elicitation and analysis) is about collecting and analyzing Business-, Stakeholder-, and Solution Requirements for the entire project and documenting the findings in a Business Requirements Document (BRD).

Since all Business Requirements are defined to the software specification level of detail at the beginning of the project, the effort to change a User Story or requirement is enormous. If the project is already in the programming phase, it may not even be possible.

Lean / Agile Software Lifecycle

Agile and Lean lifecycles, on the other hand, are a set of principles that encourage flexibility, adaptability, communication, and working software over plans and processes. In Agile, you find two important concepts – Incremental and Iterative.

Incremental product development means building something piece by piece, just as you build an image by completing a puzzle. In an incremental development method, software is developed and delivered in individual pieces (Releases).

Iterative product development means building something by successive refinements, starting from a "Minimum Viable Product", also called MVP.

An MVP has sufficient Features to attract the interest of enthusiastic customers and meet their basic needs. However, the product must be sufficiently usable to provide practical benefits. It is then refined through customer feedback.

Regardless of lifecycle, business needs analysis, meaning defining what developers should build, is a critically important activity on any software development effort.

As mentioned before, in a traditional development environment such as Waterfall, requirements are defined at the beginning of a project for the entire scope of the project. This is no longer true for Agile approaches.

> *Since Agile development is iterative and incremental, requirements discovery and analysis also must become iterative and incremental.*

To illustrate this point, let us look at how Requirements Analysis fits into an Agile lifecycle. Lean and Agile are about flexibility, adaptability, and minimizing waste. There are many different life cycle implementations around the world. To explain the timing of analysis activities in an Agile lifecycle, we use the Agile method "Scrum".

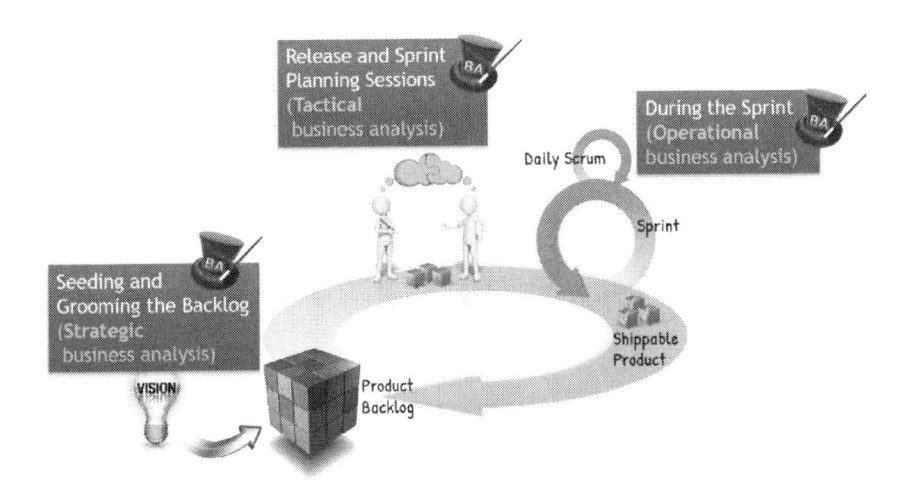

Just in Time (JIT) vs. Just in Case (JIC)

Before we delve into the Agile lifecycle, there are two important concepts that we need to define. They are **Just-in-Time (JIT) and Just-in-Case (JIC)**.

Although the Agile philosophy originated in software development, the Lean philosophy is not just focused on software it is about building anything. The key concept behind Lean is,

"Do not waste our time, money, and energy doing things that are later going to prove unnecessary or totally useless.

Do not do things too early because as the world changes, they may turn out to be irrelevant."

Just-in-Time (JIT) allows to optimize the availability of resources. In the manufacturing industry, for example, JIT means that we produce or build a part when someone orders it or needs it. We do not produce concrete blocks until someone builds a house. That is the just-in-time concept. In the Lean philosophy, all work is postponed until the "last responsible moment".

Just-in-Case (JIC) says that we will have enough concrete blocks in stock so that the construction workers can do their work without waiting (which would waste their time). JIC can be a waste of resources if it is not well planned and carefully managed.

In a Lean or Agile software environment, you need to minimize the JIC workload, but still plan for developers to have User Stories available when needed. On the other hand, you do not want to waste resources by defining details of User Stories and requirements that may never be implemented.

The Waterfall method applies the JIC concept on a broad basis. In this method, all requirements down to the system specifications are defined before development begins, i.e. before one line of code is written. There are still some projects where this process model is required, but they are rare. Most contemporary software initiatives benefit from an Agile and Lean development process that increases business agility.

JIT and JIC = Last Responsible Moment for Analysis

Another expression for JIT and JIC is "last responsible moment". But what is the last responsible moment for User Story Analysis? In Agile methods like Scrum, detailed User Stories with Acceptance Criteria and Test Scenarios or even technical specifications are created as late as possible which is usually to a certain degree during Release Planning and to a more granular level during Sprint Planning.

Just-in-time Lean Analysis means that you are no more than one or two releases ahead of the development team with detailed and flushed out User Stories. As Product Owner, or as we like to call this role, the one who wears the business analysis hat, you must analyze and prioritize the Business and Stakeholder Requirements (i.e. User Stories and Epics) for the next **1-2 Releases**.

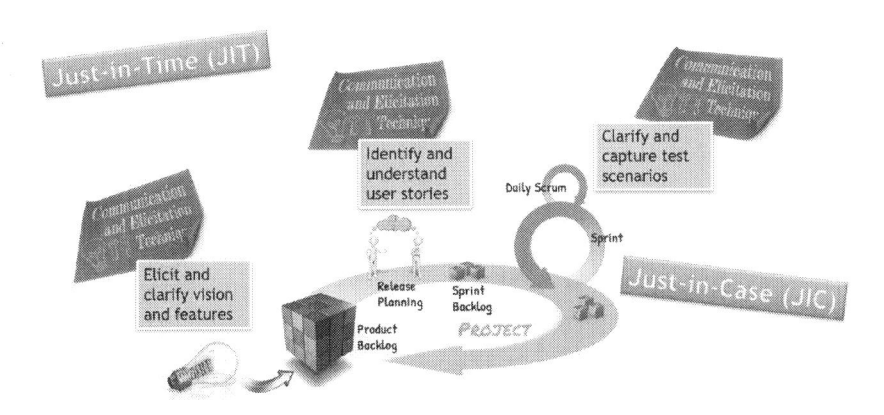

During Sprint Planning, developers need a clear understanding of the requirements at the solution level (i.e. Functional and Non-Functional

Requirements). That is when the development teams, together with the Business Analyst (or the one wearing the BA hat), the Product Owner, and the SME, create solution-level requirements (aka Solution Requirements or Specifications).

As you can see, requirements communication, elicitation, and analysis techniques are needed "just-in-time" across the entire spectrum of the product. In a few instances, you even need "just-in-case" items but keep them limited because Lean Software Development is all about not wasting time by recognizing complexities and dealing with them in the most efficient manner. It helps if all members of the Agile Team as well as the members of the Business Team(s) are familiar with Requirements Elicitation and Analysis techniques.

Since we authored this book primarily for representatives of the business community, we will only briefly introduce Release and Sprint planning to give you an idea of what they are.

Release Planning

In Scrum, designing and programming software is divided into **Releases** and **Sprints**. The goal of a Release is delivering various sets of usable Features or functionalities that provide business value to the customer. A Release has a predefined duration, typically three to six months but that can vary from one organization to the next.

Many organizations have their own rules regarding the release of their products to customers. Some choose to Release new functionality from each Sprint; others combine the results of several Sprints into one Release.

As we have already mentioned, a Lean/Agile team member (in Scrum the Product Owner) manages the expectations of customers, users, and other stakeholders. This person decides what will be developed, when it will be developed, and in what order.

During Release Planning, the Product Owner is responsible for the business side and works with the technical team consisting of developers and testers to extract out of the Product Backlog those items that the team feels they can complete in a 3 to 6-month timeframe (or whatever the organization deems the right time frame).

The driving force, in this case, is the Product Owner who presents the business needs to the developers and negotiates with them what can be done in the specified time frame. In the case of Scrum, both, the

Product Owner, the developers, and the testers are all part of the Agile Team.

Together, they decompose Epics, evaluate, analyze, and possibly break down User Stories to fit them into this Release Plan. They also determine how they will prove when a User Story is done. In Scrum, this is achieved with User Story Acceptance Criteria or Scenarios which describe the successful outcome of a User Story (we dedicated the upcoming chapter to Acceptance Testing and Scenarios).

User Stories or Features selected for an upcoming Release are stored in the Release Backlog which is simply a list of all things that need to be done for this Release. It is like a broad and complete To-Do list. When Release Planning is finished, the Agile team is ready for the next Sprint.

Sprint Planning

A Sprint is typically a period of two to four weeks in which the Agile team will deliver working software. As mentioned, this code is not necessarily going into production. It is software that is tested successfully; it is software that works, but it is not necessarily going out to the end users. A Sprint delivers working software, a Release delivers production ready software.

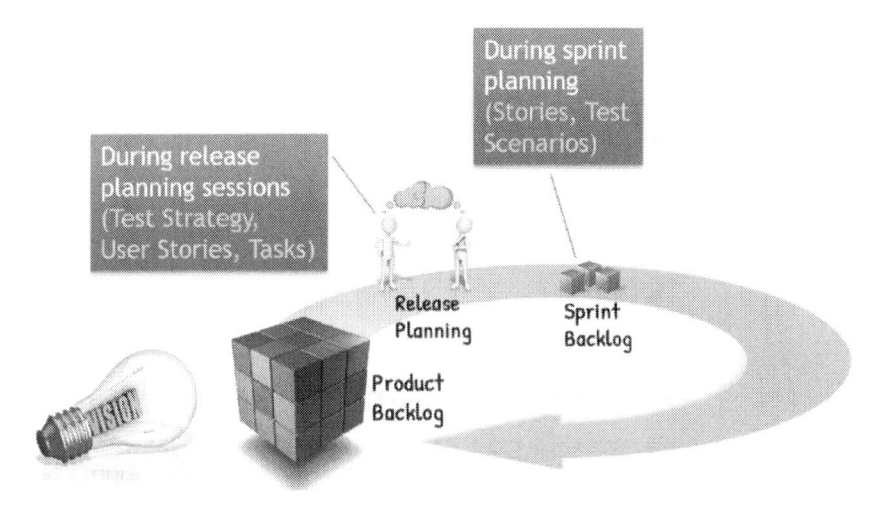

The Agile team usually starts with a Sprint Planning Session, where the technical teams (developers and testers) pick User Stories and other work items from the Release Backlog and transfer them to the Sprint Backlog. Sprint planning is similar to Release Planning; the difference is in the detail of User Stories, Features, and Acceptance Tests.

Next, the developers, together with the Product Owner and representatives from the business community, will create the necessary detail to allow the developers to confirm the effort estimate with a reasonable level of confidence. This is still not necessarily the level of detail that programmers need to write code.

If necessary, the developers will conduct more conversations with the business teams or the Product Owner during the Sprint Planning, to further clarify some stories and expand the Acceptance Criteria.

Organizations that have subscribed to ATDD (Acceptance Test-Driven Development) or BDD (Behavior-Driven Development) may already be creating Scenarios, Scenario Outlines, and Examples, or they may wait until the Sprint Planning has begun. This enables developers and end users to validate that the application delivers what the business community needs.

Ongoing Activities During a Sprint

During a Sprint, developers, the Product Owner, and/or the author of a User Story have ongoing conversations. These may quite often involve a person who has the title "Business Analyst". This person is not a member of the Agile team but part of the customer or business side team.

Traditionally, a Business Analyst (BA) captures, analyzes, documents, and validates Business, Stakeholder, and Solution Requirements. This requires an in-depth understanding of the business and its customers. The ability to analyze the different viewpoints of Stakeholders involves facilitating the negotiation between Stakeholders and the development team to define what to build.

In the early days of the Agile movement, "true agilists" claimed that the role of BA was unnecessary. But more and more companies are realizing that they need someone with business analysis skills on their Lean or Agile teams.

To solve this problem, most of the organizations we work with have at least one person for each Agile Team with skills in Business Problem Analysis, Requirements Elicitation, Requirements Analysis, and Requirements Validation. This can be a Subject Matter Expert executing the business analysis tasks (or, as we like to say, "someone who wears the business analysis hat"). It can also be a Product Owner, a Project Manager, or an End User with BA skills, to name a few. We have written the book you are reading for exactly this target group.

Every morning the Agile team starts off with a daily Scrum which gives every member about 15 minutes to report what they did yesterday and what kind of impediments they faced.

In Agile terminology, an impediment is anything that keeps a developer from getting a job done in a certain time frame. It is the job of the Product Owner to resolve any impediments. If there is no instant resolution, developers are moving on to the next work item until the impediment has been removed.

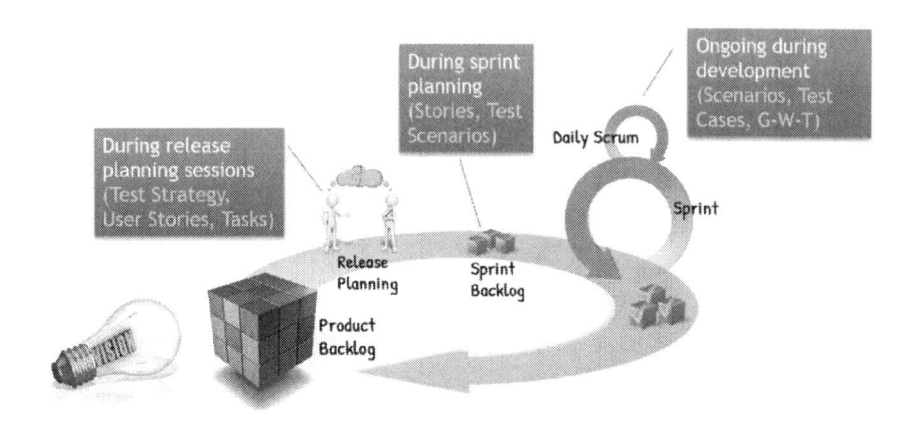

Diagram: Agile process showing "During release planning sessions (Test Strategy, User Stories, Tasks)", "During sprint planning (Stories, Test Scenarios)", "Daily Scrum", "Ongoing during development (Scenarios, Test Cases, G-W-T)", "Sprint", with Release Planning, Product Backlog, and Sprint Backlog elements.

Just as in a Release Planning Session, during the daily planning session the whole team is working together to make sure that they clearly understand each User Story before coding it.

This might involve additional business analysis techniques such as Process Analysis, Data Modeling, Timing Analysis, Story Decomp / Feature Drill-down, and many more. If they have not already done so, the Agile team also creates Given-When-Then Scenarios, Outlines, and Examples to prove that the Features and User Stories are implemented correctly.

Lean/Agile Business Analysis

That is the whole concept behind the timing of doing analysis in an Agile world. Whether you believe Business Analysis is no longer needed in Lean/Agile methods or not, its results are still necessary, even if we give the entire process a different name. In Agile or Lean environments, someone still must decide whether to devote resources to solve a particular problem or take advantage of an opportunity.

Historically, in a Waterfall environment, Strategic Business Analysis was the up-front work at the very beginning of a project or initiative. The outcome of Strategic Business Analysis sometimes was to cancel the project, at other times, it was to split it into multiple projects. At the very least, you got high-level Business and Stakeholder Requirements.

In Lean/Agile approaches, you still need Strategic Business Analysis **outcomes** which can be in the form of User Stories, high-level Features, or plain textual requirements. These will fill your Product Backlog.

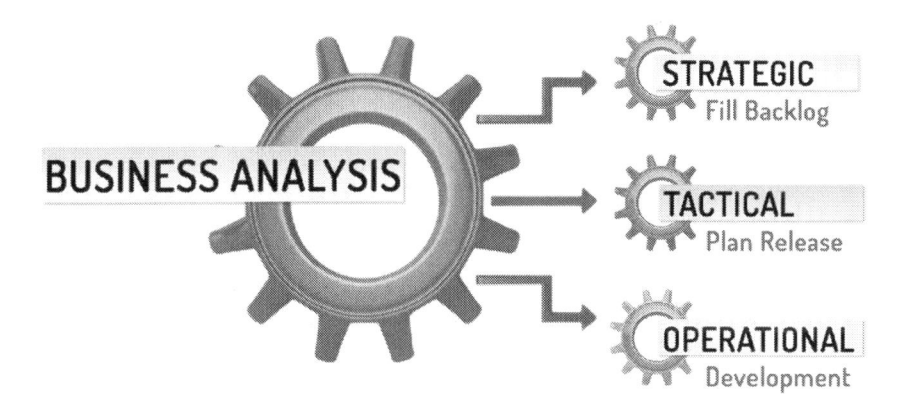

BUSINESS ANALYSIS

STRATEGIC
Fill Backlog

TACTICAL
Plan Release

OPERATIONAL
Development

At the next stage, we have Tactical Business Analysis. During Backlog Refinement, Release Planning, and Sprint Planning, you take the User Stories and other requirements down to a lower level of detail. Some organizations go down one more level to Operational Business Analysis. That is the nitty gritty detail that usually only concerns developers. It is also often referred to as Systems Analysis.

Preparing User Stories for Release and Sprint Planning

A mutual understanding of the User Story within the team is critical for their successful implementation. Anyone, from the author of the User Story to the business community, the technical team, and the testers who prove whether the User Story is working correctly, must be on the same page. Ambiguity and/or subjectivity in a User Story endangers this understanding.

Ambiguity and subjectivity are the twin killers of IT initiatives. More misunderstandings of what the product should be doing are caused by ambiguous and or subjective User Stories than any other single cause. How can you recognize ambiguity and subjectivity and what you can do to reduce them before they start to become costly?

In traditional development methods such as Waterfall, we tried to remove ambiguity and subjectivity from all requirements statements at the beginning of the project. That obviously was the cause for a lot of waste.

Some publications claim that the change to Lean and Agile software development alone removes most ambiguities due to the short iterations of 2 to 4 weeks. In our experience this is not true. Beyond that, we do not believe (contrary to some others) that User Stories should be intentionally ambiguous so that they remain negotiable. There are other ways to achieve this goal much easier and better.

As we mentioned earlier, you do **not** want to waste time removing ambiguity and subjectivity while you are seeding a Product Backlog or creating a Feature List. At that time, you have no idea if these User Stories will ever make it to a future Release. Removing ambiguity at that point would be against Lean principles.

However, it saves a lot of time during conversations with developers if there is as little ambiguity and subjectivity as possible in your User

Stories. Following Lean principles, the right time to reduce ambiguity and subjectivity is when you are preparing User Stories for the next iteration or even during Release and Sprint planning, that is - just before the programmers start to code.

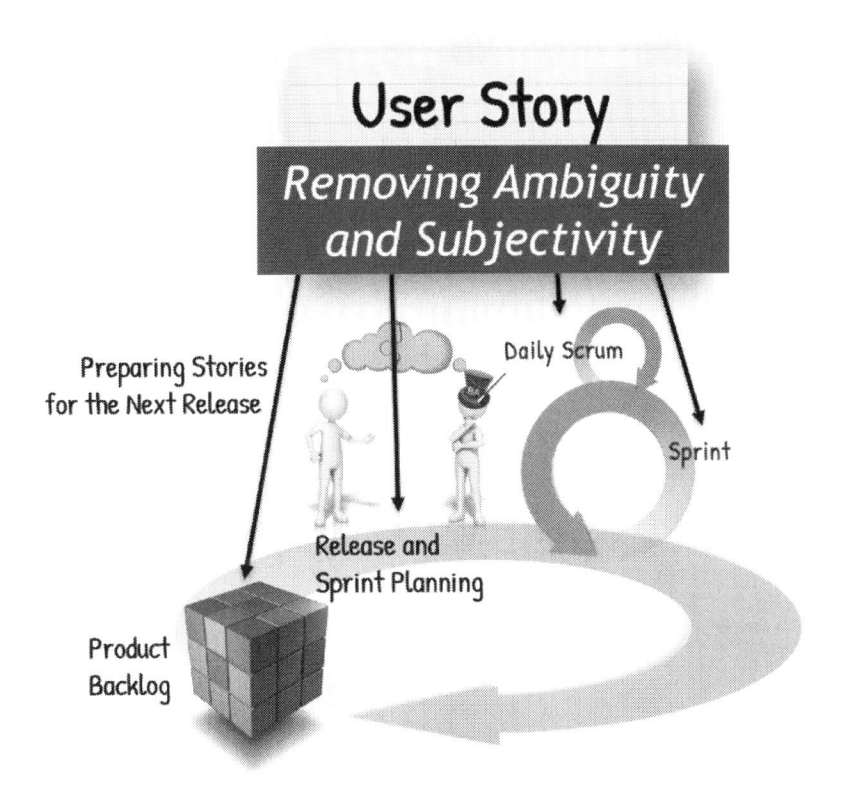

Imagine the Product Owner together with some business experts or end users would clean up ambiguous User Stories while they prepare them for the next iteration. The result? The development team would not waste time trying to understand ambiguous words and phrases. That would be LEAN!

Who Needs Clarity, Anyway?

We would like to say, "A User Story has to be clear to all target audiences", but that phrase in itself is ambiguous. What is clarity and who is the target audience?

Clarity is a mutual understanding and agreement about the meaning of a statement whether it is a User Story, a Feature, a Scenario, or any other form of Lean requirement. Achieving clarity is difficult because people take part in the process - lots of people and each with their own perception. These people make up the target audience of a User Story. They are all Stakeholders, and as we mentioned before, Stakeholders are more than just end-users.

Discovering and Writing User Stories is not for the faint-hearted. The agreements you must reach amongst so many different Stakeholders and groups are often overwhelming. Once you have an agreement, how do you know that **everyone** really has a "mutual" understanding? Here is an example.

You and the User Community

Imagine a group of end-users is interested in a specific User Story. They discuss the Story within the user community. You help them reach understanding and agreement.

Since you are the one eliciting and writing the User Story, **you** must have a mutual understanding with the **user community**. To write the Story, you need to understand the business need in detail so that you can express it in User Story format.

You also need to figure out how the user community will know that the implemented User Story is doing everything correctly. For that, you need agreement and understanding on Acceptance Criteria and/or Scenarios before the company spends the money to develop the program.

You and You

Furthermore, you must reach **agreement with yourself**. For instance, when you talk to the users and help create a User Story you think you have agreement in the user community. You know exactly what they want.

The next morning you wake up and think about that User Story and you realize that there is a nuance you had not yet considered. Suddenly, your understanding of that User Story's meaning or purpose starts to change; it morphs. You better go back to that group of users and make sure you still have mutual understanding and agreement.

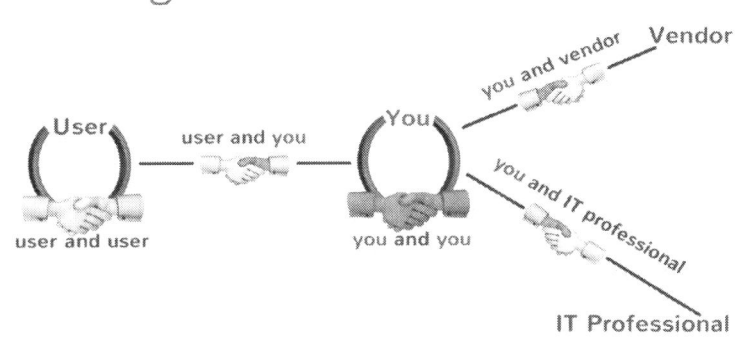

Clarity = **Common** Understanding and Agreement between:

- user and user
- user and you
- you and you
- you and vendor → Vendor
- you and IT professional → IT Professional

You and IT Professionals

If you develop the product in house, **you** must reach a mutual understanding with the **IT professionals**. They are often not familiar with the terminology of the business world. They need to understand the needs of the business community in their language (User Stories, Scenarios, Examples, Qualities, Constraints, etc.) so that they can deliver exactly what the users want.

You and a Vendor

It gets even more complex if **you** are outsourcing software development or plan to buy it off-the-shelf. You are adding another target audience or Stakeholder. The **vendor** must now share that mutual understanding. And of course, life gets a little slippery if your vendor's native tongue is not English (for example, if you outsource to a non-English-speaking country like Russia). Reaching a mutual understanding in that situation needs a lot of clarity.

To achieve mutual understanding in this situation, utmost clarity and unambiguity is needed. Foreign suppliers may not understand the subtle nuances of a language. You must therefore ensure that every word, term, phrase in the User Story or Scenario contributes to mutual understanding from beginning to end.

Ambiguity and Subjectivity Feed Misunderstanding

The challenges that we face with effective requirements are a breeding ground for failed digital solutions. With our examples, we have only scratched the surface when it comes to different Stakeholder types. There are many more and all of them speak "their own language". Communicating amongst such a diverse group of people is a noticeable challenge and clarity is our only weapon.

We should do everything we can to improve the mutual understanding of User Stories, Features, Scenarios, and other requirement communications. But do not forget!

> *You should only clarify User Stories or requirements that will be developed in the next Release.*

Now the next question is - how can you recognize ambiguity and subjectivity? First, you need to understand the difference between the two.

What Are Ambiguity and Subjectivity?

Ambiguity

Ambiguity in User Stories allows different people to interpret the Story in multiple ways. As a result, one can never be sure what the intended meaning was.

It is difficult for authors of User Stories to detect ambiguities because they have a context in mind. The ambiguity in a requirement or User Story is often only visible to stakeholders who **do not** know the context.

One of the best ways to remove ambiguity from your User Stories is by adding context to it.

For example, the statement "I saw her duck!" has many potential meanings. Does it mean you saw her duck under something, or that you saw her pet duck, or that she is being shot at and is ducking down to make sure that the shot misses her? What is really meant here? Without context you have no way of knowing the correct answer.

Subjectivity

Subjectivity, on the other hand, means that the meaning of words can be interpreted differently (legitimately) depending on individual life experience.

OBJECTIVE REALITY   SUBJECTIVE INTERPRETATION

As you can see in this picture, all three subjects see the same tree. The first person sees just the **tree**. The second person, however, is thinking of **fruit trees** and maybe even how great an apple would taste right now. The last person sees the tree as an **investment opportunity**. She could be planning a landscaping business. As you can see, if you do not add examples here, there is a potential for misunderstandings what the word "tree" means.

The best way to remove subjectivity is using concrete examples. Examples are one of the most powerful ways of clarifying the meaning of your User Story. User Story Acceptance Criteria expressed as Scenarios and Examples have become exceedingly popular. They deliver concrete examples of the outcomes of a User Story before any coding happens.

For instance, if you tell someone that,

The increasing dependence on loans as part of the financial aid package endangers the future success of today's students.

The phrases "increasing dependence", "future success", and "endangers" all express the writer's opinion and are subjective. But if you add an example, you can remove the subjectivity.

The increasing dependence on loans as part of the financial aid package endangers the future success of today's students.

Example: According to a 2013 New York Times article, 60 percent of students graduating from college in 2011-2012 left school with debt; the average amount of debt per student was $26,500,

---

Revealing and Removing Ambiguity

There are those in our industry who think that, in a Lean environment, User Stories must be ambiguous because ambiguity will allow the User Story conversation with developers to be flexible. Some authors even go as far as saying that User Stories should be intentionally ambiguous and intentionally incomplete so that the Agile Team can discuss, clarify, and figure out everything during the Sprint.

As we mentioned in the introduction to this chapter, we follow a different philosophy. Obviously, in Lean and Agile environments, you should not waste time removing ambiguity and subjectivity from User Stories that may never be implemented.

However, to avoid wasting time during Release or Sprint Planning (especially the time of the entire Agile team), you should remove any avoidable ambiguity and subjectivity when preparing for the next iteration; at the latest, however, just before the developers start coding. This is, in our opinion, what Agile and Lean approaches mean by the "Last Responsible Moment".

We mentioned earlier that you can cut ambiguity with added context, while you can remove subjectivity with concrete examples. Since subjectivity can best be eliminated with examples, we will discuss this in detail in the chapter on Acceptance Tests with Scenarios, Scenario Outlines and Examples.

Continuing this chapter, we will show you simple techniques for avoiding ambiguity in your User Stories.

Use of Pronouns

One source of ambiguity is the improper use of pronouns. Pronouns can be a source of headaches in any form of requirement whether it is a User Story, Feature, Scenario, Example, Specification, or Business Rule. If you use a word such as "it", or "they", there should be no confusion in a Stakeholder's mind about what you mean.

For example,

> **Insurance applications should be processed by underwriters within 3 business days, otherwise they will be returned.**

What does the pronoun "they" refer to? Does it refer to the applicant? Does it refer to the underwriters? It is not clear what "will be sent back" at this point. The change in the Business Rules is as follows,

> **Insurance applications should be processed by underwriters within 3 business days, otherwise the applications will be returned.**

That simple replacement reduced ambiguity. Use pronouns sparingly so as not to introduce ambiguities in User Stories. A User Story should have only one possible interpretation.

Generic Verbs and Nouns

However, there is still a certain ambiguity in our Business Rules. What about the word "processed"? The word "processed" has many different meanings. Each stakeholder may interpret a User Story expressed with generic verbs or nouns differently.

If you look at only some of the synonyms of the verb "process", it can mean: prepare, transform, treat, manage, act, refine, think, digest, argue, to name but a few. Can you imagine how many different interpretations you get when you use the word "process" in your User Story?

One of the best ways to avoid this trap is to use "strong" verbs. "Weak" verbs are generic and apply to many situations. Strong verbs are precise and apply to limited circumstances.

For example, we can further reduce the ambiguity in our previous example by replacing the word "processed". When we ask the Subject Matter Experts, we discover that when underwriters "process" a claim, they either accept or reject it. So, to further reduce the ambiguity in this business rule, you could rephrase it to read:

Insurance applications which are neither accepted nor denied by underwriters within 3 business days will be returned.

Be Specific! Avoid verbs or nouns that can be misinterpreted by anybody who reads them.

Sometimes, you will find that a generic word in a Story hides an Epic or larger User Story. We will explore this topic in the next section when we talk about splitting User Stories that have generic words.

Adding Context and Content

Although we have mentioned context several times, we will briefly go into it again because adding context is one of the easiest ways to remove ambiguity.

If you are using the User Story format, adding context is as simple as following the structure guidelines for good User Stories. If your Story has a role (As a *role*), and it has a business value (to *achieve the goal*) it already has a lot of context. Role and business value go a long way in reducing ambiguity.

In addition, Acceptance Criteria or Test Scenarios for a User Story, add even more context. We will cover User Story Validation and Testing in detail in the next chapter of this book.

What if your company expresses requirements in sentence format or just phrases? It is perfectly fine to write Features in sentence form. However, in that situation, you might be missing things like the role and business value. It becomes critical for the clarity of the Feature to add more context to reduce ambiguity as much as you can.

For example, what are you envisioning when reading, "Raymond gripped the bat tightly"? Are you thinking of a batter holding a baseball bat or of a guy from the Carlsbad Caverns in New Mexico struggling with a wild animal in his hands? When you add context, the meaning becomes easy to interpret. Changing the sentence to read, "Raymond gripped the **baseball** bat tightly." clarifies this statement.

Specificity Adds Clarifying Content

Being more specific in describing a business need can reduce ambiguity. For example,

> **Insurance applications which are neither accepted nor denied by underwriters within 3 business days will be returned.**

The term "3 business days" can be ambiguous unless you have a Business Rule, a glossary definition, or use a standard term defined for your organization (and there you learned that quantifying things makes them unambiguous – go figure!).

Assuming you have no definition for "3 business days" anywhere, you need to add some clarifying information to your User Story. If you were to say,

> **Insurance applications which are neither accepted nor denied by underwriters at the close of business on the 3rd business day after receipt will be returned.**

We have worked with the same sentence three times and each time we removed ambiguous terms. This could be a never-ending story which is a violation of Lean principles.

If you reduce some ambiguity in a User Story, this will save you and the rest of the Agile Team a lot of time in Release and Sprint Planning or with Kanban Replenishment or Commitment Meetings. **Do not shoot for perfect** here, just eliminate as much ambiguity as you can.

Undefined Acronyms

Finally, Acronyms! They save us a ton of time. They definitively fit the Lean concept. Acronyms are a phenomenal idea. However, they can also introduce ambiguity in a heartbeat. If you are using an acronym you want to make sure that the acronym can only have one single meaning within the context of the Story.

The acronym FEMA is a wonderful example. Anybody in the US who has experienced or read about a natural disaster would read that as the Federal Emergency Management Agency. But if you are from India, it could also be the Foreign Exchange Management Act of 1999. If you are a farmer, it could mean the Farm Equipment Manufacturers Association.

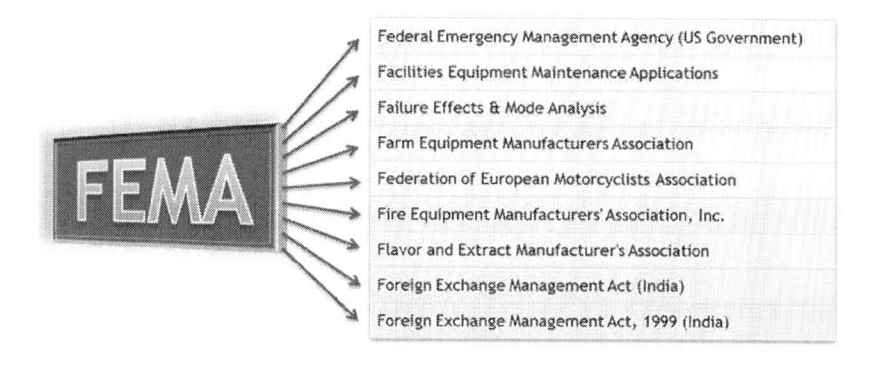

FEMA

- Federal Emergency Management Agency (US Government)
- Facilities Equipment Maintenance Applications
- Failure Effects & Mode Analysis
- Farm Equipment Manufacturers Association
- Federation of European Motorcyclists Association
- Fire Equipment Manufacturers' Association, Inc.
- Flavor and Extract Manufacturer's Association
- Foreign Exchange Management Act (India)
- Foreign Exchange Management Act, 1999 (India)

The acronym FEMA could be interpreted in many ways, unless you know for sure that it refers to a national emergency within the United States, monetary exchanges in India, the farming community, or any of the other examples that you see above.

The common recommendation is to expand any acronym the first time that you use it and then you can continue using it throughout. That is a fine recommendation if you deal with traditional requirements documents. However, in Lean and Agile environments, how can you be sure that the acronym FEMA is interpreted correctly from one Release to the next?

A better solution for Lean and Agile development is to expand all acronyms in a glossary and inform your team where they can find the glossary. An even better solution is to integrate the definition by using rollovers, popups, or links for your acronyms. If somebody wants to know what that an acronym means, they can get that information right away.

Ensuring a Common Understanding

Just like it is difficult for a writer to edit their own work, it can be difficult for the author of a User Story to find ambiguity in their own Stories. For that reason, other people should review our Stories and see whether they can clearly understand the intended meaning.

The remaining techniques to remove ambiguity are mostly used in traditional development environments, but we feel that knowing them is a valuable contribution to your bag of techniques and tricks. You never know when you end up with a User Story that is difficult to express clearly and then, these techniques might come in handy. Some of them also are great to make sure the entire Lean or Agile Team understands the Story the same way.

In addition, if you are in an environment where Acceptance Criteria and Given-When-Then Scenarios and Examples are "not a thing" yet, you can use these techniques to remove subjectivity as well. Remember, subjectivity is how different people might perceive your User Story, while ambiguity is different possible meanings of words and phrases. The following ideas help with both.

Desk Checking

A simple technique to discover ambiguities is Desk Checking. Although, the concept originated in the coding world, it can be a useful tool for discovering ambiguities in User Stories, Features, or anything you have written.

Here is how it works. If you write a User Story in the morning, read it again in the afternoon or late evening. You might interpret it differently because your mind is in a different mood. If you write it in the late afternoon wait until the next morning and read it when you are fresh.

Re-reading your Story at a different place than where you wrote it can have the same effect. If you wrote it in the workplace, read it on your ride home (DISCLAIMER: not in your car while driving, but if you commute by bus, train, or plane). Locale and the passage of time both change perceptions that you can leverage to reduce ambiguity.

Peer Reviews and Revisions

Peer Reviews are another great tool to check for ambiguity and especially for subjectivity. Give your User Story to another Stakeholder or, if you do not have access to them when you need them, give it to a peer to read.

See if they have a different interpretation than you do, talk about the Story or Feature and reach agreement on how to make it clearer. If you all agree, you have a much better chance that downstream people will understand it the same way.

Revising User Stories to Remove Ambiguity

You can even go one step further and ask a Stakeholder or a peer to rewrite a User Story using their own words. This is an amazing technique for finding ambiguity and subjectivity. We have it used many times.

Unfortunately, it can be time consuming. To follow Lean principles, you should only use it on business needs that are quite difficult to communicate. For example, we like to use this technique during User Story Discovery Workshops or Replenishments Meetings to confirm complex Features or exceptionally large User Stories (Epics).

The person rewriting your User Story or Feature needs to follow one simple rule. They cannot use any of the original words except:

- ☑ articles (i.e., a, an, the, etc.)
- ☑ prepositions (i.e., of, with, for, etc.)
- ☑ conjunctions (i.e. and, or, but, etc.)

This fosters creative thinking. If you used the word "Customer" in your User Story, the Stakeholder or peer is not allowed to use it in their rewrite. That simple rule forces them to think about a synonym or clarification of the term "Customer" in the context of this Story. They might use words like "Purchaser" or "Buyer". The new wording may lead you to rethink what your User Story really means.

You will be amazed how quickly this method reveals subjectivity in your User Stories. If you read their rewrite of your Story or Feature and you agree that it matches your interpretation - fantastic!

However, the rewrite will often cause you to question your User Story. This is a warning sign of hidden ambiguity or subjectivity. We have used this technique in many companies. To show you the process, we will share one of these experiences.

Example of the Peer Revision Technique

This is the original User Story we wrote based on an interview with the customer. The product was a travel agency booking system.

As a telephone operator, I can complete at least 12 reservations per hour during peak volume to reduce wait times for customers.

We gave this to another telephone operator and asked her to rewrite it. This is the rewrite:

As a reservationist, I am able to process a minimum of a dozen requests for travel accommodations within 60 minutes during the busiest time of the year to minimize dropped calls.

Clarification "telephone operator"

As you can see, she changed the term "telephone operator" to "reservationist". Since we are dealing with travel reservations, we decided that "reservationist" is actually a much better term for the role. A "telephone operator" could be anyone who answers phone calls whereas a "reservationist" implies someone who can help customers book travel requests.

That rewrite alone was worth its weight because it allowed us to name the right Stakeholder for the role of the User Story.

She also changed the phrase "I can complete at least 12 reservations" to "I am able to process a minimum of a dozen requests for travel accommodations". It seemed that we all agreed on the meaning here, so nothing changed.

Clarification "Peak times"

Next, she changed, "per hour" to read, "within 60 minutes". In this case, there was no difference between an hour and 60 Minutes. However, what happens if the User Story is for a scheduling system?

An hour is always 60 minutes, but does the specification "per hour" mean it must start exactly on the hour? Could it be any 60-minute interval (e.g., 8:00 to 8:59 AM versus 8:17 – 9:16 AM)? If we were dealing with a scheduling product, we might want to rethink our User Story.

The biggest revelation for us was her replacing "during peak volume" with "during the busiest times of the year". Our understanding of peak volume was deviations or differences in booking volume **during the day**. The thought that this might refer to **seasons** did not occur to us. But it made sense when we read the rewrite. There will be many more travelers during vacation time, spring break, or holidays than at other times. After more talks with Stakeholders, it turned out that "busiest time of the year" was what they really meant.

Clarification "Wait times for customers".

The last rewrite was for the phrase "to reduce wait time for customers". Seemed like a great idea to us to think about the customer perspective. But, in this case, the business value of the Use Story was to "minimize dropped calls". The organization looked at dropped calls as guaranteed lost business while longer wait times might frustrate some customers, but they are not necessarily lost business. Therefore, the reformulation was the clearer User Story.

Leverage People's Differences

If you are using the Peer Review or Rewrite techniques, here are some more ideas that have worked well for us in the past. When you pick people to rewrite you User Story, pick someone:

- ☑ with a different point of view than yours,
- ☑ with a different background than yours.

If you ask only your best buddy with whom you get along fantastic because you have a lot in common, to rewrite the User Story or Feature, you might not get the results you need.

If you had training in thinking styles such as Meyers-Briggs or similar personality assessments, use this knowledge to find the right people that you can ask for a rewrite. You will get more valuable feedback from someone who has a different way of thinking. This will allow you to recognize discrepancies in your User Stories and Features.

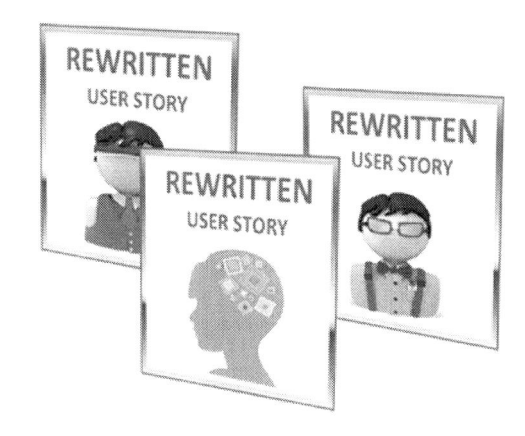

Exercise: Using Out-of-Box Thinking to Reduce Ambiguity

This exercise gives you the opportunity to try the Peer Revision technique to find and remove ambiguity in your User Stories, Features, and Scenarios.

Instructions:

Below are two User Stories. Rewrite them without using any of the nouns, verbs, adverbs, or adjectives. Your version should, however, express the same intent as the original.

User Story 1:

> As a passenger, I can view the location of my luggage on any device that is connected to the internet.

User Story 2:

> To reduce wait time at the terminal, passengers can send an electronic boarding pass to any device that our scanners can read.

Feedback User Story 1: How would you rewrite the Story, "As a passenger, I can view the location of my luggage on any device that is connected to the internet."?

Possible Rewrite: As a traveler, I can check the physical position of my checked baggage on any electronic unit accessing the world-wide web.

Feedback User Story 2: How would you rewrite the Story, "To reduce wait time at the terminal, passengers can send an electronic boarding pass to any device that our scanners can read."?

Possible Rewrite: To minimize the length it takes to check-in for a flight, flyers can have the appropriate documentation for gaining access to the plane transmitted to a readable electronic product.

5 Common User Story Splitting Techniques

Exceptionally large User Stories are known as Epics. Whether the Story is considered an Epic or just too large for a single Release or Sprint, you need to break it down into multiple, smaller User Stories. This process is called User Story Splitting or User Story Slicing. You can split Stories while grooming (aka maintaining) the Backlog. At the latest, they must be split in preparation for a Release or Sprint.

The desired size depends entirely on factors like the Agile team's experience, size, and velocity as well as the iteration length. Ideally, User Stories are sized so that the team can complete about 5-10 during an iteration. If your User Stories are larger than that, break them into smaller parts.

User Story Splitting is a critical skill for every Agile team member, but also for members of the business community. To be effective, Story splitting should be a collaborative effort. Everyone needs to work together on "intelligent" splitting.

To ensure that everyone can contribute to creating valuable User Stories, we would like to present a few simple User Story splitting techniques. The goal of each presented technique is to find the quickest path to delivering value to the business community.

Splitting to Reduce Complexity

Sometimes, a complex User Story hides a simple User Story that would provide significant business value if it could be delivered in a single Release.

If you break this simple Story out, the complex aspects of the Story could be added in later iterations or Releases. For example (and just to keep your attention, we will use the goal-focused User Story format):

To enhance knowledge sharing, instructors can assign students to groups dynamically ensuring that each group has a balanced set of skills needed to complete each exercise.

Could you split the story to do that simple core first and enhance it with later Stories?

How about:

To complete exercises, instructors can allow students to work in groups.

That is a simple User Story that delivers significant business value. Once that works, subsequent iterations could deliver the remaining User Stories:

⇨ **To balance the set of skills needed to complete an exercise, instructors can dynamically change the makeup of groups.**

⇨ To optimize the learning experience, instructors can define the skills necessary to complete each exercise.

⇨ To build effective teams, instructors can capture the skills each student has.

⇨ To build effective teams, instructors can match the combined skills of student groupings to the skills necessary to complete the exercise.

Exposing complexities in User Stories and Epics is often called a vertical breakdown of the User Story. Vertical breakdowns are the preferred method in Lean and Agile for splitting User Stories that deliver business value.

A horizontal breakdown splits a Story by developer tasks. A horizontally split Story usually does not deliver value to the end customer. Developers use horizontal splitting for technical User Stories, for example to define the architectural layers of a system, such as databases, network, security, user interface, etc.

Simple User Stories Increase Understanding

User Stories that use compound sentences do not qualify as simple in our book. Here is a Lean technique that will make them simpler and at the same time smaller.

Just as a refresher, a compound sentence often looks like this:

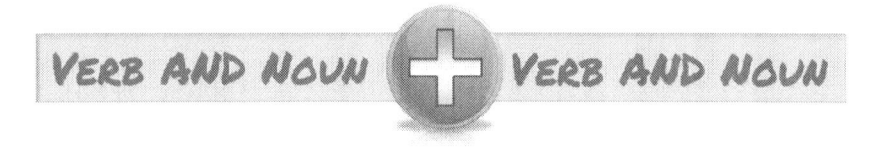

VERB AND NOUN ➕ VERB AND NOUN

You can recognize them if they have the words "if", "and", or "but" in them. A professionally written User Story avoids these constructs.

There is one exception and that is the word "and". It is a quite common word and has a ton of different connotations. There are instances when the use of the word "and" in a User Story does not create a compound sentence and then it is acceptable.

For instance, here is an example of a User Story.

**As an applicant, I can navigate to the coverage screen,
enter personal and vehicle data,
and submit the application online
to request automobile insurance coverage.**

We find the first "and" in "personal **and** vehicle data". That is allowable because it is a list. Then we read "**and** submit the application...". That usage is not ok because it creates a compound sentence. There is a verb and an object behind the "and".

To make this a simple User Story, we suggest splitting it into multiple Stories. One User Story might be,

---

**As an applicant, I can navigate to the coverage screen
to select the insurance coverage I need.**

Here, "to select the insurance coverage I need" is the business value that an applicant receives by navigating to the coverage screen. The second implied User Story is:

**As an applicant I can enter
personal and vehicle data to calculate the premium.**

By entering personal and vehicle data, the applicant learns how much the insurance company would charge him for insurance coverage. And the third Story is:

As an applicant I can submit an application online to request automobile insurance coverage.

The business value for the applicant in this case is that the Insurance Company can consider offering you the necessary automobile insurance coverage.

> **As an applicant, I can navigate to the coverage screen, enter personal and vehicle data, and submit the application online to request automobile insurance coverage**
>
> **Contains three distinct thoughts**
>
> | As an applicant, I can navigate to the coverage screen to select the insurance coverage I need | As an applicant, I can enter personal and vehicle data to compare premiums | As an applicant, I can submit an application online to request automobile insurance coverage |
> |---|---|---|

This is one example of how to make a User Story simpler by breaking it down or splitting it. This way, it is easier to understand and less subject to misinterpretation.

There are a few more words that we would like to eliminate for simplicity sake. Avoid using qualifying phrases such as, "unless" "except", or "without" in your User Stories. If you see those words, it is a sign that this Story might need splitting.

For example,

As an underwriter, I can override a coverage denial for an applicant to increase our customer base unless the denial was due to bad credit in which case, I can confirm the denial to protect our customer base.

The word "unless" makes a User Story a lot more complicated. This is a great candidate for splitting. Fortunately, when words like "unless" are used, it is easy to break the Story down. In this case, there are two implied User Stories.

As an underwriter, I can override a coverage denial for an applicant to expand our customer base.

AND

As an underwriter, I can confirm coverage denial for an applicant with poor credit to protect our customer base.

As you can see, creating two User Stories has led to a significant simplification. Moreover, each of them is now so detailed that a developer could probably code them in a few days.

These User Story splitting techniques are quite simple. Before we examine more complex techniques for splitting or breaking down User Stories, here are a few sized role- and goal-focused examples.

⇨ To save money, visitors can select the lowest fare flight that meets their travel needs.

⇨ As a visitor, I can view all available flights that match my scheduling Constraints to select the best fit.

⇨ As a policyholder, I can view the account balances on all my policies to manage my financial obligations.

⇨ To plan their career paths, students can see all classes offering required training topics for the upcoming 6 months.

These User Stories would be a reasonable start for a conversation between the developer and the author of the Story.

Splitting Stories by Data Types

Sometimes, the complexity in a User Story is caused by the variety of data types that is involved. For instance, in creating an application to help golf course professionals score tournaments, we ran across this User Story:

> **As golf tournament administrator, I can calculate players' scores to accurately distribute winnings.**

Looking at this User Story as an outsider, it sounds simple enough. Just capture the individual hole-by-hole score for each player, sum them, sort them, and calculate how much to pay each place.

Only as you learn more about golf competitions do you realize there are some tricky variations on scoring the game. In its simplest form, "stroke play", the score is simply the number of strokes each player needed to get the ball from the teeing ground into each hole for the tournament.

In that case, our first thought works well. However, some competitions involve handicapping in which you must track both gross scores (total number of strokes) and net scores (adjusted by each individual player's handicap).

Gross and Net are two different scores (or data) that each player receives at the end of an amateur tournament. Calculating gross scores is quite simple. Where it gets complex is with net scoring because it involves the established handicap of the player. Just as a side note, establishing a player's handicap deserves its own User Story (or, more realistically, Epic) because, based on personal experience, it is extraordinarily complex.

That knowledge might lead you to split the User Story into:

As golf tournament administrator, I can calculate a player's gross stroke play scores to determine their gross placement in the tournament.

And

As golf tournament administrator, I can adjust a player's net stroke play scores using their individual handicaps to determine their net placement in the tournament.

For the sake of our example, we assume that the individual players' handicaps are known, meaning establishing them is out of scope for our Stories.

We could split these Stories by more data variations if needed. Turns out there are several ways to score golf tournaments. For example, there is a scoring system called "Stableford" in which players accumulate points instead of strokes and the highest score wins. There are also team events based on the scores for teams of 2 – 4 players wherein those can be aggregated or only the best 1 – 3 scores used. Match play is a format where the only thing that matters is who has the lowest score on each hole. And there are many other formats.

Each scoring system changes how the tournament winners and losers are determined. You might just end up with a handful or more of distinct User Stories each of which covers a specific scoring method.

These types of data variations are prevalent in many situations. If that causes the User Story to become unwieldy (i.e., not doable in a single Sprint), split it to enable the Agile team to deliver a simple version and then enhance it to include the outliers.

Splitting Stories by Business Rules

Implementing Business Rules can be tricky, especially when there are multiple rules for a specific situation that may be in conflict. Implementing a User Story that enforces all rules correctly could be huge. For example, consider the User Story:

> **To increase registrations for our online courses, course administrators can grant a 30% discount to veterans, a 20% discount to students who are from Florida, a 10% discount to students from out of state, and a 5% discount to foreign exchange students.**

Just a casual glance at this story shows that there are several distinct Business Rules that change how much we will charge a new student for a class. That makes the User Story quite confusing and complex. There is, however, a simple User Story hidden in it, namely:

> **To increase registrations for online courses, course administrators can grant discounts.**

Assuming the Agile team could implement that Story in a single Release, you could later add the User Stories,

> **To entice Veterans to register for our courses, course administrators can grant a Veterans discount.**

AND

> **To increase in-state registrations,
> course administrators can grant an in-state discount.**

And so on. The various discount amounts can be adjusted in the Business Rules repository.

You now have multiple Business Rules that could potentially interfere with each other. For example, based on the original User Story, what is the discount for **a Veteran from Florida**, 30%, 20%, 50% (30% + 20%), or 44% ((X * .30) * .20)? You need a new User Story explaining how the Business Rules should be applied, like:

> **To maintain a consistent discount policy,
> course Administrators will grant new students
> the highest discount for which they qualify.**

Splitting Based on Workflow or Events

Splitting a User Story or Epic by steps in a workflow is a common method but it can be hard to split well. Making each step of the workflow a User Story is not desirable **unless the step provides a value to the end-user.**

To split a User Story based on workflow, you need to find the fewest number of workflow steps that create a business value. You can move the remaining steps of the workflow to future Releases or Sprints. For simple workflows, a technique known as "Sequence of Events" is enough. For more complex Epics or workflows, you need to develop a more detailed workflow diagram.

Sequence of Events Splitting

"Sequence of Events" is one of our favorite techniques. Here is how it works. Ask your end-users to describe the activities in the business environment that will handle this User Story. Tell them that it does not matter whether the steps are sequential or not, you would like to hear all of them.

> **As Event Manager, I can arrange for all facilities online to optimally support the event.**

Our Stakeholder might describe what happens like this:

> "I need to make all the arrangements for concerts by popular artists. I start by contacting the artists to get their requirements for the venue and dates. Once I have their needs, I contact all venues that meet the artists' requirements, select the best fit venue, book the venue for the scheduled dates, setup the event on EventBrite to sell tickets, and monitor ticket sales to ensure maximum attendance."

This explanation reveals the following actions:

1. Contact performers (artists)
2. Capture performers' venue requirements
3. Research potential venues
4. Compare venue availability, cost, and Features
5. Select best-fit venue
6. Schedule event with venue and performers
7. Add event to EventBrite
8. Monitor ticket sales

One idea would be to create a User Story for each workflow step and judge whether it delivers sufficient value to be a stand-alone story.

- ⇨ As Event Manager, I can **get venue requirements** from the performing artists to ensure that the facilities I book work for them.

- ⇨ As Event Manager, I can **contact all venues** that fit the artists' requirements, so I can select the best one that is available during the scheduled timeframe.

- ⇨ As Event Manager, I can **schedule the selected venue**, to ensure it is available for the event.

- ⇨ As Event Manager, I can **create an event on EventBrite** to sell tickets.

- ⇨ As Event Manager, I can **monitor ticket sales** on EventBrite to avoid overselling the event.

In this example, each of these User Stories provides value without considering the others. If all of them were implemented, the original User Story would be complete. Now you just need to prioritize these

User Stories together with the business community based on which Stories provides the most value.

Sequence of Events is a quick method for splitting an Epic. To recap, if the Epic is large or overly complex, try creating a quick list of the steps in the workflow to find all lower-level activities. Then turn each activity into a User Story with role and business value.

As we already mentioned, the business value changes. In some instances, the role can change as well. For example, if the web developer is the one adding the event to the EventBrite website. That would change the role in one User Story.

Detailed Workflow Splitting

Sometimes, you need a deep dive into the workflow to discover User Stories that can be delivered in a single iteration. As we mentioned before, workflows can be hard to split because it is difficult to create a slice of workflow that delivers business value to the end-user.

Workflow splitting for overly complex User Stories requires Process Modeling experience. You should know how to create Activity or Swimlane Diagrams, Data Flow Diagrams, or another form of process models. If you know any of these techniques, here is a brief overview of Workflow splitting.

Splitting User Stories using a workflow diagram is a 3-part process:

1. Define the workflow that would create the outcome of the User Story, meaning which steps would be necessary to do what the User Story describes to deliver the expressed value.

2. Identify **essential** steps or operations, meaning steps that have to be done under any circumstances in this workflow as opposed to those that are only needed sometimes. You might discover that delivering only the essential steps delivers most of the business value. You could also implement the simplest version of each essential step by focusing on the perfect world flow while rejecting unusual situations for manual intervention.

3. **Deliver only this limited value (essential steps or simplest flow) in the upcoming Release.** The rest of the workflow steps and operations are "Value-Added Operations" that you will deliver in future Releases or Sprints.

Workflow diagrams allow you to visualize the most complex workflow as a series of actions and decisions. The visibility of steps and their relationships to each other often allows you to see which steps have intrinsic value and which dependencies exist.

In line with Lean principles, we do not propose to create a sophisticated business process model that must be kept up to date forever. What we do recommend is to use the simplest models or diagrams that do the job.

For example, you can collaborate with the Product Owner, Subject Matter Expert, or author of the User Stories to draw a quick activity diagram on a flipchart. Visualizing the workflow through the diagram often leads to questions and clarifications that suggest simpler solutions. Simply drawing circles around processes and Functions that are essential and those that are value-added can help to reduce an Epic to a subset of User Stories.

When data transformation is an important aspect of User Stories, a data flow diagram fragment often reveals simpler approaches to delivering business value. Workflow analysis and process modeling go far beyond the scope of this book.

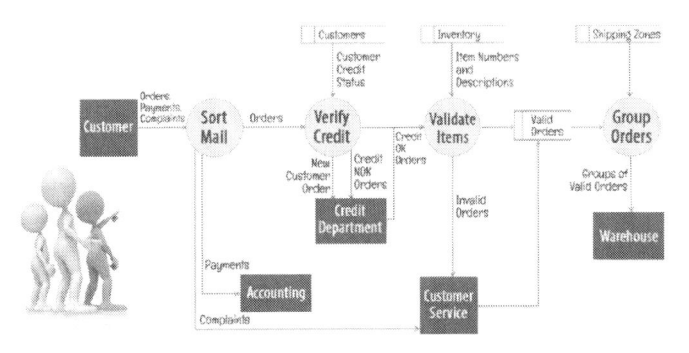

If you are interested in learning more, consider our book, "Data Flow Diagrams - Simply Put! Process Modeling Techniques for Requirements Elicitation" at http://bit.ly/LeanBusinessAnalysis (**Free** on Kindle Unlimited). If you prefer an online video course, check out http://bit.ly/EC-LeanBusinessAnalysis.

Splitting by Use Case Path

If you are familiar with Use Cases, one of the easiest ways to break down a User Story is splitting it along Use Case paths. If you have developed Use Cases to represent complex interactions, each path through the Use Case makes a great stand-alone Story.

If you currently have no Use Cases but need to split an Epic or an overly complex User Story, developing a high-level business Use Case may be the best choice.

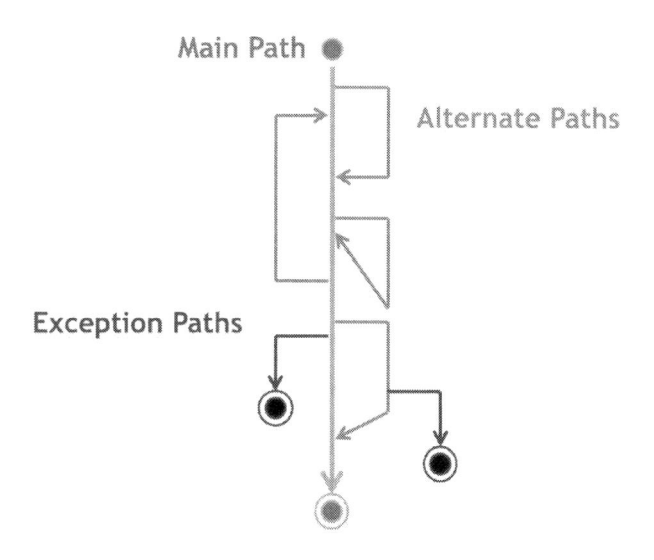

Create a Use Case for the Epic or complex User Story, then write one User Story for the Standard Path and one for each of the Alternate and Exception Paths. If the flows are too large for the next iteration and need to be split further, use the workflow analysis we described in the workflow splitting method.

Use Case modeling is too complex to be taught in this book, but if you or your developer are familiar with Lean Use Case modeling, it is a great technique for splitting Epics or complex User Stories.

You can learn how to create a Use Case in our online course: **"Lean / Agile Business Analysis: Writing BUSINESS Use Cases"** (https://bit.ly/lean-use-cases).

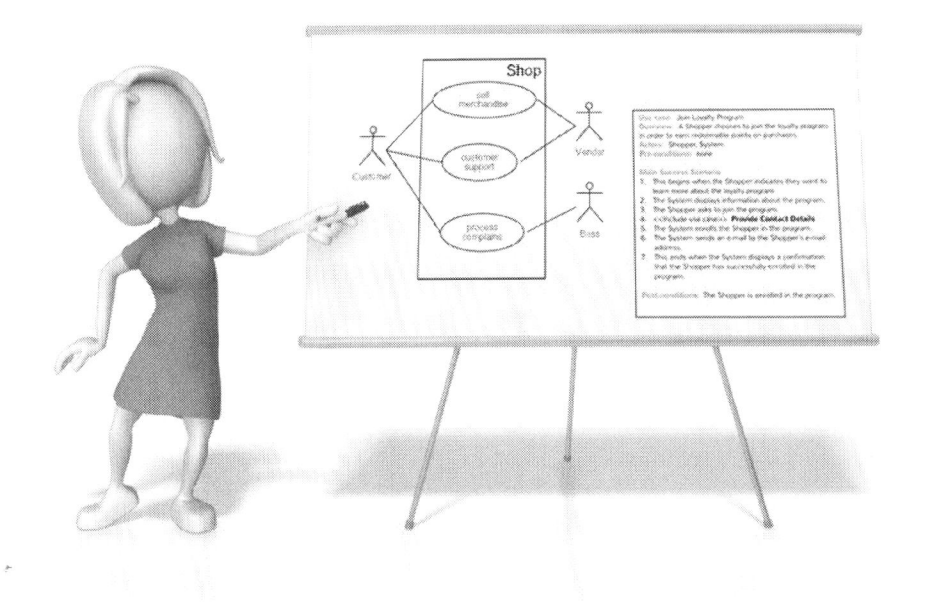

Solution Requirements

During the current iteration, sometimes a User Story must be broken down into functional items so that it can be coded. For example, in Scrum, many Agile developers prefer Sprint Backlogs that have User Stories broken down to Functional Features.

To develop a software solution that meets the defined requirements, User Stories or Features, developers need the help of the business department to achieve the right level of detail and make the best system design decisions.

Story Decomp or Feature Drill-down is a technique that system analysts and designers used in Waterfall as a tool to make design decisions. At the beginning of the project they defined Functional and Non-Functional Requirements for the entire scope of the project. Obviously, the timing is different in a Lean environment.

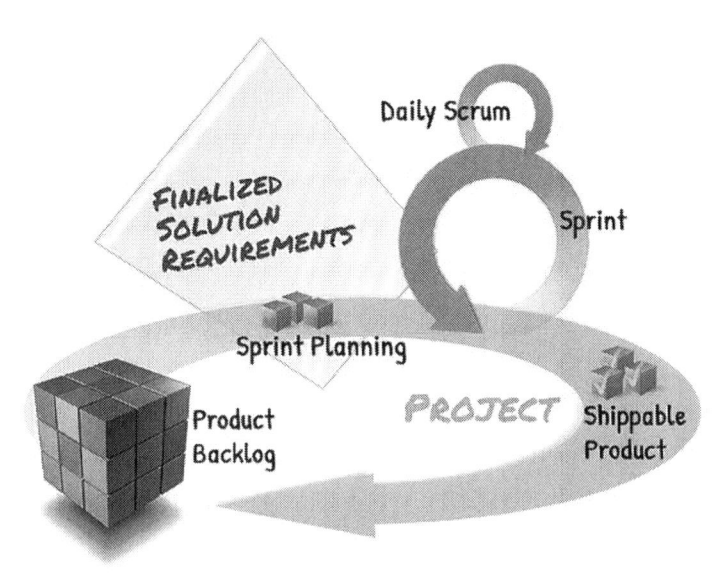

Lean practices require that you make design decisions at the last responsible moment which means that you should not define Functional specifications for User Stories that are still in the Product Backlog.

Getting to Solution Requirements

Solution Requirements provide the level of detail that developers need when designing a Product Feature. But what exactly are Solution Requirements?

In the Lean and Agile world, a **Functional Feature** encompasses Functions and related Data the solution will perform. **Quality Requirements** define the properties and characteristics which the digital solution should demonstrate. **Constraints** are absolute limitations, rules, laws, regulations, and environmental factors which must be considered in the solution.

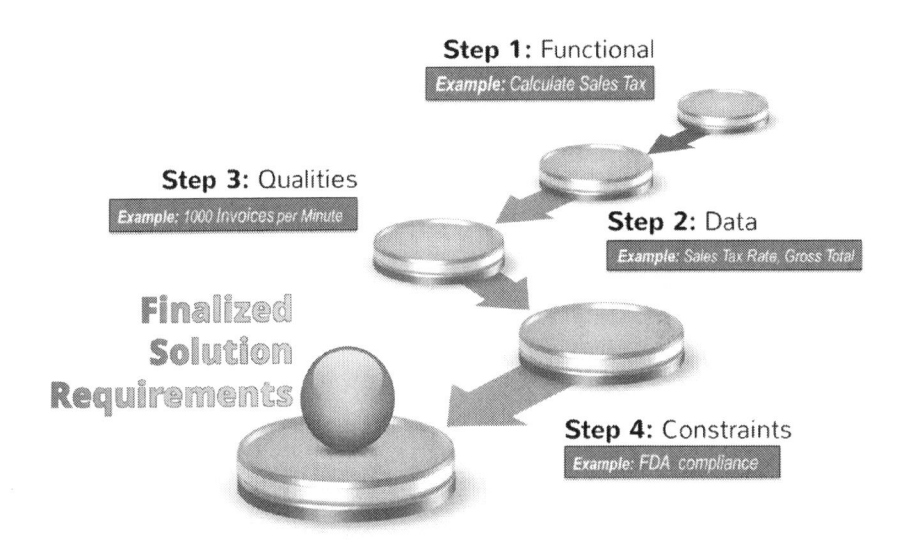

Step 1: Functional
Example: Calculate Sales Tax

Step 2: Data
Example: Sales Tax Rate, Gross Total

Step 3: Qualities
Example: 1000 Invoices per Minute

Step 4: Constraints
Example: FDA compliance

Finalized Solution Requirements

The fundamental distinction between **Qualities** and **Constraints** is what happens if they are not implemented. If a **Quality Requirement** is not met, the Stakeholder is dissatisfied with the solution. If a **Constraint** is violated, the solution cannot be implemented. Because of that distinction, you should focus on discovering as many **Constraints** as you can as early as possible to avoid rework or risk failure.

Features Include Functions and Data

The starting point to creating digital solutions is determining what the software must do. When you break down or split a User Story into its functional components, you can discover the steps or Functions the application or the product must do to enable the User Story.

Once you know what the product must **do** (Functions), look at the data. Ask questions such as:

- What data does the application need to work?
  What is the input?
- What is the outcome of the Story?
  What is the output?

To illustrate this idea, here is an example of a Feature "Enter Orders" with its input and outputs.

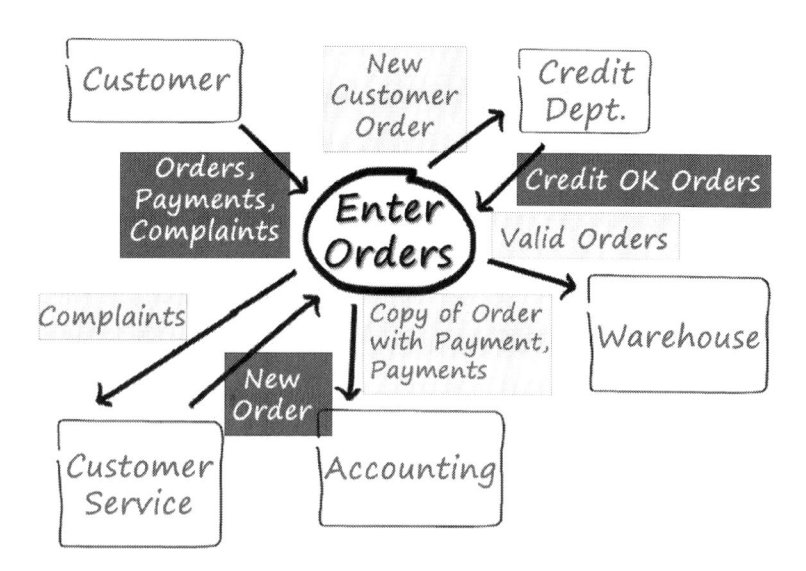

```
         New
Customer  Customer   Credit
          Order      Dept.

Orders,              Credit OK Orders
Payments,   Enter
Complaints  Orders   Valid Orders

Complaints   Copy of Order
             with Payment,  Warehouse
             Payments
           New
           Order
Customer   Accounting
Service
```

Once you know the Functions and associated data of a User Story, you can easily create Scenarios that prove the Story works correctly. We will show you how to do that in Chapter IV. Lean Acceptance Testing: The Business Perspective.

Functional Decomposition

To illustrate the point, we will use a goal-focused User Story from one of our case studies as an example:

> "To make responsible financial decisions, the Chief Financial Officer (CFO) needs the Projected Net Income (PNI) for the upcoming 12-month period."

We will use Feature Drill-down to break this Story into its Functional and Non-Functional components.

According to the Story, the CFO needs Projected Net Income (PNI). We need a function that calculates the PNI for a specified data. That function needs the "projected gross income" and "projected expenditures" as well as the "current date". We also need a User View that allows the CFO to view the PNI.

The phrase, "the upcoming 12-month period" refers to a Business Rule which we discover is a rolling 12-month period. "Rolling" means it is not necessarily a calendar year (January 1 through December 31), but can be 12 months into the future from any given date.

There also is a Security Requirement that we can infer. Access to the PNI must be limited to the Chief Financial Officer.

So far, we have:[1]

F231: Calculate Projected Net Income (**Function**)
D987: Projected Gross Income (**Data**)
D994: Projected Expenditures (**Data**)

---

[1] Legend: F = Function, D = Data, U = User View, BR = Business Rule, S = Security

D011: Current Date (**Data**)
U895: Cash Forecast Window (**User View**)
...
BR687: rolling 12-month period (**NFR - Business Rule**)
S681: Limit access to CFO (**NFR - Security Requirement**)
...

This list is obviously incomplete as you could extract many other Functional Features and Non-Functional Requirements from this User Story. It serves here only to illustrate the level of detail that many Agile development teams (depending on experience) need to write code.

Capturing Functional Features

Functions are the heart and soul of every IT solution. Unless the software **does** something, it has no value. You can name any Functional Feature using the "verb object" form. More specifically,

⇨ **use an active verb** (one that states the action)

⇨ **and direct objects** (the things the action creates or affects)

(e.g., "Calculate Sales Tax", "Verify Order", and "Identify Caller"). By naming the function this way, the name expresses what the function does.

A User Story often blatantly states or implies Functions. For example:

> To reduce order entry errors, customers can only select items that are in stock.

The following are either inferred or blatantly stated Functions:

Functions: Select Item (**blatantly stated**)
Check Item Inventory (**inferred**)
Reserve Ordered Item (**inferred**)
Track Order Entry Errors (**inferred**)

Here is another example:

> **As underwriter, I can calculate a premium discount for safe drivers to sell more insurance policies.**

This Story blatantly expresses the function "Calculate Premium Discount", so it is a good starting point. Next, look for not-so-obvious or implied Functions. By definition, a discount is a percentage taken off a base amount. That implies that the application must know the premium to be able to "Calculate a Premium Discount".

Furthermore, the Story refers to "safe drivers" as a group of people who qualify for this premium discount. How can the application recognize a "safe driver"? In discussing this with the SME, you discover that a safe driver is one who has not had an accident or traffic violation in 3 years.

Based on this information, you realize that you need a function to evaluate the driving record of the applicant to determine whether they fit this profile, ergo the function, "Evaluate Driving Record".

In each of the examples, we discovered more inferred Functions than blatantly stated Functions. In our experience, that is the norm for decomposing a User Story.

Before we get into the data side of Solution Requirements, it is time for a little practice to test your understanding. In the following exercise, you have an opportunity to recognize some of the Functions involved in User Stories.

Exercise: Functional Story Decomp

Here is your opportunity to try out what you read. As a reminder, exercises are designed to increase your retention of the presented ideas. Skipping the exercises by just reading the answers is not nearly as effective.

Keep in mind that there is no right or wrong answer. The exercises will just allow you to try out the presented concepts and techniques.

Instructions:

For each question on the next page, identify as many Functions as possible (statements about what the application or users need to do to achieve the desired results).

Express any function in the form "Verb-Object", e.g. "Order Goods", "Pay Open Invoices", etc.

Question 1:

Identify at least 5 Functions the solution would have to DO to implement the User Story:

> As an underwriter, I can view all claims filed against a policy over the past 3 years.

Question 2

Identify at least 5 Functions the solution would have to DO to implement the User Story:

> As a policyholder, I can view the status of all pending claims.

Question 3

Identify at least 5 Functions the solution would have to DO to implement the User Story:

> To ensure compliance with corporate guidelines, claim processors can view a list of all claims against all present and past policies for each customer.

Answer Question 1: Identify at least 5 Functions for the User Story: "As an underwriter, I can view all claims filed against a policy over the past 3 years."

We identified the Functions:

- ⇨ Identify Underwriter (inferred)
- ⇨ Select claims (inferred)
- ⇨ Enter effective date (inferred)
- ⇨ Show claims (stated)
- ⇨ Filter claims by policy (inferred)
- ⇨ Calculate 3-year time period (inferred)
- ⇨ Filter claims by date (inferred)
- ⇨ ...

Answer Question 2: Identify at least 5 Functions for the User Story: "As a policyholder, I can view the status of all pending claims."

We identified the Functions:

- ⇨ Identify Policyholder
- ⇨ Select policies by Policyholder
- ⇨ Filter claims by status "Pending"
- ⇨ List claims
- ⇨ Select relevant claim data
- ⇨ Confirm Policyholder credentials
- ⇨ ...

Answer Question 3: Identify at least 5 Functions for the User Story: "To ensure compliance with corporate guidelines, claims processors can view a list of all claims against all present and past policies for each customer."

We identified the Functions:

- ⇨ Confirm user credentials
- ⇨ Access role responsibilities
- ⇨ Relate claims to policies
- ⇨ Select claim
- ⇨ Find related policies
- ⇨ List claims by policy
- ⇨ ...

Data and Information Requirements

Data is to Functions like food is to people. You have identified Functions, meaning something the product or people using the product must do expressed in the "active verb / direct object" format. The direct object specifies the outcome of the function, which in the world of IT is typically data.

In the example we used at the beginning of this section,

> **"To make responsible financial decisions, the Chief Financial Officer (CFO) needs the Projected Net Income (PNI) for the upcoming 12-month period.",**

the function calculates the Projected Net Income (PNI). The PNI is data or information that the Function produces.

There are two distinct levels of informational components:

- → A **Data Element** is atomic data, meaning data in its simplest form such as a Customer Name, a Street Address, a City, and so on.

- → A **User View** is simply a collection of Data Elements. For example, a User View like "Customer Address" in the United States typically consists of a Street Address, City, State, and Zip Code. This User View allows anyone to locate a customer geographically. It is the Customer Address, i.e. the User View, that is the business value that the user needs.

> **Customer Address** *(User View)*
> **Customer Name** *(Data Element)*
> **Street Address** *(Data Element)*
> **City, State, and Zip Code**
> *(each a Data Element)*

To discover User Views and Data Elements, you need to ask two simple questions for each function:

- What data does the function produce when it is performed?
- What data does the function need to deliver the outcome?

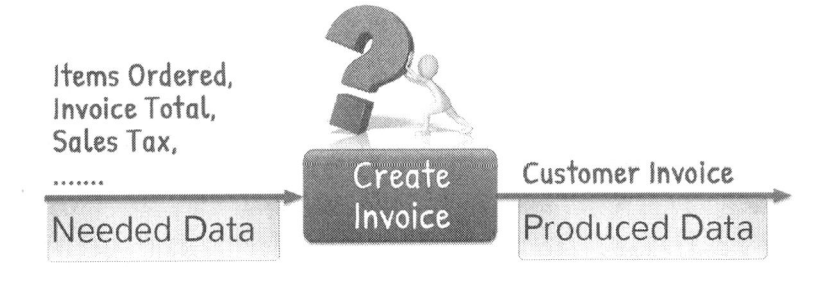

Needed Data: Items Ordered, Invoice Total, Sales Tax, ……… → **Create Invoice** → **Produced Data:** Customer Invoice

Example: Extracting Data

The "Calculate Premium" Function could require a thundering herd of Data Elements and User Views. For this example, assume that it will need the applicant's date of birth (DOB) — since automotive insurance is usually considerably higher for younger drivers.

If the policy includes collision and comprehensive coverage, the function will also need vehicle data, like the age, current value, and replacement value of the vehicle.

User Story: As underwriter, I can calculate a premium discount for safe drivers to sell more insurance policies.
Function: Calculate Premium
Data: Applicants DOB
User View: Vehicle Data

These Data Elements might not be as obvious as the earlier example, so they may need both some analytic legwork and domain knowledge.

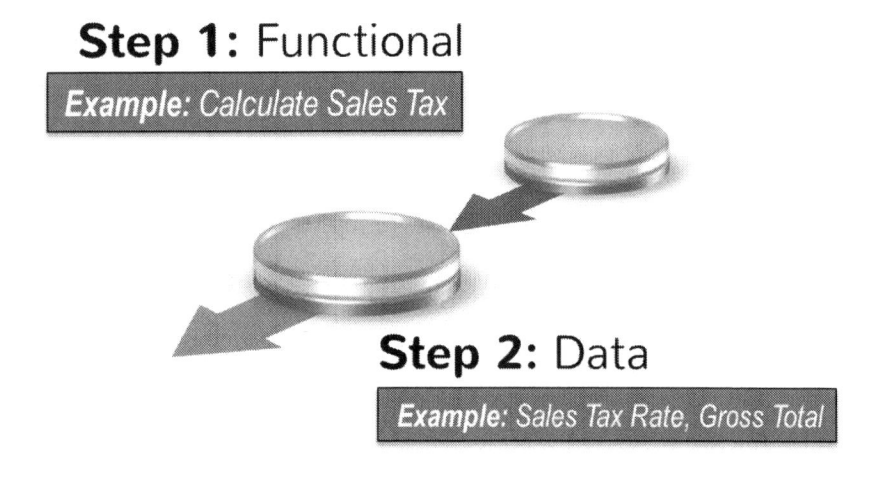

Step 1: Functional

Example: Calculate Sales Tax

Step 2: Data

Example: Sales Tax Rate, Gross Total

Exercise: Data Decomposition

Here is your opportunity to try out what you read. You will get the most out of this book if you do the exercise **before** reading our answers.

Keep in mind that there is no right or wrong answer. The exercises will just allow you to try out the presented concepts and techniques.

Instructions:

Based on a list of Functions, brainstorm the Data Element each listed function needs or creates.

Question 1:

What data does the function "List claim by policy" need and what data does it create?

Question 2:

What data does the function "Confirm policyholder credentials" need and what data does it create?

Question 3:

What data does the function "Filter claims by date range" need and what data does it create?

Answer Question 1: What data does the function "List claim by policy" need and what data does it create?

- ⇨ Claim ID
- ⇨ Claim Date
- ⇨ Policy ID

And you could name many more if you consider what data needs to be presented to the end users.

Answer Question 2: What data does the function "Confirm policyholder credentials" need and what data does it create?

- ⇨ Policyholder Name
- ⇨ Policyholder ID
- ⇨ Policy
- ⇨ Rules for Confirmation

And you could name many more if you consider what data needs to be presented to the end users.

Answer Question 3: What data does the function "Filter accident claims by date range" need and what data does it create?

- ⇨ Claim Filing Date
- ⇨ Claim Payment Date
- ⇨ Start Date of Range
- ⇨ End Date of Range

And you could name many more if you consider what data needs to be presented to the end users.

Defining Data Accuracy and Algorithms

Once again, the crucial insight in a Lean and Agile world: **Don't waste time and resources**! You could discover a vast number of Data Elements and defining each one could be a gigantic task.

> *Only the **entire Lean or Agile Team** can judge whether a Story Drill-down to Function and data level is a Lean approach for the running iteration.*

Even if the team decides that Story Decomp is the right approach, look for other data sources first. For example, many modern companies have a Data Administration Group responsible for company data. Other organizations have Data Analysts whose sole responsibility is to ensure consistent definitions of all Data Elements.

The number and variety of attributes defining each Data Element are too numerous to list here. However, we would like to mention two critical attributes that the business community needs to define (either the Product Owner / business expert or the respective data group). The two are **algorithms** for Data Elements and their respective **accuracy**.

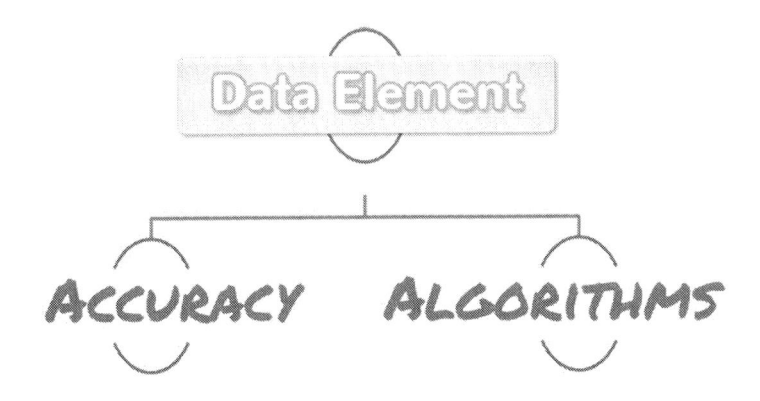

Algorithms for Derivable Data

Developers need to know the business algorithm for any Data Element your application calculates - in technical terms "Derivable Data".

For example, APPLICANT_AGE is derivable given the Applicant's date of birth and today's date. That formula is simple, but unless you specify it in the definition of the Data Element APPLICANT_AGE, the developers might have their own interpretation. Just as a side note, we have worked with organizations that are legally required to calculate age by rounding it up if you are less than 6 months from your next birthday. That begs the question, "How old are you really?

An example from our earlier User Story:

> As underwriter, I can calculate a premium discount for safe drivers to sell more insurance policies.

The business algorithm is:

Discount Amount = Eligible Premium X Discount Percentage

Data Accuracy and Currency

The business community also must define the acceptable **accuracy** of their business data — nothing is 100% accurate. To be considered accurate, each Data Element has to contain the most up to date (current) value at the required level of **precision** that satisfies the business need.

Currency of the Data

In the world of data, the term "**currency**" is a measure of time. It measures how quickly any data changes must be available from the business perspective. When a car dealer sells a vehicle, how quickly must the inventory be adjusted? Data has a lifetime that begins with the creation of a Data Element and ends when the values of the Data Element become irrelevant. Currency also means knowing when the information is out of date.

For example, for the "On-Hand-Quantity" to be current in an inventory control application, you might need to reduce the value as soon as a sale is final and increase it as soon as the Receiving Department has processed a shipment containing that item.

Another example: in an accounting application, it is typically sufficient if the accounts are updated monthly whereas in a cash-forecasting model, it might be current enough if the data reflects income from the last quarter.

Precision of the data

Accurate data is at the level of **precision** the company requires. If you are dealing with financial data for accounting purposes, it is usually necessary to specify them to within 2 decimal places.

On the other hand, if you are dealing with financial data for sales forecasting, it might be good enough to specify amounts to the nearest thousand dollars (3 digits before the decimal point), because anything more accurate would be irrelevant.

In summary, the exact precision that is required depends on the product under development:

⇨ Accounting applications are typically **precise** to the nearest cent (i.e. two places beyond the decimal point).

⇨ Manufacturing applications may require data **precise** to the nearest gram, or pound, or ton, obviously dependent upon what they manufacture and in what quantities.

⇨ Cash forecasting applications may require precision to the nearest million dollars.

Determining the level of precision for each Data Element is a business decision. Knowing when to round calculated results and when to truncate them are both key to reaching the required level of precision.

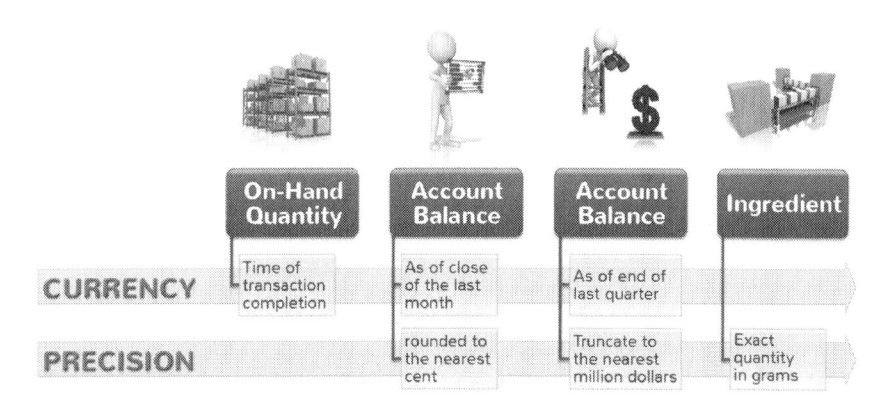

	On-Hand Quantity	Account Balance	Account Balance	Ingredient
CURRENCY	Time of transaction completion	As of close of the last month	As of end of last quarter	
PRECISION		rounded to the nearest cent	Truncate to the nearest million dollars	Exact quantity in grams

If you already have precision and currency defined from an earlier function that used this Data Element, confirm with your SME that the answers have not changed. This way, if distinct Functions require different degrees of accuracy or currency, you will be able to quickly identify this and get a resolution from the business community.

Non-Functional Requirements, Qualities & Constraints

You now have identified Functional Features, meaning things the software will do (Functions) and information it needs or creates (Data). You still need to explore the other part of solution-level requirements, namely Non-Functional Requirements (NFR). Sometimes these are called Quality Requirements or Qualities, and Constraints.

Missing and misunderstood NFRs are all too often the cause of project failure. There are a multitude of examples in the annals of IT projects where applications delivered everything they were required to do. However, they did not do them even close to well enough to meet the customers' needs.

Anyone who experienced the original rollout of the Affordable Care Act (Obamacare) website can relate to this reality. The website crashed constantly and when it was available, wait times often were measured in hours.

That is an example of what happens when you do not pay enough attention to the quality dimension. The website could process the requests once they were entered; it just took way too long to get to that point.

NFRs that are relevant to the entire product should be defined at the beginning of an initiative. NFRs that are unique to a User Story or Feature should be defined during the iteration when they get implemented. Before we show you how to drill down on a User Story to identify NFRs, we will give you a short introduction.

Fundamentally, an NFR defines criteria, properties, or conditions that an individual function or the entire application must meet before it is acceptable to the business or end-user community.

The following is a legitimate example of an NFR or Quality Requirement:

> **The nuclear power plant radiation monitor must be available 24/7/365**

It implies that the function can never be allowed to fail. Given the gravity of the situation should it ever fail, this is a pretty reasonable request on the part of the business community.

Another NFR would be:

> **Only personnel with paygrade E8 and higher can update the Andromeda File**

The next example of an NFR is technical in nature as it lists which specific technologies must be used to enforce access security.

> **Access will be controlled with retinal scan, fingerprint, and voice recognition**

Qualities and Constraints do not just affect Functions. They can also affect the data as you can see in this statement.

A customer ID must be a unique *(meaning non-recurring)*, **15-digit** *(the specific length)*, **positive** *(cannot be below 0)*, **real number** *(cannot be an irrational or an imaginary number)* **that identifies a single customer**

Those are examples of Non-Functional (quality) attributes that an application needs to enforce.

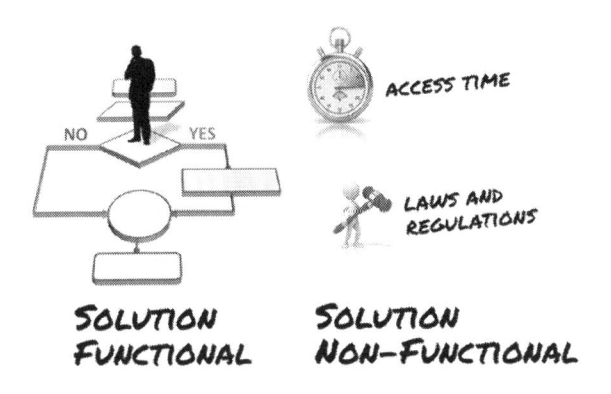

SOLUTION FUNCTIONAL   **SOLUTION NON-FUNCTIONAL**

ACCESS TIME

LAWS AND REGULATIONS

Types of Non-Functional Requirements

To get you started in defining NFRs from User Stories and Features, we will define four common types of NFRs with examples of each. We will suggest questions that we have used for discovering each type over the years in our consulting practice. These questions have proven for us to be a great start to discover critical Non-Functional Requirements.

Here are the four common types of NFRs:

- → External Constraints
- → Performance Requirements
- → User Experience Requirements
- → Architectural Capabilities

External Constraints

Digital solutions do not exist in a vacuum. There are many external forces that can influence or pose limitations on your product. Each of those are external Constraints and we can only give you some general groupings to think about.

Ignoring external Constraints is a recipe for disaster on any product or initiative and you should define them as early as possible to avoid wasted work. Some examples of external Constraints include:

Natural Limits Enforced by Nature

Physical limits like the speed of light are fundamental Constraints. For instance, if you develop an app for the web that requires satellite access, you need to consider latency, that is the time it takes a signal to go from the source to the satellite and back down to the recipient.

Other physical limits are the temperature and the environment in which the product must function. For example, if you are developing an application that needs to be used in a cold room, a germ-free room or similar environments, these are environmental Constraints. These types of Non-Functional Requirements are critical in real-time systems.

Laws and Regulations Enforced by External Agencies

Laws and regulations are a common form of Constraints, and arguably often overlooked. We suggest that you make yourself aware of relevant laws and regulations if you are a fan of your personal freedom. As the one defining the requirements, you should be aware of any organization that has the authority to impose legal limits upon what your application can do because they are important Constraints.

Ask all Stakeholders, "What are the laws and regulations as they pertain to this project, function, requirement, or application?" You are interested in any regulatory body that has the authority to stipulate or mandate rules that your application must follow.

Remember, Constraints are externally mandated conditions that limit what any solution can or cannot do. "External" means that nobody on the project team has the authority to determine whether the application should or should not adhere to them.

Policies and Rules Enforced by the Organization

Business Rules and policies are internal Constraints and your team is not authorized to change them. They are Constraints for your project unless your project is directly involved in the definition, maintenance, and/or enforcement of Business Rules and policies.

Business rules are created within your organization but usually not within your project. You must make sure that whoever has the authority in the organization has signed off on all of the Business Rules. If your organization has the Business Rules documented or in a central location, you need to get access to the Business Rules so that you can incorporate them into your application.

Security: Limiting Access and Protecting Data

One of the components of IT Security is authorized access, meaning how can any authorized user, manual or automated, interact with the application under development. Security has become a topic for headlines in recent years as more and more data is stored about more and more people in more and more places.

Data breaches are becoming a daily topic in the news and we doubt there is anyone left on the planet that has accessed the Internet in the past 5 years and not had sensitive data exposed. As our appetite for data grows, so must the robustness of our devices for protecting personal data from unauthorized access.

To reveal Security needs, ask:

 ◈ Who should have access to the application?

- Who can add, change, or delete the data?
- What are the risks of unauthorized use?
- How sensitive is the data?
- What are the costs if this data is hacked?

Distribution of Function and Data

Physical distribution is another type of Constraints. It deals with the location of functionality (where are things done) and data (where is data maintained). For performance reasons, large companies need CDNs (Content Delivery Networks) and VPNs (Virtual Private Networks) to respond to customer requests in a timely and secure manner.

As organizations continue to increase in size and complexity, this type becomes increasingly relevant. Anything having to do with the ability of a business solution to work in distributed environments falls into this type of Constraints.

Performance Requirements

In the performance category, there are limits to the speed and efficiency of the application and the entire business solution. The main problem with performance is not the difficulty in achieving it, but the cost of measuring it. Modern applications can achieve amazing levels of performance if they are necessary and the business is willing to pay for them.

Frequency: How Often Is the Feature Used?

Frequency is one of the primary performance issues. It is a measure of how often a Functional Feature will be needed in a given timeframe (per second, per minute, per day, etc.).

For example, assume that you are developing an application that calculates the sales tax for an invoice. If you are dealing with a business that produces a handful of invoices a day (for example, a truck dealer or a high-paid consultant), it would not be a wise investment to spend thousands of dollars trying to reduce processing time to the lowest nanosecond. On the other hand, if the application processes millions of invoices per minute, those thousands of dollars might be a reasonable investment.

You might need to find out what triggers this function to answer the question of how often this event will happen. You might also be interested in whether transactions are done in one fell swoop, ad hoc, or during peak times; is there a variation in the frequency such as sometimes it is low and sometimes it is high.

Urgency: Response Time vs. Update Time

Response Time

Urgency is another dimension of performance. Urgency has two sides. The one most often discussed is the Response Time, i.e. the time a person can wait for a response from the application before he or she can no longer perform his or her work.

One could also consider Response Time as a measure of the time a typical user is willing to wait for data from the application before he or she is frustrated enough to bypass the application and do the job differently.

Update Time

The other side of urgency is the Update Time, i.e. how long the application can wait for input from an external actor (e.g. an end user) before the application fails.

For example, suppose your application shuts down the nuclear reactor when a radioactivity threshold is detected in the control room. You probably do not want to design the application to wait for input from a human to tell it that the threshold has been reached. This is a situation that clearly requires a real-time system that receives its input directly from devices that detect radioactivity levels and reacts at once.

In Summary

To determine the Response Time of the end users, ask:

When must the data be available?

The question for the Update Time is:

How long can the system wait for new data?

Volume of Information

The Volume dimension deals with data. How much data does a function need and how much data does it create each time it is executed?

Obviously, processing immense amounts of data takes longer than processing single bits, so high-volume applications need to be more efficient. Even if an application is seldom used (i.e., low Frequency), a high-volume of data might constitute a reason for investing in higher efficiency.

To reveal issues with data volumes, ask the following questions for each Functional Feature:

1. How much information (pages, screens, records, transactions, etc.) is produced?

2. How much data needs to be captured and stored?

The volume of data question is critical. If an application must process vast amounts of data, developers must spend more time making sure that it is efficient and can process the data in the allotted time.

Precision and Currency of Information

We have already explained in the section "Defining Data Accuracy and Algorithms" how to define the precision and timeliness of data. Here we will only mention that both can be Non-Functional Requirements (Constraints) that are defined either for the entire product or for each Feature individually.

User Experience Requirements

The User Experience is a non-functional dimension that has become ever more critical with the advent of the WWW. This is where technology meets real people and, like any touch point between opposites, it can be tricky.

Many of your Non-Functional Requirements will come from this category. You might discover User Experience Requirements regarding your users' abilities, their location (where will they use the application), their training needs, or maybe their cultural needs and desires.

Level of Interaction

Some applications offer an immersive experience while others are only valuable for quick reference. For instance, search engines need simplicity and speed while games need to be engaging to keep the user's attention.

To define this NFR, you need to know how your users will interact with the product you are developing. Will they need:

- **cursory** (quick in-and-out, just looking for one piece of information)
- **broad** (browsing through various user views that cannot be predetermined)
- **in-depth** (drill-down capabilities including Features like breadcrumbs to keep the user from getting lost)?

Corporate and National Cultures

Culture is an aspect of the user experience with which international organizations deal every day. We maintain that this not only encompasses national identities but also corporate cultures.

Every group of people is unique; every organization is unique; finding the sweet spot of interaction between the two is an on-going challenge for anyone involved in defining, designing, or delivering digital solutions to the world.

Major corporations have Localization or Globalization groups whose sole responsibility is to define the needs of each target market and ensure that their products and services are suitable to the culture of customers and prospects.

IT Architectural Capabilities

If the application is web-based, does it have to be responsive to every device a user might use, such as a smart phone, tablet, PC, Laptop, etc.? Again, the answer is simply one of money as the more devices your application needs to support, the more it will cost.

The architectural capabilities of Non-Functional Requirements deal with the ability of the application to react to changes in its business and technological environment. This includes changes in the hardware capabilities, software, competitive environment, or any combination of these.

Maintainability defines how quickly your application should react when conditions change.

Portability is about how quickly you could migrate the application from one hardware platform to another.

Scalability defines how easy it must be for the application to grow over time.

Availability is about when the application is accessible for its users.

Reliability specifies how dependable the application must be based on the potential cost of failure. This dimension is typically defined in the twin metrics "Mean Time Between Failures (MTBF)" and "Mean Time to Repair (MTTR)". It is most commonly a factor in life-critical, real-time applications such as Emergency Room Support Systems, nuclear power plants, automated manufacturing systems, etc.

Minimum acceptable time?
Mean Time Between Failures

MTBF

Maximum acceptable time?
Mean Time To Repair

MTTR

Split Stories with NFR's

So how can you use Non-Functional Requirements to split a User Story? Some User Stories define a simple function that is challenging to develop due to performance or constraining requirements (a.k.a. Non-Functional Requirements). If that is the case, split out the User Story expressing the simple core function from those that address the non-functional needs.

> As security admin, I can grant application access rights to user roles that will go into effect within 10 seconds for all impacted users.

A Performance Requirement like this can be critical for satisfying the end-user community. Most of us have experienced applications that take forever to respond, and life is too short for that. Unfortunately, ensuring short response times can be challenging.

Getting the function to work could be easy but achieving the desired performance could be a challenge. Consider splitting the User Story into:

> As a security admin, I can grant application access rights to user roles.

and the Performance Requirement:

> Changes to application access rights will go into effect within 10 seconds for all impacted users

That would allow the Agile team to deliver the functionality and then do whatever is necessary to ensure compliance with the performance requirements.

This concludes the topic of Solution Requirements.

Functional and Non-Functional
SOLUTION REQUIREMENTS

IV. Lean Acceptance Testing: The Business Perspective

Testing is crucial for any software development methodology (SDM), whether it follows a Lean (e.g. Kanban), Agile (e.g. Scrum), DevOps (e.g. Continuous Delivery), or traditional (Waterfall or RUP) approach. Unfortunately, testing is very time consuming. Studies of IT projects have shown that testing accounts for up to 45% of the effort required to implement a digital solution.

There are many types of Testing needed between conception and deployment of an application. Developer-driven Testing (aka Unit, Integration, System Testing) focuses on proving that the software code works. Business-driven Testing (aka Acceptance Testing) confirms that the application delivers the promised business value and should be done by the business community.

In traditional software development environments, developing and running Acceptance Tests starts late, often after the design phase, sometimes even after coding is completed. To make matters worse, End-user Acceptance Testing is often neglected in traditional methods due to time and budget Constraints. This changes with Lean and Agile approaches.

Since this book is primarily intended for the business community, we will only deal with Acceptance Testing.

Topics covered in this chapter

In this chapter, we cover ATDD (Acceptance Test-Driven Development) and BDD (Behavior-Driven Development), two new testing concepts associated with Lean and Agile software development. We will start with explaining what they are, how they work, and why they are important.

ATDD/BDD are complex methods. As Business Analysts, we only need to be well-versed in a subset of the new testing approach, namely Scenarios (the new Acceptance Criteria) which are written in the Gherkin language (GIVEN-WHEN-THEN).

In the early days of Agile, Acceptance Criteria were written on the back of a User Story card. When a company adopts ATDD/BDD, Acceptance Criteria are defined as Scenarios, Scenario Outlines, and Examples which are typically stored and maintained in automated tools. In this chapter, you will learn how to find, analyze, structure, and write these new forms of Acceptance Tests.

To assess the outcome of a User Story, you need test data. Scenarios and Scenario Outlines describe the steps that lead to the business value of your User Stories. We demonstrate how to optimize test data using Scenario Outlines together with Examples. To reduce waste and minimize the number of Scenarios or Examples, we also show you test data Engineering methods.

In ATDD/BDD, automation is the final and highly recommended stage. However, the topic of test automation is too large to cover in this book. In addition, there are many good books and courses already available. The largest investment in time is finding and writing GWT Scenarios and Outlines. That is the focus of this chapter.

The New Acceptance Test Paradigm

With Lean and Agile software development a new testing paradigm has emerged. It is also amazingly effective for traditional approaches to software development. ATDD (Acceptance Test-Driven Development) and/or BDD (Behavior-Driven Development) represent a significant change in thinking compared to previous development methods, as they require the business experts or Test Engineers to develop Acceptance Tests *before* developers write a line of code for the application! ATDD and BDD focus on improving the quality of the software product.

In Lean and Agile development, User Stories must have Acceptance Criteria (aka Conditions of Satisfaction). These define Functional, Non-Functional, and informational requirements that the story must fulfill to be accepted by stakeholders. They determine when a User Story is done and functions correctly.

Acceptance criteria can be written in natural language, in numbered lists, tables, GIVEN-WHEN-THEN (GWT) Scenarios, or other standards chosen by your organization.

Many Lean and Agile teams use the GWT Scenarios because it makes the transition to automated testing much easier. For example, Cucumber is an open-source software testing framework that supports tests written in Gherkin. It reads the Gherkin Scenarios stored in Feature Files to enable automated testing.

Lean/Agile approaches recognize that the Scenarios developed for Acceptance Testing **ARE** the actual requirements from the developers' point of view. For this reason, developing Scenarios **BEFORE** writing the code is crucial for the success of Agile/Lean undertakings.

ATDD/BDD Explained

In ATDD (Acceptance Test Driven Development) and BDD (Behavior-Driven Development), the business or customer side team and the technical team work together to develop acceptance tests before the developers write one line of code. Collaboration in creating these tests is critical to ensure that all the different perspectives are covered.

These joint discussions are often referred to as the 3-Amigos Meeting (although they are often attended by many more people). The participants represent three different and equally critical perspectives:

⇨ **Customers** (supported by Business Analysts): What do we need?
⇨ **Development**: How can we deliver?
⇨ **Quality Assurance** (aka Testing): Does it really work?

Developers use these tests to guide them when programming. If the code produced by the developers passes the Acceptance Tests, it meets the requirements of the SMEs or customers. This places the responsibility on the stakeholders who define the acceptance tests to ensure that their tests are complete.

A critical success criterion for effective ATDD or BDD approaches is knowing how to create acceptance tests without knowing exactly how the product or application will work in the future. This is one of the most challenging steps you need to take to ensure that IT delivers the technology that customers need.

How Does ATDD/BDD work?

ATDD and BDD have their roots in a concept called Test-Driven Development (TDD). TDD was one component of a software development approach called eXtreme Programming (XP) which predates Agile.

The concept was so successful that most Agile and Lean methods use it today in their software development approaches. In the early years, TDD was used exclusively for Unit Testing. Based on Functional (solution) requirements, developers would create simple Unit Tests and then create the code to pass the tests.

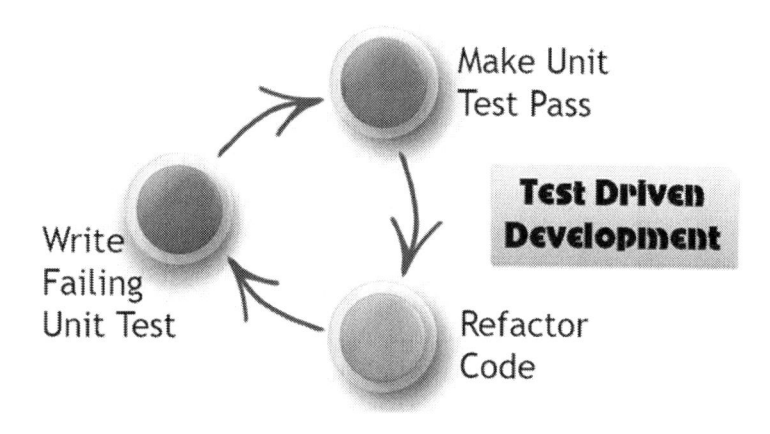

Make Unit Test Pass

Test Driven Development

Write Failing Unit Test

Refactor Code

Once a test passed, the developer worked on the next Unit Test and kept going in cycles until all the code passed all Unit tests. After many success stories, people realized that this was a phenomenally effective technique. There was only one problem. The industry had gone backwards in terms of stakeholder involvement. Interpretation of business needs was again exclusively in the hands of developers. Then, ATDD and BDD came to the rescue.

ATDD/BDD ends the need for developers to interpret vague, wordy user requirements by giving them Acceptance Tests called "Scenarios" that **ARE** the IT requirements. In ATDD/BDD, domain experts develop Scenarios and Scenario Outlines with Examples. Developers create code that will pass these easy-to-understand tests instead of trying to interpret hard-to-understand requirement statements.

The Subject Matter Expert (business expert, Product Owner, Project Manager, Line Manager, Test Engineer, etc. with developer guidance, if required) writes as many "failing Acceptance Tests" or Scenarios as a User Story or Feature needs. The number and level of detail of the tests or Scenarios depends on the complexity of the Story or Feature, the cost of failure, and the experience of the developers.

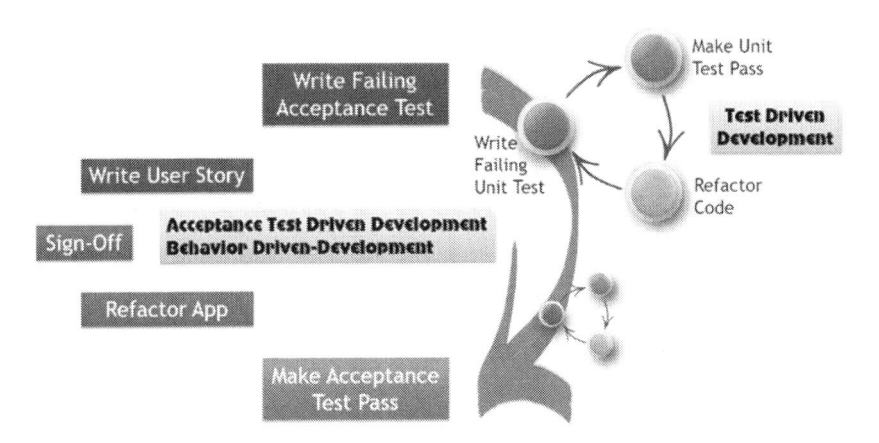

Developers then take a Scenario and write "Failing Unit Tests" to test the functional parts of the coded Scenario. They then repeat the test-driven development cycle (Write "Failing Unit Test", "Make Unit Test Pass", "Refactor Code" etc.) until all Unit Tests have been successfully completed.

Once they have proven that their code passes all Unit Tests, the Acceptance Test or Scenario comes back for Acceptance Testing ("Make Acceptance Test Pass"). If accepted by the quality group, the developers integrate that code into the application. This involves a process known in geek-speak as "Refactoring". As those wearing the business analysis hat (i.e. everyone who defines requirements, User Stories or Features), we do not need to know anything more about this topic.

Although there are several different approaches to writing and structuring acceptance tests (e.g. unstructured Acceptance Criteria for User Stories), most organizations we work with use Scenarios written in Given-When-Then syntax. In the next subchapter we will discuss Gherkin Scenarios and Scenario Outlines in detail.

The Future of IT - DevOps with Continuous Integration and Delivery

With this approach, we are setting the stage for a concept called DevOps or Continuous Delivery which is currently the holy grail of Information Technology (IT). The name speaks for itself.

Continuous Integration and Delivery basically means that the IT department can change infrastructure and applications or add functionality at any time. They continuously maintain the product or software. However, it does not mean that if a user discovers an application failure, it will be fixed today. A responsible person from the business community must set priorities for upcoming fixes, enhancements, and changes.

In our (the authors') opinion, this is the future of software development, and an important prerequisite for this is test automation. One of the key factors for the success of this new approach will be the quality of Scenarios and acceptance tests.

Acceptance Criteria as Given-When-Then Scenarios

The purpose of the Acceptance Criteria is to verify that the code works as intended. For example, if you wanted to test whether the User Story "place an order" works in an e-commerce application, you need to define Acceptance Criteria, i.e., conditions that must be met in order for the User Story to be considered correctly implemented.

In Agile / Lean Methods, developers, business/domain experts and testers are responsible for creating Scenarios (a form of User Story Acceptance Criteria) before they even know how the program will actually work.

Scenarios Are the Ultimate Requirements

A User Story is not a "requirement" as we used to understand it in IT or requirements engineering. A User Story is a trigger for a conversation between someone representing a stakeholder (users and others) and a developer. It is not a specification. When the technical and business teams come together to talk about a User Story or Feature, the goal is to ensure that all parties **really** understand the intent.

Developers, testers, SME's, and the Product Owner who might be involving a Business Analyst get together and discuss the Story. Since it is much easier to show an example than to specify an abstract business need, the discussion revolves around the results of the User Story also known as Acceptance Criteria of the Story.

Acceptance Criteria can take many different forms; however, Scenarios have become one of the most wide-spread. The team members discuss the Story and determine the Scenarios that will prove to them that the User Story works correctly in the product

Scenarios follow the Gherkin syntax (GIVEN-WHEN-THEN). Gherkin enables business teams (e.g. Product Owner, SME, end-user, Business Analysts, etc.) to document acceptance tests in a language that the business community, developers, and testers can all understand. This promotes collaboration and mutual understanding of the required tests. Scenarios use the GWT structure to express the business logic and are often kept in a Feature file.

As mentioned above, automated Acceptance Testing is a critical success factor for some of the new software development philosophies. Currently, many teams still have difficulties in implementing automated testing, but Lean and Agile teams still use Scenarios to control their programming work.

Next, we will show you the evolution of a Scenario based on an example from one of our products – training classes.

Scenarios

Scenarios describe the steps, events, and interactions between a user and the software. To show you how to develop a Scenario using an example based on a common event, here is a simple goal-oriented User Story that we created for a training company:

To plan their career development paths, students can see classes they still need to take because of their BASE scores.

To clarify this Story, you need to know that BASE is a Business Analysis Skills Evaluation. BASE scores are the building blocks for creating a custom business analysis training plan for each student based on their current skills.

If you start to think about what Scenarios you need to verify the correct implementation of this User Story, you realize that there is an obvious one: "Student (let's call him Fred) requests class schedule." That is the whole purpose of this User Story. Next, we want to express the business logic in GIVEN-WHEN-THEN format.

GIVEN is anything that must be set up for this Scenario to deliver the results that you need. We could also say that you are defining the "pre-conditions" for this Scenario. If there is more than one pre-condition, you use the connector "AND" in Gherkin. (The "AND" statement can be used in Gherkin to for additional GIVEN, WHEN, or THEN statements.)

SCENARIO: Fred requests class schedule and he has unfinished classes

GIVEN Fred is logged into the website
  AND Fred has completed BASE
  AND Fred has unfinished classes
WHEN Fred requests class schedule
THEN Fred's customized training plan is viewable

In this Scenario Fred, our student, is logged into the Web site, he has completed BASE, and has unfinished classes.

Whereas GIVEN describes the pre-conditions, the WHEN action "Fred requests class schedule" triggers this Scenario. The THEN specifies the outcome of this Scenario meaning Fred's customized training plan is viewable. Before we move on to Scenario Outlines, let us expand on the content of each statement.

In the GIVEN clause, you should express any kind of setup data that is necessary for this test to succeed. This encompasses hardware conditions as well as data, files, or records that must have a specific condition for the test to run.

The WHEN clause defines any actions or events that initiate the Scenario. It is the interaction between a Stakeholder of the system and the system itself. For example, if you are dealing with a web site the WHEN statement lists the type of user interaction such as "enters value", "clicks a button", "submits a form", etc. However, if you are dealing with an API, for example, the Stakeholder interaction might be "responding to a call".

The THEN clause defines the result(s) that determines whether the test was successful. If the THEN result is achieved as defined, the test succeeds otherwise it fails. This is often a calculated result with a certain value, but it can also be any other outcome.

> **EXAMPLE**
>
> To plan their career development path, students can see all classes that offer necessary training topics for the upcoming six months.

> **Scenario:** Fred requests recommended training topics
>
> GIVEN Fred is logged in to website
>   And Fred has completed BASE
>   And Fred has unfinished training topics
> WHEN Fred requests training plan
> THEN Fred's customized training plan is viewable

That is the basic concept of Scenarios written in Gherkin's GIVEN-WHEN-THEN (GWT). There is, however, one more keyword that can come in handy and save you a ton of work.

Defining a Gherkin BACKGROUND

Sometimes, you discover that many Gherkin SCENARIOS require the same setup conditions. Fortunately, there is a simple solution and a great time-saver. The BACKGROUND statement in Gherkin allows you to define setup criteria that will be used for a group of Scenarios.

All Gherkin statements between the BACKGROUND statement and the first SCENARIO will be executed as the first step for each SCENARIO in a Feature file. That means 2 things:

1) You can only have one BACKGROUND statement for a given set of SCENARIOS.

2) The BACKGROUND must precede all SCENARIO statements for testing a given User Story, Feature, etc.

For example, let us expand the Scenario you defined in the previous section.

BACKGROUND
GIVEN Fred is logged into the website
AND Fred has completed BASE

> SCENARIO: Fred requests class schedule and has unfinished classes
> GIVEN Fred has unfinished classes
> WHEN Fred requests class schedule
> THEN Fred's customized training plan is viewable
>
> SCENARIO: Fred requests class schedule and has finished all required classes
> GIVEN Fred has no unfinished training topics
> WHEN Fred requests class schedule
> THEN Fred is offered a certificate of completion

Scenario Outlines

In our last example we focused on "Fred". Of course, not every Scenario will be about Fred. What happens if we want to test a Scenario several times with different data? Do we have to create a Scenario for each data set? That would be a lot of wasted effort - definitely not LEAN!

This situation is extremely common in testing. Typically, a single test is insufficient to prove that the application reacts as we intended. We need to prove that the application reacts correctly under a variety of circumstances. Rewriting Scenarios with many different data values quickly becomes tedious and repetitive. Scenario Outlines together with Examples reduce this effort considerably.

Scenario Outline: A user withdraws money from an ATM

GIVEN <Name> has a valid Credit
And their account balance

WHEN they insert their card
And withdraw <Withdrawal

THEN the ATM should return <
And their account balance
And the outcome is <Resu

Name	Old Balance	Withdrawal Amount	New Balance	Result
Tom	$125	$25	$100	Dispersed
Fred	$15	$25	$15	Amount not available
Nancy	$10,287	$1,000	$10,287	Daily limit exceeded
NoAccount	N/A	N/A	N/A	Card returned

A Scenario Outline also uses the GWT syntax. However, it uses variables instead of constants to allow for the execution of a multitude of tests with a single Scenario statement. It avoids constant values like "Fred", but instead refers to a "Person". The Scenario Outline is followed by an Example Table that contains the various values assigned to each variable. Each row in the Example Table represents a single test.

Here is a common example of a Scenario Outline that many are familiar with: "A person withdraws money from an ATM".

OUTLINE: A person withdraws money from an ATM
GIVEN <Person> has a valid Credit or Debit card
  AND their account balance is <OriginalBalance>
WHEN <Person> inserts the card
  AND withdraws <WithdrawalAmount>
THEN the ATM disperses <WithdrawalAmount>
  AND their account balance is <NewBalance>
  AND the outcome is <Result>

In the GIVEN clause, you see the less than and greater than signs around the word <Person>. That is a placeholder known as a variable. Cucumber (a framework that supports the Gherkin language) stores the values in Example Tables (more on that in a minute) and automated testing tools that are compatible with Cucumber use them during test execution.

This Scenario Outline has a second condition expressed with an "AND" which reads, "AND their account balance is <OriginalBalance> (again a variable).

There are two actions or WHEN statements in this Scenario Outline:

> **WHEN** <Person> inserts the card
> **AND** withdraws <WithdrawalAmount>.

The second action or AND statement uses another variable for "Withdrawal Amount".

In the THEN statement, we find three post conditions or outcomes for this scenario:

> **THEN** the ATM should disperse <WithdrawalAmount>
> **AND** their account balance is <NewBalance>
> **AND** the outcome is <Result>

As you can see, we have several variables that are part of that process. That leads us to the Example Table mentioned earlier.

Examples

An Example Table shows concrete, specific outcomes that the developing product must support, so it is no longer necessary to understand or interpret a requirement. You can learn more about how to create Examples in the chapter on identifying Scenarios.

When you set up an Example Table in Gherkin, list each variable in your Scenario (Person, OriginalBalance, WithdrawalAmount, NewBalance and Result) as a column header. The names of each column must EXACTLY match one of the declared variables and every declared variable must have a column of that EXACT name (capitalization matters). Each row represents a specific test with different data values that you want to test.

Person	Original Balance	Withdrawal Amount	New Balance	Result
Tom	$125	$25	$100	Dispersed
Fred	$15	$25	$15	Amount not available
Nancy	$10,287	$1,000	$10,287	Daily limit exceeded
NoAccount	N/A	N/A	N/A	Card returned

Examples, by definition, contain specific data values for executing one unique Scenario. You can have one Scenario and any number of Examples that you need to execute to prove that the application performs correctly under all the circumstances for which you are testing.

In our table above, we have four different Examples that are executed using the same Scenario.

This way, I can make sure that whether the "OriginalBalance" is $125, $15, $10287, or "N/A", the application will process all four Examples and achieve the expected "Result" in each.

Some of you have might have experienced the flood of Examples that can be identified for a given Scenario Outline. We have good news for you. In the next section, you will learn several techniques that will allow you to limit the number of Examples. We call these techniques Test Data Engineering.

To Summarize Gherkin,

- ☑ A SCENARIO has constants and NO variables.
- ☑ With a BACKGROUND you can minimize redundancies in Scenario statements.
- ☑ A Scenario OUTLINE has variables that are created using an Example Table in Gherkin.
- ☑ Each row in the EXAMPLE Table will be executed as one Scenario.
- ☑ A Scenario outline can have an unlimited number of Examples.
- ☑ All Gherkin statements are stored in Feature Files.

To stay within the guidelines of Lean and Agile, it is important to have a minimal number of Examples to validate a Feature or User Story. You want to optimize the data values, so you do not have multiple tests when one test will suffice. This leads us to Test Data Engineering which is the topic of the next chapter. But first, we recommend the following practice exercise.

Exercise: Expressing Scenarios in GWT Format

Here is your opportunity to try what you have read. Again, you will get the most out of this book if you do the exercise before you read our answers.

Remember that there is no right or wrong answer. The exercises only allow you to try out the concepts and techniques presented.

Instructions:

Expressing tests in the GWT format requires a slightly different way of thinking. Create one or more Scenarios to validate the following User Story.

Question 1:

What Scenario(s) can you identify to test this User Story:

> As a visitor, I can view all flights available for my travel date and destination to select the best option.

Answer Question 1: What Scenario(s) can you identify to test the User Story, "As a visitor, I can view all flights available for my travel date and destination to select the best option."?

A couple of potential answers:

BACKGROUND
GIVEN Visitor is on the "View Available Flights" page of the BP Air website

SCENARIO: Visitor picks departure airport, destination airport, and travel dates
WHEN Visitor requests available flights
THEN Visitor views all flights for selected dates and airports

SCENARIO: Visitor wants to see flights from alternate departure airports to the destination
GIVEN No flights available for the selected dates and airports
WHEN Visitor requests alternate departure airports
THEN Visitor can pick alternate departure airports

Of course, there are many more Scenarios you could find, and you would have to test them thoroughly. The more Scenarios you identify, the more likely it is that the Function will deliver exactly the results you want.

However, to be a useful tool in a Lean and Agile world, you need to perform **as many acceptance tests as necessary, but as few as possible.** In the next chapter you will learn techniques to ensure that you have the smallest number of Examples or Scenarios, but still achieve the desired test coverage.

Engineering AGILE Test Data

The purpose of Test Data Engineering is to:

- ☑ minimize the number of Examples
- ☑ make the process of testing repeatable
- ☑ support Regression Testing

Beyond saving time by developing as few Scenarios as possible, Regression Testing is yet another reason we need to engineer test data. How does Regression Testing work?

Regression testing is the process of running Scenarios repeatedly. Each time a developer makes a change to the application, all verified scenarios previously executed to test the product or application are re-run. This process is called Regression Testing. It proves that not only have we correctly added the new functionality, but that we have not broken anything else. This is a critical and often overlooked goal of Acceptance Testing.

Test Data Engineering is about identifying the best data values for your Scenarios and Examples. If you randomly pick data input values, you will end up with a thundering herd of Scenarios. You have no idea whether you covered the most critical outcomes. Test Data Engineering makes the testing process Lean and repeatable which results in effective Regression Testing.

Data Types for Test Data Engineering

The GIVEN-WHEN-THEN format provides information about the types of test data you need to consider in Test Data Engineering.

The GIVEN includes all data, files, records, databases, hardware configurations and everything that must be in a certain state prior to executing the respective Scenario. Check that the data you have set up is optimal for the Function or Scenario.

The WHEN specifies data that defines any values or actions required to perform the test. For example, if you are dealing with a Web site, this affects your data entry and the actions that are required to perform the test. Again, you want to optimize the data so that one test is sufficient (more on this later in this chapter).

The THEN is the result or outcome of the GIVEN and the WHEN and can have its own set of data values.

Minimizing Scenarios and Examples

Have you ever experienced the frustration of not knowing how many tests are enough to verify a User Story or Feature? In our experience, having a thundering herd of Scenarios can be just as detrimental to the success of your newest Release as having not enough.

In our instructor-led classes, we have been asked many times "How can we select the best values for Scenarios or Examples. We would like to illustrate our answer using a User Story from one of our case studies.

> To increase the number of applications,
> Insurance Underwriters can apply a safe driver discount

This User Story might need several Scenarios for Acceptance Testing. To demonstrate Test Data Engineering, we chose the following Scenario, which is on a functional detail level.

Scenario: Calculate Premium Discount for Safe Drivers
GIVEN a premium of $1,500
   AND a discount percentage of 5%
   AND policyholder qualifies for discount
WHEN policyholder requests a discount
THEN discount amount = $75
   AND new premium = $1,425

Every time this test runs, it returns with $75 discount and $1,425 total new premium unless the application has an error. However, these numbers are seemingly random. Why $1500, why not 2 million dollars or one dollar? Why is the discount percentage 5%? How many different Examples would we need to cover all potentially correct results?

If you want to test the application thoroughly and make sure that later in Regression Testing a new change has not broken things that used to work, you should use various Examples with different Test Data for this Scenario.

However, we cannot test all possible input values, because the number of Scenarios or Examples would be huge. How can we reduce an infinite number of Examples to a finite number, while ensuring that the selected Examples are still effective in covering all possible data values? This is where the concept of Test Data Engineering comes in.

Test Data Engineering encompasses three specific concepts.

- ☑ **Equivalence Class Partitioning**
- ☑ **Boundary Value Analysis**
- ☑ **Probable Error Identification**

These are three data value identification techniques that will minimize the number of your Scenarios and Examples you need to thoroughly test an application.

Equivalence Class Partitioning

This technique divides data inputs into groups that you expect to have a similar behavior, meaning if one member of the group works, they all work. To reduce the total number of Scenarios, you select one input from each group and create a Scenario or Example for it.

For instance, if you are testing the validity of a field that displays a numeric month, how many Scenarios would be enough? Do you need 12 Scenarios to test the 12 months? Do you need another thundering herd of Scenarios to test for invalid months? Fortunately, no! All you need is **four** Scenarios or Examples to have Equivalence Class coverage. So, how does this work?

Equivalence class
(Don't test the same old, same old over and over)

Any set of data that will produce a similar result
Valid months (1 - 12)
Invalid months (< 1, > 12, not numeric)

First, you divide outcomes into valid and invalid results. In our numeric month example, you have a valid outcome which is a range from 1-12, and an invalid outcome which is a month that is smaller than 1, larger than 12, or not numeric. This gives us four Equivalence Classes. Next, select one representative from each Equivalence Class and create four Scenarios. For instance:

Valid result	**5**
	(a number between 1 and 12)
Invalid Result	**-1**
	(a number smaller than 1)
Invalid Result	**43**
	(a number larger than 12)
Invalid Result	**Not numeric**
	(alpha-numeric)

However, you could get even better test coverage by optimizing those month values. You can refine your Examples by applying Boundary Value Analysis.

Boundary Value Analysis

Equivalence Classes and **Boundary Values** are linked and can be used together or individually. Boundary Values are the edges of an identified Equivalence Class, meaning the first and last items in the set. The theory is that most defects are around the edges of a class.

Each boundary of an Equivalence Class has a **valid** boundary value and an **invalid** boundary value. For example, if you are confirming a numeric month input, the numbers 1 and 12 are Boundary Values for **valid** outcomes. 0 and 13 are Boundary Values for **invalid** outcomes.

> *Boundary values*
> *(Edges are much more dangerous than flat surfaces)*
>
> On, above, or below the edges of equivalence classes
> Valid months (1, 12)
> Invalid months (0, 13, XX)

In the table below, you can see how Boundary Value Analysis changed the data input values that we established using the Equivalence Class Partitioning technique.

Valid result	~~5~~ **1**
	(between 1 and 12 bottom boundary)
Valid result	**12**
(added using Boundary Analysis)	*(between 1 and 12 top boundary)*
Invalid Result	~~-1~~ **0**
	(smaller than 1 bottom boundary)
Invalid Result	~~43~~ **13**
	(larger than 12 top boundary)
Invalid Result	**Not numeric**
	(alpha-numeric, no change)

However, there is no fixed rule to take only one input from each Equivalence Class. Based on your needs and previous experience you should decide the inputs.

Equivalence Class Partitioning and Boundary Value Analysis are great tools for creating Gherkin Example Tables or individual Scenarios that need data values, but they are not fool proof. Always trust your own intuition and experience. Add more Scenarios with different test data as needed.

Probable Error Identification

Finally, **Probable Error** is based on the idea that you will test for things that have gone wrong in the past. The expectation is that because they went wrong in the past, there is a higher likelihood that they will fail again whenever the app is modified. Although this sounds counterintuitive, this behavior has a nasty habit of always proving itself.

For instance, instead of using a number in the month field, you leave it blank. Another idea is, as opposed to leaving it blank, you add a number and then delete it which turns out to be possibly a null as opposed to a blank. Applications can react differently to a null versus a blank.

The numbers 99 and 100 could be Probable Errors, even though you are trying for 1 to 12. In this scenario, February is always a very weird month because of the 28 or 29 days. That might be a Probable Error to consider for a Scenario. Another Probable Error might be entering a single digit in the month field or adding a space in front or behind it. Each of them could be a Scenario or Example.

Probable error	Situations more likely to find a bug based on experience (yours or someone else's)
(If it's happened before, it'll happen again. Unfortunately!)	(Blank, null, 99, 00, _1, 1_)

By identifying "probable" errors, you can identify additional Scenarios that will find most of the errors in testing the input to a numeric month. Equivalence Classes, Boundary Values, and Probable Error are easy techniques to minimize the number of Scenarios and Examples while maximizing the probability of detecting errors. Test Data Engineering is particularly effective when there is a large pool of input combinations.

Test Data Engineering Is Lean

In our example, we identified about eight different Scenarios or Examples. These eight will find most errors in testing a numeric month. Considering that you are testing a tiny little field "numeric month", eight Scenarios/Examples seems a lot. However, imagine the number of Scenarios/Examples you would end up with if we had not applied Boundary Values, Equivalence Classes, and Probable Error testing.

Test Data Engineering reduces the number of Scenarios/Examples that you need down to the minimum. In addition, engineered test data is more likely to succeed in finding errors in the software AND it is reusable because it always returns the same results.

Exercise: Engineering Test Data

Here is another opportunity to try out what you read. Keep in mind that there is no right or wrong answer. This exercise tests your ability to apply Equivalence Classes, Boundary Values, and Probable Error to engineer your Test Data.

Instructions:

Read the description for the Loan Request process. Then answer the questions.

Process Loan Request

If the customer's current debt load plus the credit request is greater than 4 times their gross income, then deny the request unless their credit is excellent, and they have been on the same job for over 5 years. If this is the case, approve the request but require a co-signer.

If the total new debt is less than 4 times their gross income, and their credit is excellent or good, approve the request.

If they only have good credit and have been in their current job less than 5 years, approve with a co-signer. Otherwise, reject the order.

Intentionally left blank

Question 1:

What are the **Equivalence Classes** in "Process Loan Request"?

Question 2:

What **Boundary Values** can you find in "Process Loan Request"?

Question 3:

What **Probable Errors** can you find in "Process Loan Request"?

Answer Question 1: What are the Equivalence Classes in "Process Loan Request"?

- ☑ People whose current debt plus the request exceeds 4 times their gross income
- ☑ People whose current debt plus the request is less than 4 times gross income
- ☑ People who have been on the job for more than 5 years
- ☑ People who have been on the job for less than 5 years
- ☑ People with excellent credit
- ☑ People with good credit

NOTE: What about people whose current debt plus the request is exactly 4 times their gross income or people who have been on the job for exactly 5 years? These are questions that the business community needs to clarify before you can assign them to an Equivalence Class.

Answer Question 2: What Boundary Values can you find in "Process Loan Request"?

- ☑ New debt = 4 times gross income
  New debt = (4 times gross income + $1)
  New debt = (4 times gross income - $1)

- ☑ Job history = 5 years
  Job history = 5 years + 1 day
  Job history = 5 years - 1 day

NOTE: These boundaries assume that the gross income to new debt ratio is calculated to the nearest dollar and the length of time on the same job is determined to the day. You need to confirm these assumptions with the business community before continuing.

Answer Question 3: What Probable Errors can you find in "Process Loan Request"?

- ☑ People whose current debt plus new request is $1 less or more than their current income
- ☑ People with excellent credit requesting a loan that exceeds 4 times gross income who are making the request on the 5th anniversary of their employment
- ☑ People who have marginal credit
- ☑ People who do not have a credit record

Lean Analysis to Find Gherkin Scenarios

Where do you start identifying Scenarios? As we discussed in earlier chapters, you should have created User Stories, a Feature list or requirement lists, or at least have access to them. For example, in a Scrum (Agile) initiative there are User Stories for which Scenarios are needed in either the Release or Sprint Backlog. In other approaches, the User Stories are located on the Kanban board or in a Feature list.

Finding the right Scenarios for acceptance tests is one of the challenges to be overcome. In this section, we show you different techniques for finding Scenarios based on a variety of sources, including User Stories, Features, Decision Tables, Problem Statements, Use Cases, and other artifacts.

We will also show you how to create Scenarios using Functional Features and NFRs from the results of Story Decomp (Feature Drill-down), a technique you learned in an earlier chapter. In our experience, this technique is an ideal tool for identifying Scenarios that are already planned for a Sprint and that developers need to understand better.

From User Stories to Scenarios

We will start with the most common method which is creating Scenarios based on a User Story. Good User Stories answer (in some format) three fundamental questions:

- ☑ WHO needs something?
- ☑ WHAT do they need?
- ☑ WHY do they need it?

For example, the User Story:

> **As a Visitor, I can view all available flights that fit my scheduling Constraints to select the best fit.**

In this User Story, the "WHO" is clearly stated (a Visitor). "WHAT" they need is the ability to view flights in some manner. The final phrase "select the best fit" answers the "WHY" question (business value) and gives you the final criteria for an end-user Acceptance Test. The challenge now is how to extract Scenarios from this User Story without knowing how the developers are going to code it.

Here is a simple, step-by-step approach for discovering Scenarios based on a User Story that has worked well for us in the past.

Step 1: Use the "WHY" in the User Story

Start at the end - the business value (the "WHY" statement). Brainstorm for 5 minutes and list all possible needs of the website visitor that would confirm that the product delivers the promised business value.

As a visitor, I can view all available flights that fit my scheduling Constraints **to select the best fit**.

For example, the "WHY" statement in this User Story is "select the best fit". This implies finding a flight that gets the visitor from the point of origin to the desired destination with some caveat. Based on flying experience, we would consider the following Scenarios:

For a Visitor, the best fit can be:
1. the lowest cost flight available as soon as possible
2. the lowest cost flight within the next 3 months
3. the flight with the fewest stops
4. the flight that leaves close to a specified time
5. the earliest possible flight for a given departure date
6. the last possible flight for a given arrival date
7. ...

Evaluate each item on the list with the team to determine if it should become a Scenario. Stay Lean! Do not just create a Scenario because you can. Always ask yourself if you create this Scenario:

- Does it add value?
- Does it matter if this Scenario fails or succeeds?
- How much does it matter?

For instance, if this situation only happens once every 10 years, it might not be worth a Scenario.

Once you have made that decision, write a Scenario for each selected item. For example, if you decided that #3 is a suitable candidate, you could create the Scenario:

Scenario: Fred views a flight with the fewest stops
GIVEN Fred is on the booking page of the website
WHEN Fred requests to view flights with the fewest stops
THEN Fred views flights sorted by number of stops

Step 2: Use the "WHAT" in the User Story

Next, look at the business process (the "WHAT" statement). Brainstorm for 5 minutes and list all different situations that you can think of that would confirm that the product does what it should do.

As a visitor, I can **view** all available **flights** that fit my scheduling Constraints to select the best fit.

For example, "view flights" implies that the visitor may need a variety of ways of seeing the offers. Again, based on my experience, I would contemplate the one where I can

As a Visitor, I can:

1. Get an email with a list of suitable flights
2. See a list of flights sorted by time
3. See a list of flights sorted by price (low to high or vice versa).
4. View the list on my **PC**
5. View the list on my mobile device
6. ...

Again, stay Lean! The team should decide which items should become Scenarios and then write a Scenario for each selected item. Here is another example. #1 seems to be a reasonable candidate, so the team could create the Scenario:

Scenario: Fred requests an email with a list of suitable flights
GIVEN Fred is on the booking page of the website
WHEN Fred selects the email option
THEN Fred receives an email with a list of suitable flights

Step 3: Use the Qualifiers in the User Story

Finally, analyze all qualifiers for the "WHAT" and the "WHY". Add more situations you can think of in 3 – 5 minutes that confirm that the Story meets the qualified business outcome.

> As a visitor, I can view **all available** flights that fit my scheduling **Constraints** to select the best fit.

The first qualifier in our User Story is "all available".

"all available" flights should include the one where:
1. No flights are available from my selected departure airport
2. There are two or 3 flights from the same airport
3. There are flights from multiple departure airports
4. Flights to multiple destination airports
5. Flights that have seats available
6. Flights that offer standby seating
7. ...

NOTE: Here, I need a discussion with my Subject Matter Experts to clarify the qualifier "all available". Should it include charter flights, private jet service, military flights, etc. The answers to that could significantly increase the number of Scenarios.

The second qualifier in our User Story is "fit my scheduling Constraints".

> As a Visitor, I can view all available flights that **fit my scheduling Constraints** to select the best fit.

"fit my scheduling Constraints" should include:

1. Flights that allow arrival at the destination within a predetermined time (i.e., to attend a meeting at 10 am in New York City would include leeway for transportation from the airport to the meeting location)
2. For religious reasons I cannot fly on certain holidays
3. ...

Business Rules Identify Scenarios

We have already mentioned Business Rules several times. To extrapolate Scenarios from Business Rules, we have to delve deeper into them.

In their simplest definition, Business Rules are guidelines that define (or restrict) business activities. Business rules are an integral part of requirements analysis. They describe the processes, definitions and Constraints that apply to an organization. They can relate to people, processes, business behavior and computer systems and are set up to help the organization achieve its goals.

What is the difference between a business rule, a Business Requirement, and a Scenario?

- ⇨ **Business Rules** give you the criteria and conditions for a decision.

- ⇨ A **Business Requirement** enables the implementation and compliance with a Business Rule.

- ⇨ **Scenarios** are used to validate whether the Business Rule or Business Requirement is implemented correctly.

Business rules are a form of requirements that must be implemented regardless of the technology and that the business community can easily change at any time.

For example, if the marketing department wants to offer a 10% seasonal discount to students living in Florida, they want to do so without the involvement of a programmer. Marketing needs to be able to make these changes spontaneously to adapt to current market changes and remain competitive. Business Rules give them this ability. Unfortunately, Business Rules can be quite complex and therefore difficult to decipher. Here is an example of a poorly designed business rule:

Business Rule:
Process Loan Request

If the customer's current debt load plus the credit application is more than four times his gross income, reject the application unless the credit is excellent, and the customer has more than 5 years of work experience. If this is the case, approve the application but request a co-signer. If the total new debt is less than four times their gross income and their credit is excellent or good, approve the application. If they have only good credit and have been in their current profession for less than 5 years, approve the application with a co-signer. Otherwise, reject the application.

This Business Rule can easily lead to multiple Scenarios. You could define Scenarios that cover all outcomes to ensure that the new software takes these conditions properly into account. However, it is extremely difficult to extrapolate the different possible outcomes from this text.

Decision Tables allow you to express complex Business Rules that require combinations of conditions to ensure that you test for relevant ones. Explaining how Decision Tables are created is beyond the scope of this book. However, there are many courses available online where you can learn how to create a Decision Table. Next, we show you how to use the Decision Table to identify Scenarios.

On the next page is a Decision Table that illustrates the business rule from the last page. Remember that "new debt" is the existing debt amount **plus** the requested credit amount.

Conditions							
New Debt > 4X Gross Income	Y	Y	Y	N	N	N	N
Job Experience > 5 years	Y		N	Y	Y	N	N
Credit Excellent	Y	N		Y	N	Y	N
Credit Good					Y		
Outcomes							
Approve Loan	✓			✓	✓	✓	
Request Co-Signer	✓				✓		
Deny Loan		✓	✓				✓

The Decision Table lists all relevant conditions in the upper 4 rows and all outcomes in the lower 3 rows. The check marks show which combination of conditions leads to the individual outcomes.

Once you have created a Decision Table, it is easy to identify critical Scenarios or Scenario outlines.

Each column in a Decision Table is at least ONE Scenario!

In the first column of the Decision Table for the approval of loan applications we find the answer "Y" 3 times. These are the conditions (GIVEN) of a new Scenario. The applicant:

- ☑ has a new debt that is more than four times the gross income
- ☑ has been working in this job for more than five years
- ☑ has an excellent credit score

The lower half of the Decision Table (in the same column) shows you the outcomes (THEN) of your new Scenario. In this case, the request:

- ☑ is approved and
- ☑ requires a co-signer

Agile Business Analysis: Getting and Writing Lean Requirements

Now look at column 2, we see the conditions - a "Y" and a "N". This leads to a GIVEN in which the requester's:

- ☑ new debt that is more than 4 times the gross income, and
- ☑ the credit score is NOT excellent

Conditions							
New Debt > 4X Gross Income	Y	Y	Y	N	N	N	N
Job Experience > 5 years	Y		N	Y	Y	N	N
Credit Excellent	Y	N		Y	N	Y	N
Credit Good					Y		
Outcomes							
Approve Loan	✓			✓	✓	✓	
Request Co-Signer	✓				✓		
Deny Loan		✓	✓				✓

In this case, we do not care if the requester has been on the job for more than five years. If the credit is not excellent and the debt is more than 4 times gross income, we will:

- ☑ deny the request.

This Decision Table shows seven combinations of conditions (columns), each of which leads to one or more actions or outcomes.

To illustrate this point, following are the Scenarios for the Decision Table using the "Background" format that you learned earlier.

Conditions

New Debt > 4X Gross Income	Y	Y	Y	N	N	N	N
Job Experience > 5 years	Y		N	Y	Y	N	N
Credit Excellent	Y	N		Y	N	Y	N
Credit Good					Y		
Outcomes							
Approve Loan	✓			✓	✓	✓	
Request Co-Signer	✓				✓		
Deny Loan		✓	✓				✓

BACKGROUND

GIVEN new debt is greater than 4 times the gross income

SCENARIO: Customer applies for loan (Column 1)

GIVEN applicant has been on the job for more than 5 years
   AND credit is excellent
WHEN customer submits loan request
THEN approve loan
   AND request Cosigner

SCENARIO: Customer applies for loan (Column 2)

GIVEN credit is NOT excellent
WHEN customer submits loan request
THEN deny loan

SCENARIO: Customer applies for loan (Column 3)

GIVEN applicant job experience is not more than 5 years
WHEN customer submits loan request
THEN deny loan

BACKGROUND
   GIVEN new debt is not more than 4 times the gross income
       AND applicant has been on the job for more than 5 years

   SCENARIO: Customer applies for loan (Column 4)
   GIVEN credit is excellent
   WHEN customer submits loan request
   THEN approve loan

   SCENARIO: Customer applies for loan (Column 5)
   GIVEN credit is good
   WHEN customer submits loan request
   THEN approve loan
       AND request Co-signer

BACKGROUND
   GIVEN new debt is not more than 4 times the gross income
       AND applicant job experience is not more than 5 years

   SCENARIO: Customer applies for loan (Column 6)
   GIVEN credit is excellent
   WHEN customer submits loan request
   THEN approve loan

   SCENARIO: Customer applies for loan (Column 7)
   GIVEN credit is not excellent
   WHEN customer submits loan request
   THEN deny loan

You could extend the test coverage with the help of Boundary Value Analysis and Scenario Outlines if this would make sense for your User Story or Function.

The beauty of this approach is that very often the people who define Business Rules or the developers themselves create a Decision Table to ensure that their specifications are complete. You may not even have to be the one to create the table. If you have access to a Decision Table, it is a phenomenal tool for finding Scenarios.

Problems and Symptoms Are Great Test Scenarios

We introduced Problem Analysis as a tool for finding User Stories in the chapter on discovering User Stories or Features. During Problem Analysis, we separated the "real problems" from the symptoms which resulted in a "Problems and Associated Symptoms" list.

If you chose this approach, you could now use the results to create Scenarios. The primary test of any implemented User Story or Function is that the problems and associated symptoms disappear when the application is working correctly.

To prove that a specific symptom has disappeared, use this three-step process to set up a GIVEN-WHEN-THEN Scenario or Scenario Outline. For each symptom or problem on your list, answer the following questions.

1. Find the GIVEN
To create your setup data, ask:

- What caused the problem?

- What business situation do you need for the symptom to become visible?

Use the answers to create the set-up data (GIVEN) for your Scenario.

2. Find the WHEN
To formulate your WHEN question, ask:

- What actions do I need to take to trigger this problem?

- What events take place if this problem occurs?

The answers to these questions will be your WHEN.

3. Find the THEN

To formulate your THEN, ask:

- What is the right outcome of the actions?
- How would I know that the problem is solved?

The answers to these questions will be yours THEN.

Problems faced by the business community usually have the highest pain point. If you test the Scenarios based on the results of the Problem Analysis, you will have proof that the pain point has disappeared. You will be the hero.

The Technique Applied

We will use an example of a case study from one of our seminars. The symptom is:

> **Safe driver discounts are incorrectly calculated when combined with homeowners' discounts.**

During our analysis, the SME gave us the business rule that policyholders will get the highest discount for which they qualify, meaning multiple discounts do not apply.

One of the Scenarios we could create is:

Scenario: Calculate automobile insurance premium for a customer who is entitled to a homeowner discount and a discount for safe driving.

What is the setup state (GIVEN) here?

To apply a safe driver discount, we need a premium amount to which we can apply it. This leads us to the following GIVEN statement:

GIVEN A policy with an annual premium of $1,500

Since the customer is entitled to a discount as a homeowner and receives a discount as a safe driver, the Function (as we know from our Business Rules) should apply the larger of the two discounts available for this policy. This leads us to the following WHEN statement:

WHEN the policyholder is entitled to a 7% safe driver discount
AND the policyholder is entitled to a 5% homeowner discount

To get to THEN, we do some calculations. If the premium is $1500 and the safe-driver discount is 7% (the larger of the two discounts), the total discount amount is $105, so THEN reads:

THEN the discount for safe drivers is $105

This is an example of how to move quickly and with minimal effort from Problem Analysis through Symptom Reduction to the GWT Scenario. This technique gives you better Test Scenarios because you can prove that this Scenario solves a business problem.

Creating a Scenario Outline

To take this one step further, you might need more than one Scenario to test different data values. We already explained how to get from a Scenario to an Outline with associated Examples. However, just as a refresher, we will turn this Scenario into an Outline. You can also create an Outline right away and save yourself some time.

Just replace all values in your Scenario with variables, like:

Scenario Outline: Calculate automobile insurance premium for a customer who is entitled to a homeowner discount and a discount for safe driving.
GIVEN A policy with a <premium> per year
WHEN Policyholder qualifies for <safe driver discount>
AND Policyholder qualifies for <homeowners discount>
THEN Total safe driver discount is <discount amount>

Then create an Example table with engineered test data (Equivalence Partitioning, Boundary Value Analysis, and Probable Error) as we discussed in the section on Test Data Engineering.

From Use Cases to Scenarios

A Use Case is another phenomenal tool for getting to Scenarios. It is a simple transition. However, just like with Decision Tables in one of the earlier chapters, "how to create a Use Case" is too complex to explain in this book. We offer a Use Case course on Udemy.com and a book is also in the making.

However, we will give you a brief overview of what Use Cases are. Maybe they will pique your interest to learn more about this fantastic tool. Skip "What is a Use Case" if you are already familiar with the concept.

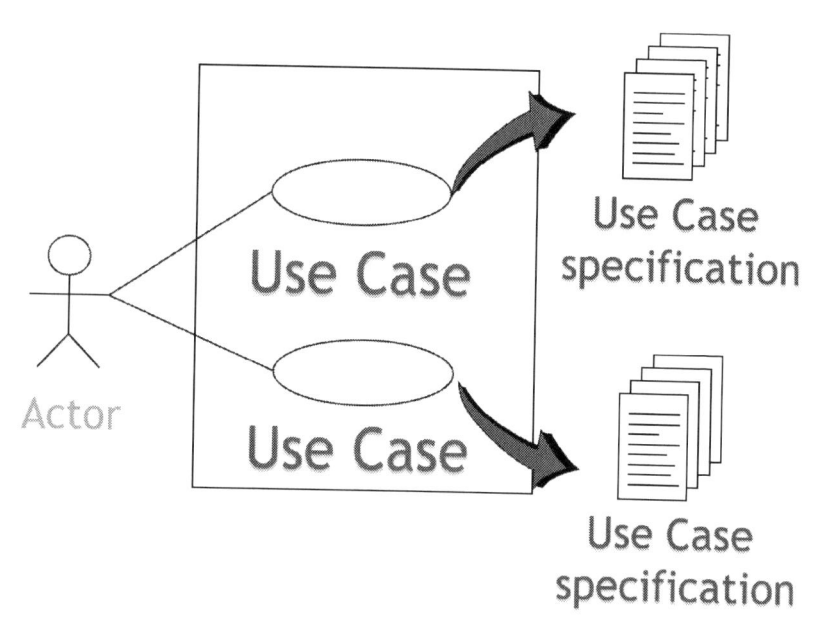

What is a Use Case?

Fundamentally, Use Cases represent the Functional requirements of a product. A Use Case describes interactions between a user and software. The parts of a Use Case are:

- ☑ A **Name** which identifies the Use Case and describes the purpose

- ☑ A **Description** (optional) about the business value that this Use Case delivers.

- ☑ **Business Rules** (optional) defining Constraints or Non-Functional Requirements that apply to this Use Case.

- ☑ A **Trigger** which causes the Use Case to become active.

- ☑ A list of the **Actors** (people or other applications) that are involved in the Use Case.

- ☑ **Precondition(s)** that must be met before the Use Case can be executed.

- ☑ A **Standard path** showing the sequence of events that happen under most circumstances.

- ☑ **Alternate paths** (optional) that will always create the same post-condition as the standard path.

- ☑ **Exception paths** (optional) leading to a different post-condition than standard and alternate paths. The purpose of exception paths in a Use Case is to deal with errors and unsuccessful outcomes.

- ☑ **Post-condition(s)** which are the desired outcomes of the Use Case.

There are a few more items but they are irrelevant for creating Scenarios from Use Cases. Just as a word of caution, Use Cases also can have scenarios and it is easy to mix up the definitions of Test Scenarios and Use Case Scenarios. A Use Case Scenario is a single path through a Use Case and can be converted easily into a GWT Scenario.

Here is an example of a Use Case using a Samsung smart phone:

NAME: Check missed calls

TRIGGER: User turns on phone to check missed calls

PRE-CONDITION: The phone is powered off

STANDARD PATH
S05 User presses power button
S10 Phone displays the home menu
S15 User requests call history
S20 Phone displays all calls
S25 User clicks on last missed call
S30 Phone displays the caller's contact info

POST-CONDITION: User can return a missed call by pressing the "call" button.

ALTERNATE PATH
A01: @S05, the phone does not turn on
    A01.05 User locates an electrical outlet
    A01.10 User plugs the phone into the outlet
    A01.15 Phone displays the "Charging" symbol
    A01.20 **RESUME** @S05

EXCEPTION PATH
E01: @S30, phone displays "UNKNOWN CALLER"
    POST-CONDITION: User cannot return the call

From Use Cases to Scenarios

When you analyze a Use Case for Test Scenario development, you can create a positive Scenario for each Standard, Alternate, and Exception Path to prove that they work. The purpose of a positive Scenario is to prove that Standard and Alternate Paths deliver the same Post-conditions and that each Exception Path delivers its Post-conditions.

You can also create negative Scenarios. A negative Scenario ensures that your Feature or application gracefully handles incorrect Pre-conditions, invalid data input or unexpected user behavior. Use your creativity to imagine what an end-user could do wrong.

For example, if you are testing the calculator function of a smart phone, it should not be possible to enter alpha-numeric characters (e.g. letters). The purpose of negative Scenarios is to ensure that the software has sufficient error handling.

Sample Scenario from a Use Case

The Use Case "Customer cancels policy" comes from a case study that we have used many times in our training classes. It is a simple Use Case (they can be much more complex!) that shows what happens when a policyholder cancels the insurance coverage for his automobile.

In a Lean and Agile environment, the timing and purpose of Use Cases has changed. We no longer create a vast number of Use Case Diagrams or Use Case Narratives to demonstrate the full functionality of the entire product or application in its final form.

We only create the Use Cases that help us in Release and Sprint Planning to define either Functional Specifications or Scenarios for Acceptance Testing. Some Agile Teams handle large Epics with Use Cases during Backlog Refinement.

The following Use Case example is taken from an automobile insurance company and shows the workflow when an insured person cancels the insurance coverage for his vehicle.

NAME: Customer cancels policy

PRE-CONDITIONS: Customer has an account

MAIN PATH
1. Customer logs in
2. System displays menu
3. Customer selects "View Active Policies"
4. System displays active policies
5. Customer selects policy and chooses "Cancel" action
6. System requests confirmation
7. Customer confirms
8. System cancels policy and notifies Underwriting
9. System displays menu
10. Customer logs off

POST-CONDITIONS:
1. Policy is "Pending cancellation" status
2. Policy is assigned to Underwriting

ALTERNATE PATHS:
A01 @4 Customer has no active policies
    A01.01   System displays "No active policies available"
    A01.10   Resume @ 2

As you can see, just like in our first example, this Use Case is a dialog between an actor, in this case the Customer, and the system or Feature that we are testing. The Use Case has a Standard Path that applies to most Customers, and we have added one Alternate Path that happens when the Customer does not have an account.

This simple Use Case leads us to several Scenarios. Starting with positive tests, we create at least one Scenario for the Standard Path and one for the Alternate Path.

In our example, two Scenarios would probably be sufficient since we are not dealing with data input. However, if we were dealing with data values that the user could enter, we could create a Scenario Outline and apply Data Engineering techniques (see the earlier chapter) to create an Example Table testing different input data.

But back to the positive tests of our simple Use Case. Looking at the standard path, one Scenario would be:

> **Customer in good standing with active policy cancels coverage**

Since we have only one Alternate Path and no Exception Paths in this Use Case, our positive tests would identify just one more Scenario.

> **Customer has no active policies and cancels coverage**

In this case, we would expect the Alternate path to kick in and inform the user that there are no active policies.

Our next step is creating negative tests for the Use Case. We start with a negative Scenario that uses an invalid precondition.

> **Customer does not have an account**

Since we do not have data input in this Use Case, this would be the bare minimum of Scenarios. You might need more Scenarios if you want to test what happens if a customer still owes money, or if a customer wants to quit in the middle of the cancellation process, and so on.

For example, you could add the Scenarios:

1. **Customer has policy with overdue amount**
2. **Customer chooses not to cancel policy**
3. **Customer does not confirm cancellation**

In a fully developed Use Case, these situations would be covered in more Alternate and Exception Paths. However, in a Lean world, these paths might not have been important enough to be documented in which case adding new Scenarios to cover the situation is probably a good idea. Only create additional paths if they are part of this iteration/Release.

If you are creating Scenarios from Use Cases, always be creative and think about what the user could do or what could go wrong **in each step of each path**.

Exercise: Discovering Scenarios from Use Cases

Here is your opportunity to try out what you read. As always, keep in mind that there is no right or wrong answer. The exercises will just allow you to try out the presented concepts and techniques.

Instructions:

Before starting the assignment, read the Use Case below.

Use Case Name: Withdraw Funds from ATM
Pre-Condition: ATM is operational
Trigger: Cardholder inserts bank card into ATM
Main Path:
    10 ATM displays authorized operations
    15 Card Holder selects "Withdraw Funds"
    20 ATM offers common withdrawal amount and account
    25 Card Holder accepts offer
    30 ATM requests authorization from Card Holder's bank
    35 Card Holder's bank authorizes withdrawal
    40 ATM releases Card Holder's card
    45 Card Holder removes card
    47 ATM notifies Card Holder's bank of dispensed funds
    50 ATM dispenses money
    55 Card Holder removes money
    60 ATM prints requested receipt
    65 Card Holder removes receipt
    70 ATM returns to ready state

Assignment 1:

What Scenario(s) can you identify for step 47 in the main path, "ATM notifies Card Holder's bank of dispensed funds"?

Answer Assignment 1: What Scenario(s) can you identify for step 47 in the main path (ATM notifies Card Holder's bank of dispensed funds)?

A couple of potential Scenarios to validate whether **step 47** will be executed or not:

SCENARIO: Cardholder withdraws money at the ATM of their own bank
GIVEN Cardholder's bank owns the ATM
WHEN Cardholder's bank releases funds
THEN ATM dispenses money

SCENARIO: Cardholder withdraws money from another bank's ATM
GIVEN Cardholder's bank does NOT own the ATM
WHEN Cardholder's bank releases funds
THEN ATM dispenses money
   AND ATM notifies Cardholder's Bank of Dispensed Funds

Find Scenarios Using Acquire, Abolish, Affirm, Avoid

It is always a promising idea to have many different techniques for coming up with Scenarios in your toolkit. In an Acceptance Test Driven Environment (ATDD), it becomes a critical success factor.

The next technique that allows you to find more Scenarios has to do with the reality of change. (On a side note, this is also a great technique for discovering User Stories and Features.)

There are capabilities, behaviors, functionality, and data, in the current system that a **user has**; there are also capabilities, behaviors, functionality, and data that the **user does not have** in the current system.

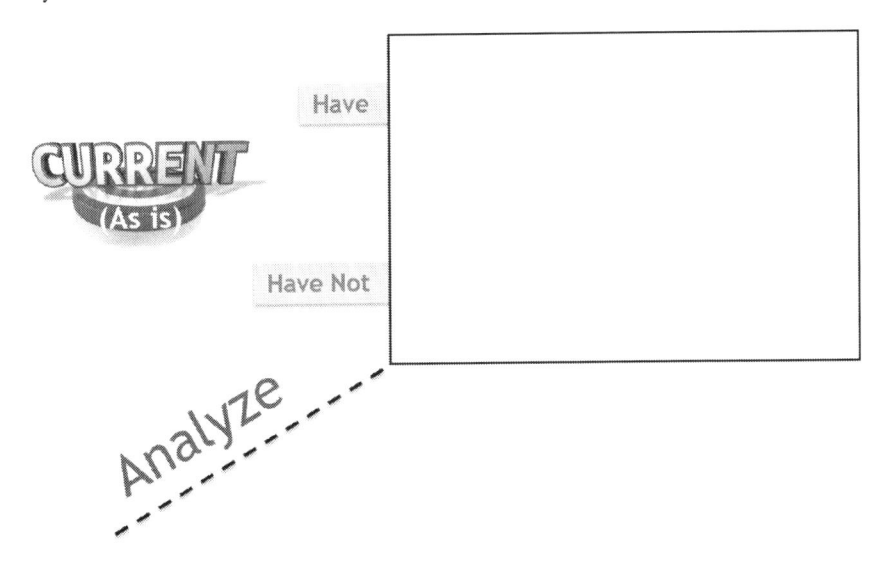

The whole concept of analyzing the current "as is" is about looking at what you have and do not have, what you know and do not know. Analysis can do nothing more than deliver knowledge about the current system (manual or automated) or your current situation.

To get to the future (i.e. reach a target state) you need User Stories, Features, or other requirement types to define what the future will look like. Requirements define what the business community needs or wants or does not need or want. The major difference between need and want is a question of priority.

To summarize, the users currently have capabilities that exist (Have) or are missing (Have Not), and capabilities that they Want (Need) or Don't Want (Don't Need) in the future.

This gives us four distinct domains or perspectives to discover Scenarios as well as User Stories, Features, and other requirement types. The domains are named:

- **Acquire / Acquire** (Do Not Have, but Want)
- **Abolish / Abolish** (Have, but No Longer Want)
- **Confirm / Affirm** (Have and Want to Keep)
- **Avoid / Avoid** (Neither Have nor Want)

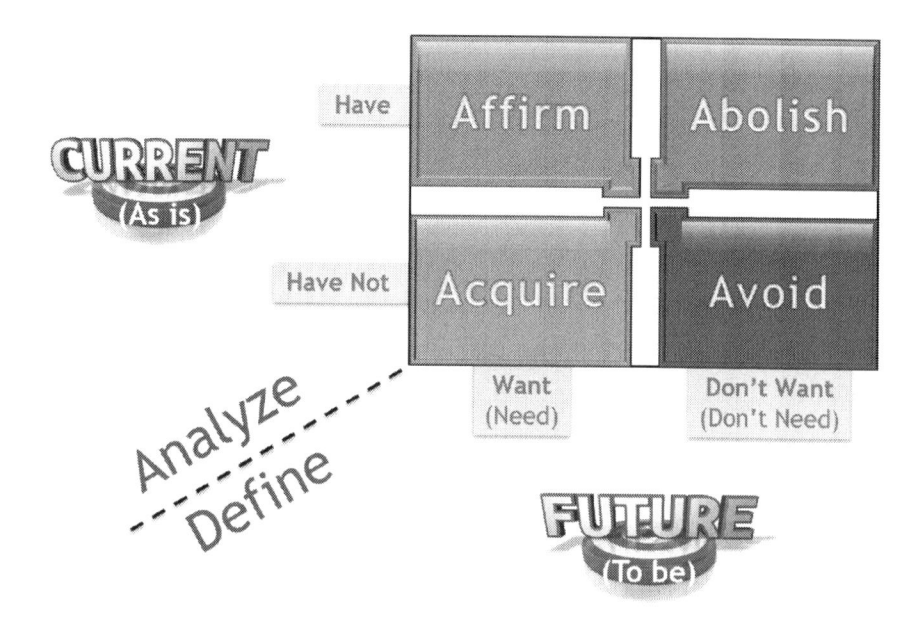

Acquire Capabilities

If used as a technique during Discovery, the "Acquire" domain allows you to define User Stories, Features, and other requirements that the business does not currently have but needs in the future.

For finding Scenarios, this is gold. For everything that you can think of that the customer wants to "acquire", you need to set up Scenarios or Scenario Outlines with Examples (test data) to prove that the application delivers what the business wants to have or know in the future. Most Scenarios in this category should be covered by User Stories that you already identified during Discovery.

Abolish Capabilities

The "Abolish" domain is about functionality or data that the business currently has and no longer wants. Maybe they do not want to have it in the future because it causes problems, or the business just wants to save some money.

This is also a great perspective to discover User Stories or Scenarios. Define how to eliminate the things the business no longer wants. Do they need to replace what they currently have with something else? You need Scenarios that test what happens if the abolished data or functionality is no longer available.

User Stories and Scenarios from the two domains "Acquire" and "Abolish" are common and most end-users have no problem letting you know what they want and do not want. However, the other two domains are slightly more challenging.

Affirm Capabilities

For, the "Affirm" domain, ask if there is something that the customer currently does a certain way and wants to keep doing the same way in the future; it could also be certain data they currently have and need in the future.

The risk here is that the end-user assumes that they will always have this functionality, behavior, or information because why on earth would you take it away? If there is no Scenario, User Story, or Feature defined to keep certain functionality or data, there is at least a risk that it might disappear.

Again, this is a great perspective for discovering Scenarios. This is an area that we often neglect in testing because why would we want to test something that was not changed. In reality, Regression Testing is all about making sure that what you currently have and want to keep stays the same and does not get eliminated.

Avoid Capabilities

The fourth domain is "Avoid". This domain is a little tricky because it deals with things that the business does not have currently **and** does not want in the future. Why on earth would you even talk about it if you do not have it and you do not want it?

Developers and designers are highly creative people. In developing and designing software, they often are inspired with a great new Feature or idea. Sometimes, the idea can have consequences that will force people to do things in an undesirable way.

The biggest problem with this domain is that it is infinite. You could write hours and hours of User Stories and Scenarios covering all the things that you do not want in this new product. The key here is to focus on things that have happened in the past either to the developers or the users. This is where you can create Scenarios to prove that your solution does not add or change functionality that the user wants to keep as is.

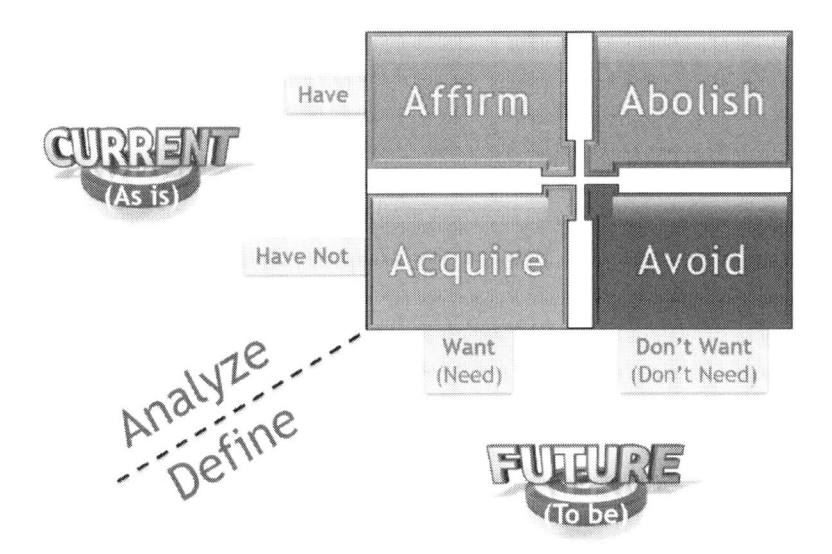

Agile Business Analysis: Getting and Writing Lean Requirements

	Have	Affirm	Abolish
CURRENT (As is)	Have Not	Acquire	Avoid
		Want (Need)	Don't Want (Don't Need)

Analyze --- Define

FUTURE (To be)

The four domains "**Acquire**", "**Abolish**", "**Confirm**" and "**Avoid**" can deliver a flood of Scenarios, User Stories, Features, and even Non-Functional Requirements. To stay Lean, do not waste time developing useless Scenarios. Weigh the effort of creating test Scenarios against the risk of failure and then decide how many Scenarios you need (and which ones are important).

Functional Features Reveal Scenarios

In an earlier chapter, you learned how to break User Stories and Features down to a lower level of detail with a technique called "Story Decomp / Feature Drill-down". Now, we will use the results of this technique to discover Scenarios. This is a powerful method for finding Test Scenarios once the team is working at a low level of detail, meaning just before coding.

As we mentioned in the chapter on Story Decomp / Feature Drill-down, many developers create functional items for User Stories that they will code in the next iteration. Check with your technical team whether they have Functional specifications (Functional Features) for you.

If you want to create your own functional requirements to identify Scenarios, make sure that the User Story warrants the effort. Decomposition can be time-consuming, so we only recommend using it when there is no simpler technique to get your Scenarios.

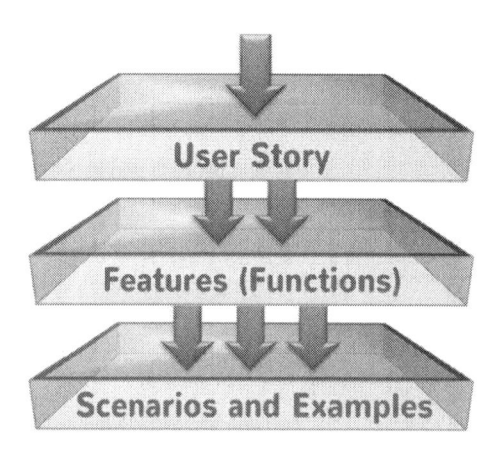

User Story

Features (Functions)

Scenarios and Examples

Our discussion about how to get from a list of Functions and data to Scenarios is based on the following User Story which has been decomposed.

Example for Decomposing User Stories

User Story: As golf tournament director, I can adjust a player's net stroke play scores using their individual USGA handicaps to determine their net placement in the tournament.

Features: Capture Strokes per Hole (inferred)
Capture Player's Handicap (inferred)
Adjust Hole Score for Handicap (blatantly stated)
Calculate Total Net Score (inferred)
Determine Ranking (blatantly stated)
Resolve First Place Ties (inferred)
...

Data: Player Name
Strokes per Hole
Player's Handicap
Hole Handicap
Total Score
Ranking (placement in tournament)
...

Note: You can use Data Elements to create Example Tables for Scenario Outlines

NFR: A player's handicap must be a valid USGA handicap
...

Once you identified all of the Functions needed by the User Story, you need to define Scenarios for testing each function. Do not reinvent the wheel here! Functions often are used for multiple User Stories, so you might avoid wasted effort by checking whether Scenarios to test any of these Functions already exist.

If you do need to develop new Scenarios, here are some examples for the Functions listed above:

Potential Scenarios

Function: Capture Strokes per Hole

⇨ Enter valid score per hole (Outline with Examples: numeric, >0, <=max number of strokes allowed)

⇨ Enter invalid score per hole (Outline with Examples: non-numeric, <1, > max number of strokes allowed)

⇨ ...

Function: Capture Player's Handicap

⇨ Enter valid handicap / default (Outline with Examples: numeric, >=lowest handicap allowed, <=max handicap allowed)

⇨ Enter invalid handicap (Outline with Examples: non-numeric, < lowest handicap allowed, > max handicap allowed)

⇨ ...

Function: Adjust Hole Score for Handicap

⇨ Calculate net score for Fred who scored 8 on "Hole Handicap Rank (HHR) 9" and has a "12" handicap

⇨ ...

Note: The calculation of the net score in golf can be extremely complicated if you follow the official USGA rules. Therefore, an exceptionally large number of Scenarios is possible. You have to use Test Data Engineering together with Scenario Outlines to get the fewest examples.

Function: Calculate Total Net Score

⇨ Calculate tournament net score for Lisa, who had a gross score of 79 and has a handicap of "11"

⇨ ...

Function: Determine Ranking

⇨ Lisa wins with a net score of 68,
Paul takes second place with a net score of 69,
Emilie third place with a net score of 72.

⇨ ...

Function: Resolve 1st Place Ties

⇨ Angela and Tom tie for 1st place and have a different gross score on handicap hole 1

⇨ Emilie and Andrea share 1st place and have the same net score on handicap hole 1

⇨ ...

Note: One of the most challenging Functions in our list is the "Resolve 1st Place Ties" function when multiple competitors tie for first place. Whereas a playoff is preferred, it is not always practical due to time and weather Constraints.

The most common alternative is to determine the winner by comparing hole-by-hole scores starting with the most challenging hole (Hole Handicap 1) and working down to the easiest (Hole Handicap 18). The competitor with the best score on the highest Handicap Hole Rating that is **not** tied wins.

As you can see, this seemingly simple function "Resolve 1st Place Ties" is surprisingly complicated. We would not have known that based on the User Story:

> "As golf tournament director, I can adjust a player's net stroke play scores using their individual **USGA** handicaps to determine their net placement in the tournament."

The complexity only became clear through User Story Decomp to the Functional Feature level. That is the power of this approach. This Function requires more Scenarios than you might think at first glance.

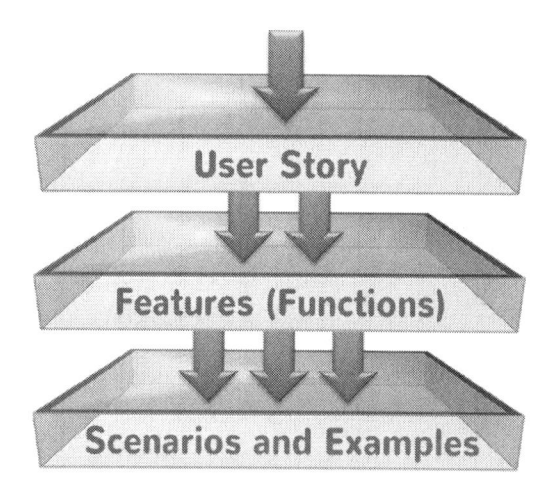

User Story
↓↓
Features (Functions)
↓↓↓
Scenarios and Examples

Scenarios for Non-functional or Quality Requirements

Testing Non-Functional Requirements can be extremely time- and resource-intensive. Advanced organizations have specialists whose primary job is performance testing, security testing, usability testing, etc.

As the one wearing the business analysis hat, you may or may not be involved in that process. We offer here guidance for those unlucky souls responsible for ensuring that the product meets all NFRs before it can be released into production.

As a refresher, NFRs express conditions such as how many, how often, how fast, how friendly, etc. Any of the four common types (Constraints, Performance, User Experience, or Volatility) should be tested.

If any of the NFRs are important to the success of the product or Feature, you need to define Acceptance Criteria (e.g. GWT Scenarios and Examples) that will instill the confidence that the Non-functional Requirement has been met. Most Scenarios test the functionality of the product, but non-functional testing is as important as functional testing. If you want to ensure customer satisfaction do not neglect writing Scenarios that test NFRs of the product as well.

Global NFRs impact multiple User Stories. They are often implemented early in an initiative. Therefore, check to see that the NFRs extracted from a User Story are not covered by an existing Regression Test before you define any Scenarios. Perhaps there is an existing automated or manual Acceptance Test to verify these NFRs.

You can create tests for NFRs in the form of Acceptance Criteria, Scenarios or simply as artifacts. NFRs should never be dependent on a single User Story because they often need to be tested at different points in time during the product lifecycle.

Writing Scenarios for NFRs

In the last section we found Scenarios based on the functional items of the User Story using the example of the evaluation of a golf tournament. This time we need the non-functional component. The User Story was:

> **As golf tournament director, I can adjust a player's net stroke play scores using their individual USGA handicaps to determine their net placement in the tournament.**

The Story Decomp (in Chapter III, "Non-Functional Requirements, Qualities & Constraints" revealed the following NFR:

> **A player's handicap must be a valid USGA handicap**

There are definitively two Scenarios needed for this NFR. One where the player has a valid USGA handicap and another where she or he does not.

For example, if the player has proof of her or his USGA handicap, the Scenario reads:

Scenario: Fred registers with a valid USGA handicap
GIVEN Fred has signed-up for the tournament
   AND Fred registers on the day of tournament for play
WHEN Golf Pro requests proof of USGA handicap
   AND Fred shows an official USGA handicap card
THEN Fred is assigned a tee time

And if the player has no official USGA handicap:

Scenario: Fred registers without a valid USGA handicap
GIVEN Fred has signed-up for the tournament
   AND Fred registers on the day of tournament for play
WHEN Golf Pro requests proof of USGA handicap
   AND Fred does not have an official USGA handicap card
THEN Fred leaves in tears because he is not allowed to play

You could have more Scenarios. For example: What if a player from Europe participates? Handicaps in Europe are regulated by the R&A (Royal and Ancient Golf Club, based in St. Andrews, Scotland). This may require another Scenario unless an R&A handicap is accepted by the USGA as "official" handicap.

Exercise: Testing NFRs

Here is your opportunity to try out what you read. You will get the most out of this book if you do the exercise **before** reading our answers.

Keep in mind that there is no right or wrong answer. The exercises will just allow you to try out the presented concepts and techniques.

Instructions:

Create GWT Scenarios for the following NFRs. Write at least one Scenario for each presented NFR using the format GIVEN (pre-conditions) WHEN (event occurs) THEN (Evaluation conditions)

Question 1:

What Scenarios can you identify for this NFR?

> **Only authorized users can modify personnel records.**

Question 2:

What Scenarios can you identify for this NFR?

> **Experienced underwriters should require no more than a one-day introductory seminar to process Internet applications.**

Answer Question 1: What Scenarios can you identify for the "training" NFR: "Only authorized users can modify personnel records"?

Scenario: Authorized user updates records
GIVEN A user is authorized to modify personnel records
WHEN A user updates personnel record
THEN The records are updated

Scenario: Unauthorized user tries to update records
GIVEN User is not authorized to modify personnel record
WHEN User attempts to update personnel record
THEN The record is not updated
   AND security is notified of the unauthorized attempt

Answer Question 2: What Scenarios can you identify for the NFR Requirement: "Experienced underwriters should require no more than a one-day introductory seminar to process Internet applications"?

Scenario: Experienced Underwriter with one-day seminar issues policy
GIVEN An Underwriter with 3+ years' experience processing insurance applications
WHEN An Underwriter is assigned a valid application submitted via the Internet
   AND the Underwriter had a one-day introductory seminar to process Internet applications
THEN The Underwriter issues a policy

Scenario: Experienced Underwriter with one-day seminar denies coverage
GIVEN Underwriter with 3+ years of experience is processing applications
WHEN Underwriter is assigned an invalid application submitted via the Internet
   AND Underwriter had a one-day introductory seminar to process Internet applications
THEN Underwriter accurately issues a coverage denial notice

V. Implementing Lean and Agile Practices

You now have many new techniques for capturing and communicating business needs within Lean and Agile teams. The challenge for you is how to start using these approaches. As mentioned in the preface, we do not expect you to read the book from cover to cover and put everything we propose into practice. Change does not happen this way.

However, we suggest that you look for opportunities to try one or two of the techniques. If you are just starting a new initiative with a Lean or Agile team, consider the value of a Question File as described in Chapter II. Requirements Elicitation and Backlog Seeding" in the section: **"Track Your Progress with a Question File"**.

If you are wondering whether you have fully identified all stakeholders, consider using some of the ideas in the same chapter in the **"Identifying Stakeholders"** section.

Because it is a novel and revolutionary idea, we strongly recommend finding a way to adopt Cynefin as a tool for evaluating the relative complexity of a proposed change, an Epic, a User Story, or a Feature before you commit. You can find it in the same chapter in section **"Using Cynefin to Deal with Uncertainty"**.

Another technique we think you should try is Lean Problem Analysis, as described in Chapter II section: **"Reveal User Stories with Business Problem Analysis"**. We have used this approach in almost every project we have ever undertaken and have been amazed at how effective this technique is at drawing a group's attention to a particular problem.

We are so convinced of its value that we even use it regularly in our private lives to discover and understand everyday problems. Read our blog post: **A Proof of Concept: Business Analysis Techniques Work - Part 1: (http://bit.ly/Problem-Analysis)**

If you are invited to participate in a 3 Amigos meeting, you should analyze the ambiguity and subjectivity of your User Stories before the meeting. The more you can do to improve the clarity of your User Stories, Features, Scenarios, and Examples, the more efficient and time-saving your User Story discussions will be for the entire team. That is Lean! Read more in Chapter III in the section **"Preparing User Stories for Release and Sprint Planning"**.

Another technique that many of our students have adopted is the **"Solution Requirements"** technique (Chapter III). This simple technique contributes more to exposing potential misunderstandings than any other technique we have tried. However, you may need to change your mind about who should do what in IT initiatives.

Most of the organizations we work with already use Gherkin's GWT approach to testing. In fact, all the larger organizations we have in our client base have already moved to automated testing. A prerequisite for this is a certain standardization of Test Scenarios. It seems that Gherkin will win the battle for the best solution. More on this topic in the section **"Acceptance Criteria as Given-When-Then Scenarios"** in Chapter IV.

Whether you are responsible for Unit Testing or End-user Acceptance Testing, you will benefit from the techniques described in **"Engineering AGILE Test Data"** (Chapter IV). This approach to test data selection can significantly reduce the number of Scenarios required to verify the digital solution.

Finally, if you have the task of finding Scenarios, check your sources and then select the appropriate section from Chapter IV **"Lean Analysis to Find Gherkin Scenarios"**. From User Stories to Use Cases and Non-Functional Requirements, you should find some food for thought on how to create Scenarios and Scenario Outlines that prove whether the solution has the required quality. Remember that Lean is not just about reducing waste, it is also about building quality in from the start. In closing, wherever your Lean and Agile journey takes you, we hope that you enjoy the ride.

ABOUT THE AUTHORS

Angela and Tom Hathaway are authors and providers of numerous classroom training courses, video courses, books, and other publications for Business Analysts around the world. They have facilitated hundreds of workshops on requirements and User Story Discovery for information technology projects under various acronyms (JAD, Story Workshop, Requirements Discovery, etc.).

Like all good IT stories, theirs began many (many) years ago with a project. Tom was the super technician, Angela the super Subject Matter Expert. They fought their way through a three-year development of a new underwriting and claims system for a prominent German insurance company.

They vehemently disagreed on many aspects but discovered a fundamental truth about IT projects. The business community (Angela) was to decide on business needs, while the technical team (Tom) was to ensure that technology delivered what the business needed. A revolutionary idea! All that remained was to learn how to communicate without bloodshed to make the project a resounding success. Mission accomplished.

They decided that this epiphany was so important that the world needed to know about it. As a result, they made it their mission (and their passion) to share this groundbreaking concept with the rest of the world.

To achieve this ambitious goal, they married and began the mission that still defines their lives today. After living and working together day and night for over 30 years, they are still enthusiastic about helping the "victims of technology" (aka users) to demand and receive the IT solutions they need to do their jobs better. More importantly, they have fallen in love with each other with more enthusiasm than ever before!

Tom and Angela love to share their experience, knowledge, and expertise with the world. They have taught face-to-face classes to thousands of students, published numerous how-to books on business analysis, authored over 10 courses on Udemy.com (with over 42,000 students – and still counting) and enriched the global community with 1.6 million views on their YouTube channel.

Their goal is to provide everyone "who wears the business analysis hat™" or anyone who needs to create requirements from the business perspective with high quality, cost-effective training materials and business coaching to implement what they learn. If you want to know more, please contact us:

⇨ Phone: (USA) 1-702-625-0146
⇨ E-Mail: Tom.Hathaway@ba-experts.com
⇨ Web: https://businessanalysisexperts.com

Printed in Great Britain
by Amazon